Micr

For the IBM PC
and Compatibles

Microcomputer Graphics Using Pascal

For the IBM PC and Compatibles

RICHARD HALPERN
Bergen Community College

1817

HARPER & ROW, PUBLISHERS, New York
Cambridge, Philadelphia, San Francisco,
London, Mexico City, São Paulo, Singapore, Sydney

Sponsoring Editor: John Willig
Project Coordination: Total Concept Associates
Cover Design: Sullivan Studios
Text Art: Textbook Art Associates
Production: Willie Lane
Compositor: Ampersand
Printer and Binder: R.R. Donnelley & Sons Company

Microcomputer Graphics Using Pascal: For the IBM PC and Compatibles

Library of Congress Cataloging in Publication Data

Halpern, Richard P.
Microcomputer graphics using Pascal for the IBM PC and compatibles.

Bibliography: p.
Includes index.
1. IBM Personal Computer—Programming. 2. PASCAL (Computer program language) 3. Computer graphics.
I. Title.
QA76.8.I2594H35 1985 001.64'43 84-29022
ISBN 0-06-042584-9

85 86 87 88 9 8 7 6 5 4 3 2 1

Contents

Preface

Welcome to the world of computer graphics! If you know little about the subject and wish to learn more, I think you will find this book useful. In this introduction, I will briefly discuss what this book is about and what you should know to make good use of it.

What Is Computer Graphics Good for, Anyway?

The simplest answer to this question is that it's good for quite a bit. Computer graphics is used in many different fields. It is a phenomenon that is bound to increase as the price of good graphics equipment continues to drop. The following are representative examples of computer graphics applications:

Business. *Bar graphs* and *pie charts* are often used in business, usually to summarize large quantities of data that would otherwise be time-consuming and painful to read.

Science/Research. Various plots, such as *line graphs, scatter diagrams,* and *histograms,* are used to summarize patterns and tendencies found in research results. *Contour plots* are ideal candidates for computers; not only can the computer plot the desired quantity, but it can also do the complex calculations often associated with these plots. *Simulations* of physical phenomena, such as fluid flow, can be carried out and observed by means of computer graphics.

Engineering/Design. A wide variety of projects, from large power plants to delicate optical systems, are designed with the aid of computer-generated drawings. Not only can something be designed, but its performance can be simulated using the computer. If need be, the design can be modified and redrawn, and this process can be repeated as often as necessary.

Image Processing. Computers can be programmed to analyze the information content and enhance the quality of certain images. The most widely publicized examples of this are pictures sent back from space probes. The computer can remove spurious information that is inevitably present in long-range transmissions and improve contrast. In a more down-to-earth application, computer-assisted tomography—the CAT scan—allows a physician to assemble a three-dimensional model derived from X rays taken from various perspectives.

Computer-Generated Movies. The slick commercials on television that are characterized by space-age effects are mostly computer-generated. So are such films as *Tron.*

Games. Computer games are examples of clever graphics programming. At first available only on arcade machines, they can now be played on very inexpensive home machines. This is a good example of how plummeting prices make graphics-related equipment available to a wider audience.

What Can You Expect from This Book?

The purpose of this book is to explain the *principles* behind computer graphics. The chapter summary that follows will give you a rough idea of what lies ahead. Note that the book is *not* a compendium of graphics programs. Although numerous ideas are illustrated with Pascal routines, it is up to you to do the vast bulk of the programming. The book will give you the foundation and the framework; you must build the rest of the house.

Chapter 1 is a discussion of hardware. A knowledge of how a system puts an image on the screen is very useful, especially if you want to exploit the features of the system through advanced programming. The chapter doesn't discuss specific brands of hardware. Rather, it answers general questions: How does a CRT project an image on its screen? How can a computer store an image? What are the major input and output devices, and how do they work?

Chapter 2 introduces the essential core of graphics commands that are needed to apply the principles covered in the book.

Chapter 3 presents two types of graphs that provide points of departure for the discussion of two important problems. The line graph introduces a discussion of how to handle the wide variety of coordinate systems that exist in the real world. The bar graph is used to introduce the general problem of drawing polygons. This chapter also discusses the problem of filling polygons—that is, lighting all the interior pixels.

Chapter 4 discusses two-dimensional transformations. These are the mathematical operations that allow us to execute certain changes on an object, such as enlargement or various types of movement.

The focus of chapter 5 is the organization of graphics data: How do we arrange graphics information in the memory so that we can use it to make a picture? How do we store a picture on a disk and retrieve it from the disk?

Chapter 6 discusses the concepts of windows and viewports. You will learn how to restrict your attention to a particular area of a picture and how to limit your drawing to a certain part of the screen.

Chapter 7 begins the treatment of three-dimensional graphics. After some mathematical preliminaries, which extend familiar two-dimensional concepts to three dimensions, the chapter discusses projections that enable us to represent real-world objects on a two-dimensional screen.

Chapter 8 continues the discussion of projections, extending your capabilities to include viewing an object from various positions.

Chapter 9, the last chapter, is devoted to the task of hidden line removal. This is important because only the parts of an object that we can see should be projected on the screen.

Finally, appendix A provides a review of mathematics; appendix B presents additional p-System Turtlegraphics commands; and appendix C provides a discussion of Turbo Pascal.

What Does This Book Expect from You?

Needless to say, to do computer graphics, you need a graphics-capable computer. This book assumes that you have an IBM PC with graphics capability and that you can program in Pascal. IBM provides for Pascal graphics in its version of the UCSD p-System. There are also other systems, such as version 2.0 of Turbo Pascal (see appendix C) from Borland. Although the p-System was used in developing this book, it is not absolutely essential that you have it. *Any system that can execute the equivalent of the graphics commands described in chapter 2 is adequate.* I have been careful throughout the book to build the routines on a small group of basic commands. Readers who wish to explore the entire Turtlegraphics system should refer to appendix B.

Most areas of computer graphics require some mathematics. At the very least, you should feel comfortable with basic algebra and trigonometry. In addition, you should either understand or be able to learn about vectors and matrices. If you have any doubts about these areas, you should read appendix A first.

The surest way to become proficient in computer graphics is to *do* computer graphics. A book can teach you the principles, but it cannot convey the many details and subtleties involved in developing a useful graphics project. At the very least, try the exercises at the end of each chapter. They provide a good review of what you have learned (or think you have learned). Better yet, think of some projects that are interesting to *you*. Such projects tend to be the most motivating, and they will often stimulate you to probe beyond what you have already learned. Let your imagination go free—and have fun!

Richard Halpern

Microcomputer Graphics Using Pascal

For the IBM PC
and Compatibles

Chapter 1

Hardware Fundamentals

When you have finished this chapter, you will understand how a microcomputer can produce an image from dots on a cathode ray tube (CRT). You also will have been introduced to various useful computer graphics hardware devices.

Objectives

1. To understand the essentials of microcomputer operation.
2. To understand the operation of raster scan and vector scan displays and DVST systems.
3. To understand the operation of hard-copy output devices.
4. To understand the operation of various graphics input devices.

BASIC COMPUTER OPERATION

Although a microcomputer may appear to be a jungle of integrated circuits, we can think of it as composed of three distinct units: a **memory unit**, a **central processing unit (CPU)**, and an **input/output (I/O) unit**. Basically, the memory stores information, the CPU does the calculations, and the I/O unit acts as the interface between computer and human. We will elaborate on each of these units shortly. For electronic communication, the units are linked together by many parallel wires called a **bus**. A schematic diagram of a computer system is shown in figure 1.1.

How is information in a computer represented? If we could investigate the voltage at every point along the computer's lines of communication, we would turn up only two possible values: 0 and a fixed value, such as 5 volts. This situation is represented most naturally by the binary number system, whose values, called **bits**, are 0 and 1. The 0 represents the absence of a voltage, and the 1 represents the presence of a voltage. Therefore, all information in a digital computer can be represented as a series of 1's and 0's.

Computers handle bits in groups called **words**. A word usually has 32 bits for large computers, 8 or 16 bits for smaller computers. It is important to note that two words that have the same combination of 1's and 0's do not necessarily have the same meaning. Computers interpret words differently in different situations. Consider the word 0 1 1 0 1 0 0 1. At times, it is interpreted as the binary number 105. At other times, it is interpreted as the character *i*. Fortunately, computers are designed to provide the correct interpretation of words at all times.

Memory

The function of a computer's memory is simply to store information. The memory unit consists of thousands of tiny electronic cells, called **locations**,

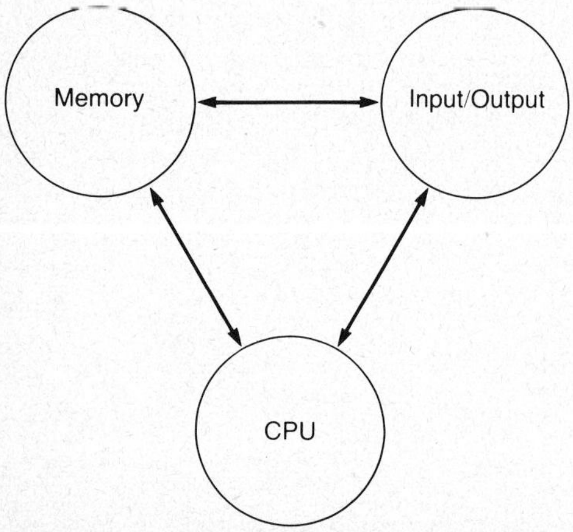

Figure 1.1 Schematic diagram of a computer. Arrows symbolize the bus, or wires, connecting the units.

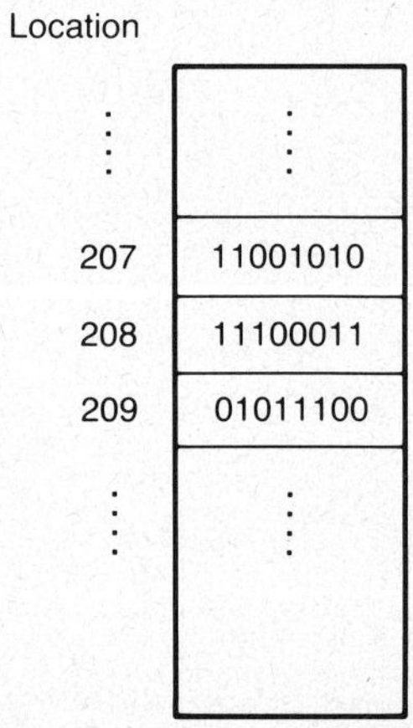

Figure 1.2 Memory locations and their contents.

each capable of storing eight bits, or one **byte**, of information. Every location is identified by a unique number, called an **address**, that indicates physical location within the memory. Figure 1.2 is a schematic diagram of a section of memory. Stored information, referred to as the **contents** of a location, falls into one of two categories: **instructions**, which tell the computer what to do and are normally stored in consecutive locations; and **data**, which consist of information that is processed in some way according to the instructions.

Two types of operations can be performed on a memory location: a **write** operation, during which the contents of a location are replaced by a different byte (figure 1.3); and a **read** operation, during which the contents of a location are copied, but not changed, by other units of the computer (figure 1.4). In either case, the memory unit must be sent signals indicating the address of the desired location and the nature of the operation (read or write). The memory is equipped with special circuitry that decodes these signals and responds accordingly. Note that all locations of the memory can be addressed with equal facility; this capacity is known as **random access.**

Memory that can be used for both read and write operations is called **random access memory (RAM)**, but it should be thought of as read-and-write memory, since, as noted, all machine memory is random access. When the power is turned off, the contents of RAM are lost. Memory with instructions permanently in place is called **read only memory (ROM)**. One cannot write to or alter ROM. Note that ROM retains its contents even if the power goes off. It is usually desirable to keep certain information permanently in memory. For example, a particular set of instructions is needed by the

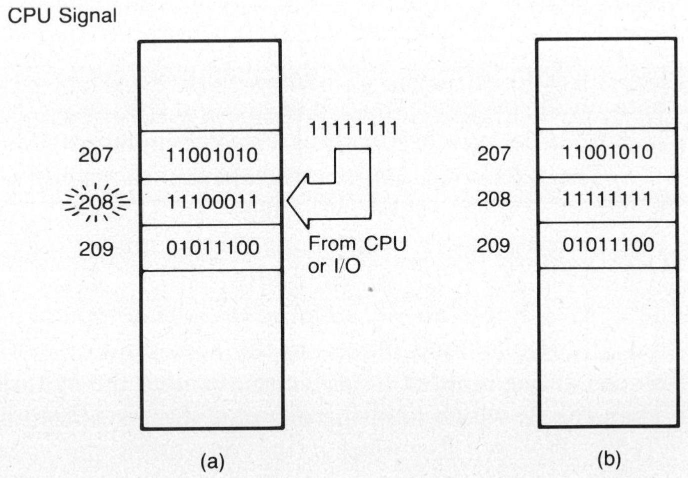

Figure 1.3 The write operation. (a) Just before writing to location 208. (b) After writing; note new contents of location 208.

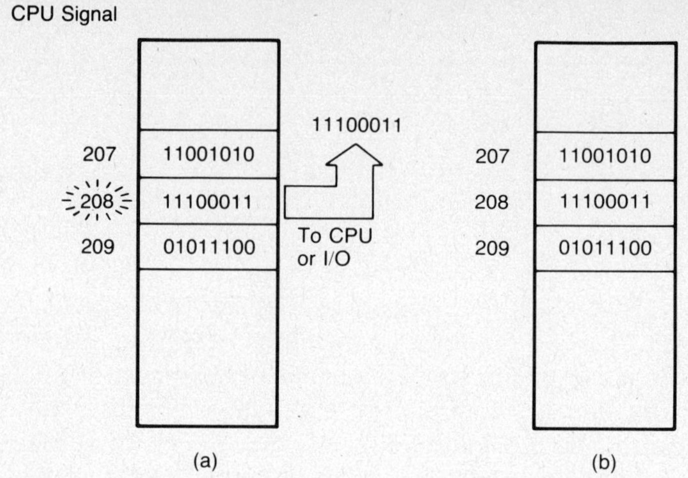

Figure 1.4 The read operation. (a) Reading location 208. (b) Memory after reading: location 208 still has its original contents.

computer to decode a keypress. Manufacturers make these instructions a permanent part of the computer so that each time a key is pressed, the instructions in this permanent memory are carried out and the keypress is decoded.

Central Processing Unit (CPU)

The CPU is the "brain" of the computer. It performs various arithmetic, logic control, and decision-making functions. Basically, the CPU divides its time between two **modes**, or phases, of operation. In the **fetch** phase, the CPU reads a byte from memory and then interprets it as either an instruction or data. In the **execute** phase, it carries out the instruction, or, if the fetched byte is data, processes it according to a previous instruction.

The CPU does its job with the aid of several special-purpose memory locations called **registers**, which are located in the CPU itself. The **instruction register** holds an instruction until it is decoded by a logic circuit. Another register, the **accumulator**, is used to carry out operations on two quantities. For example, suppose that the computer has to add 3 and 7. First, the 3 is fetched and placed in the accumulator. Next, the 7 is fetched and placed at one input of a CPU circuit called the **arithmetic-logic unit (ALU)**. Then the 3, which is in the accumulator, is placed at a second input of the ALU. The ALU performs the operation and stores a 10 back in the accumulator. The CPU can then use the 10 for another operation or store it in the memory.

How does the CPU step through a list of instructions? It is assisted by another register, the **program counter**, which always contains the address of the next byte to be fetched by the CPU. In the fetch phase, the CPU signals the memory for the address given by the contents of the program counter. Then the program counter is incremented by one. This crucial step ensures that when the next fetch takes place, the CPU gets the next address on the list. If the program counter is initialized to the address of the first instruction, and the last instruction is an `END` command, the CPU automatically executes all the instructions, and no more.

In graphics systems, specially designed processors have registers that are devoted solely to graphics functions. For example, by simply changing the contents of a color-mapping register, a programmer can rapidly change the colors of large areas of the screen. (After studying the raster scan system later in this chapter, you will appreciate the power of this capacity.)

Input/Output (I/O) Unit

Computers would not be useful if they were not able to communicate with the outside world. Such communication is the function of the I/O unit. There are several ways to manage I/O, but only one is of particular interest for computer graphics: **memory-mapped I/O**. The concept of memory mapping is quite simple: each input or output device is connected to a unique memory location, and the CPU reads from or writes to that location. For example, suppose that a keyboard is connected to location 10. When a key is pressed, its bit code is placed in location 10, and the CPU can determine what key was pressed by reading from location 10. Similarly, suppose that a video display is connected to location 20, using circuitry that flashes the contents of that location on the screen. To produce a byte of visible output, the CPU simply writes to location 20. Thus, input and output operations appear to the CPU as ordinary data transfers.

A given I/O device can be connected to more than one memory location. For example, a video display that can show twenty-five lines of eighty characters each represents 2,000 unique areas on the screen, each of which can be assigned its own memory location. Then a character can be made to appear in any screen area by writing its code to the corresponding memory location (see figure 1.5).

OUTPUT DEVICES

For our purposes, the most important output device is the video display. This is basically a television set that can display characters and graphics with great clarity. The heart of a video display is the **cathode ray tube (CRT)**.

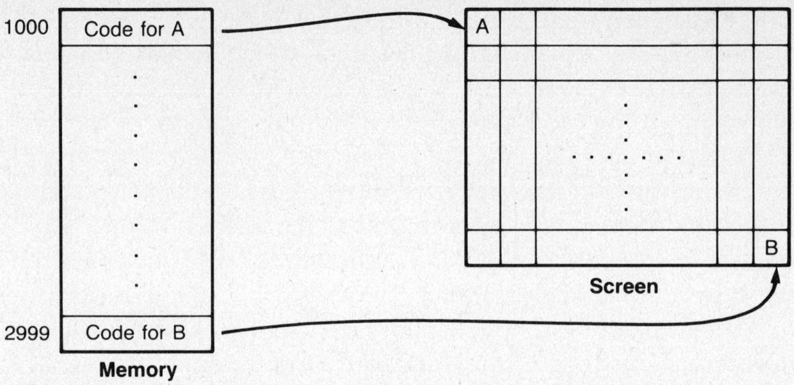

Figure 1.5 Hypothetical memory-mapped video display. The first byte of a 2,000-byte section maps to the upper left; the last byte maps to the lower right.

Basically, a CRT produces electrons at one end and accelerates them toward a phosphor-coated screen at the other end. The phosphor glows wherever electrons strike it.

Figure 1.6 shows the various elements of a CRT. A component called a **cathode** emits electrons when it is heated. Another component, the **anode**, is maintained at a high positive voltage. The anode attracts the electrons and causes them to accelerate rapidly toward the screen. A third component, called a **focusing device**, concentrates the electrons into a beam so that by the time they reach the screen, they have converged to a tiny, dotlike area.

An image is created by causing dots to light at selected points on the

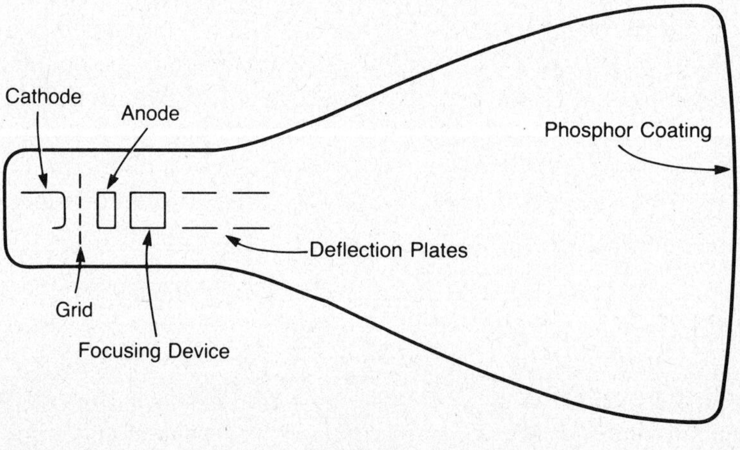

Figure 1.6 A cathode ray tube (CRT).

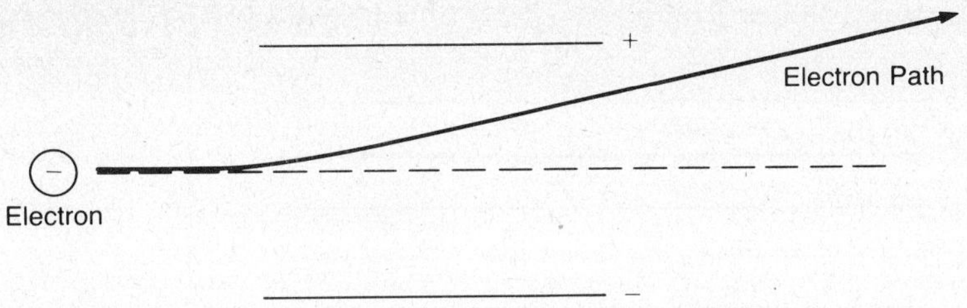

Figure 1.7 Deflection plates. The electron, initially headed in the direction shown by the dashed line, actually follows the path of the solid line because of the attraction of the positive plate and the repulsion of the negative plate.

screen. (This is similar to a newspaper picture, which, upon close examination, is seen to be made up of dots.) To accomplish this, the CRT must have two additional capabilities: it must be able to direct the beam to any point on the screen, and it must be able to turn the beam on and off as needed. Moving the beam around is the function of two pairs of **deflection plates** (see figure 1.7). The plates are connected to voltages of equal magnitude but opposite sign. When an electron passes between the plates, it is attracted to the positive plate and repelled from the negative plate. The amount of deflection depends on the magnitude of the voltage. One pair of deflection plates provides horizontal deflection; the other pair provides vertical deflection. The beam can light any dot on the screen, provided that the right combination of vertical and horizontal deflection voltages is applied to the plates.

Turning the beam on or off is the function of the **grid**, which is basically a metal cup located between the cathode and the anode and connected to a variable negative voltage. The negative grid creates a situation in which the grid repels electrons while the anode simultaneously attracts them. By varying the voltage on the grid, we can control the relative magnitude of the attracting and repelling forces, thus controlling the intensity of the electron beam. If the grid voltage is sufficiently negative, the beam is effectively turned off.

Raster Scan Displays

We have seen that the CRT has all the components it needs to put a dot of light anywhere on the screen. How do we harness this ability to draw an image? One way is the so-called **raster scan** technique. Imagine that both deflections are initially set to light a dot at the upper left corner of the screen. Assume that a sinusoidal voltage is connected to the horizontal deflection plates so that the beam goes back and forth between points A and B (see figure 1.8). If the beam is turned off at B and on again at A, a viewer would think that

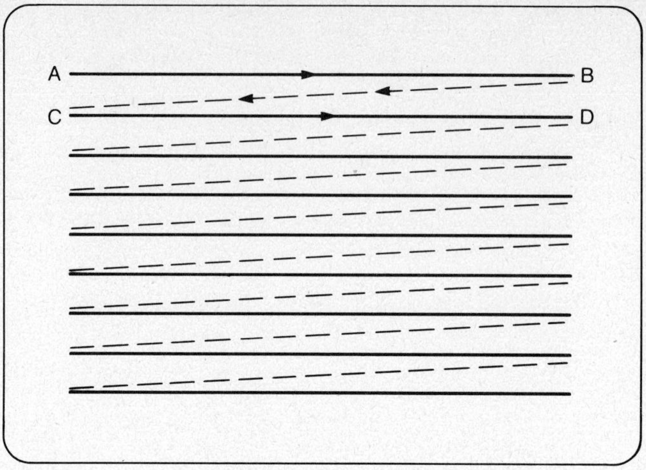

Figure 1.8 Scanning lines. The solid lines indicate that the beam is on; the dashed lines indicate that the beam is off.

a line of light is being drawn repeatedly from *A* to *B*. Suppose, now, that on the leftward trip only, the voltage on the vertical deflection plate is set so that thc bcam is displaccd downward a bit. Then, after going from *A* to *B*, the beam appears to go from *C* to *D*. In that case, a viewer would think that two lines of light have been drawn—first *AB*, then *CD*. Clearly, we can continue this process so that evenly spaced lines are drawn over the entire screen. The process of sweeping the beam across the screen is called **scanning**; the horizontal parts of the sweep are called **raster lines**.

If a CRT were limited to the foregoing process, the only image it could draw would be a screen full of lines. In fact, however, the system has a way of turning the beam on and off at selected points along the raster lines. The display is memory-mapped so that a particular bit location of the memory corresponds to a unique dot on the screen. (The section of memory that is used in this way is called the **frame buffer**.) As the beam scans, the computer reads the contents of each bit of the frame buffer sequentially and signals the beam to go on for a 1 and off for a 0. Each dot on the screen is turned on or off according to the contents of its corresponding bit in the frame buffer. Figure 1.9 illustrates this process for a highly simplified buffer. Essentially, a programmer creates an image simply by storing some combination of 1's and 0's in the frame buffer.

Unfortunately, phosphors remain lit for only a few tens of microseconds after they are hit by electrons; an image does not last very long. To compensate for this situation, the video circuits **refresh** the display; that is, they repeat the scan thirty or sixty times a second. Even though the phosphor

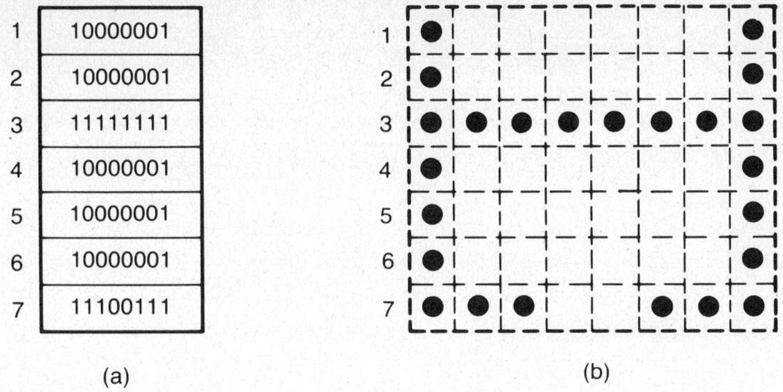

Figure 1.9 (a) Frame buffer. (b) Corresponding screen image.

is still off most of the time, the eye is fooled into thinking that the image is steady.

How much detail such a system can show depends on how densely packed the dots are. Systems with many dots per unit area are called **high-resolution** displays. There are different considerations for vertical and horizontal resolution. In the vertical direction, resolution depends on how many scanning lines the circuits can produce. Obviously, one cannot have a dot in an area that is not scanned by the beam. Therefore, vertical resolution improves as the number of scanning lines increases. In the horizontal direction, resolution depends on how rapidly the beam can be turned on and off as it sweeps across the screen. The more rapid the switching rate, the smaller the width of the dot and the higher the horizontal resolution. Switching rates depend on the bandwidth of the video amplifier; a wide bandwidth means high resolution.

The area on the screen taken up by a dot is called a **pixel**. In practice, resolution is denoted by the number of pixels that make up the horizontal and vertical extent of the screen. For example, the IBM system, which is a medium-resolution raster sytem, has a resolution of 640 pixels horizontally and 200 pixels vertically. In general, the greater the number of pixels, the smaller their size and the better the resolution.

An unavoidable characteristic of raster scan systems is that any line segment that crosses raster lines looks discontinuous (see figure 1.10). The lines are created by lighting up all the pixels between the endpoints, but both the vertical and diagonal lines show the effects of the spaces between the raster lines. There is no way to eliminate the jagged look, but the lines are somewhat smoother when they are created on a higher-resolution display. Horizontal lines, however, look continuous even on a lower-resolution display. Pixels are slightly elongated in the horizontal direction due to the horizontal motion of the beam.

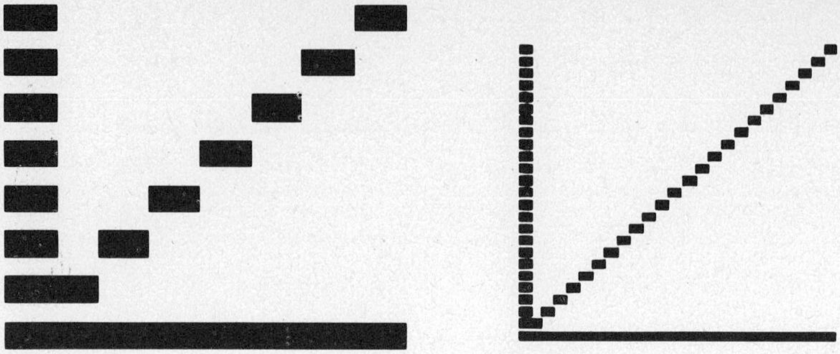

(a) (b)

Figure 1.10 Vertical, diagonal, and horizontal lines in (a) a low-resolution raster system and (b) a high-resolution raster system.

Vector Scan Displays

Raster scanning is not the only way to create an image with a CRT. The so-called **vector scan display** uses a CRT with the same construction as shown in figure 1.6, but the beam is used differently to produce an image. A vector scan display does not create an image from a group of pixels; instead, it draws line segments by simply moving the beam between the two endpoints. For example, the triangle in figure 1.11 consists of three segments that are drawn by turning the beam on at *A*, moving it to *B*, then to *C*, and finally back to *A*. Note that the beam does not crisscross the screen as it does in a raster scan. Instead, it moves only the amount needed to produce the image. In addition, the beam is never off when it is between two endpoints of a segment. Hence, regardless of the orientation of that segment, the line that results is continuous. A vector scan system uses less display memory than a raster system. For a given line segment, only the endpoints need be stored, not the points between. As in the raster scan system, however, the segments must be refreshed.

Vector Versus Raster Displays

Most contemporary graphics systems use raster scan displays. This makes good sense, given the advanced state of the art and the low cost of television technology. However, the raster system is not without its disadvantages. First, there is the problem of coarse-looking vertical and diagonal lines. Although this is minimized in a high-resolution system, the use of such a

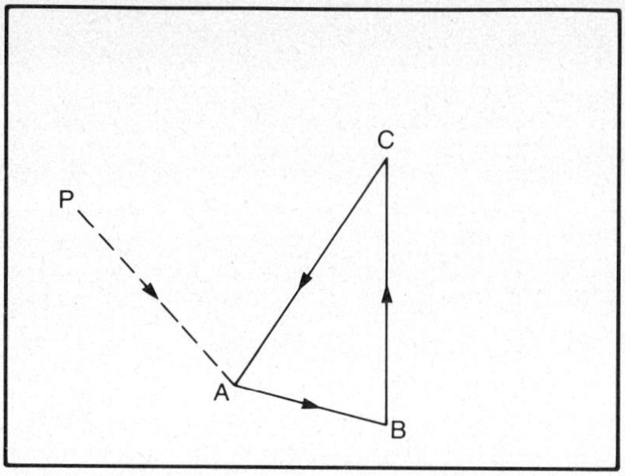

Figure 1.11 Vector scan system. From an arbitrary point P, the beam is moved to A, turned on, and then moved to B, to C, and back to A.

system creates problems of its own. A good system has a screen with, say, 1,024 by 1,024 pixels, which requires more than 130,000 bytes for the frame buffer. Aside from the cost of memory, which we can safely assume will drop, there is a price paid in performance. For example, we will see later that for animation, one creates a sequence of screens, each of which is slightly different from the preceding one. Displaying the new screen soon after erasing the old creates the sense of movement. If screens cannot be erased and recreated rapidly enough, the animation appears slow. To change the image in a raster system, a program must go through—and possibly change—each bit in the frame buffer. The more bits that must be changed, the more time it takes. Hence, images created from many pixels may not lend themselves to the rapid changes necessary for good animation.

A vector system overcomes these problems. We have already seen that line segments, the building blocks of the vector image, are free of any dotted effects. Since vector systems don't need as much display memory, changes in that memory can be made more rapidly; thus, animation looks better on vector systems than on raster systems. Unfortunately, however, the vector system has its own inherent problems. For example, refreshing the display can be troublesome, because the time available for refreshing each segment depends on the complexity of the image. If the image is simple (few segments), the beam can retrace all segments frequently enough for proper refreshing. If the image is complex (many segments), it may take a relatively long time for the beam to retrace all the segments. Then the refreshing time per segment is inadequate and the image will start to flicker. Note that in a raster scan, the scan rate (hence, the refreshing rate) is fixed, regardless of image complexity.

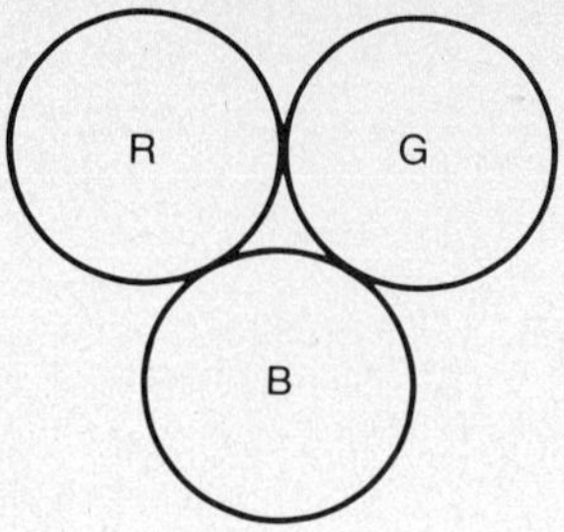

Figure 1.12 A triad. The three areas glow red (R), green (G), or blue (B) when they are struck by electrons.

Color Displays

Up to a point, a raster scan color CRT works according to the princples we have already discussed. The basic concepts of scanning the screen and lighting pixels according to a bit pattern in the frame buffer still hold. However, the color CRT has features that are not found on monochrome tubes. First, the inner surface of the screen is not coated uniformly with a single type of phosphor. Instead, the coating is a mosaic of tiny regions called **triads**. A triad is a set of three adjacent circular areas, each of which is coated with a different phosphor (see figure 1.12). The area labeled *R* in figure 1.12 glows red when it is struck by a beam of electrons; the *G* and *B* areas glow green and blue. If the areas are small enough and close together, the eye perceives one overall area whose color is a combination of the three. The exact color depends on the combination of intensities of the beams. The simplest case is when each circular area can be either on or off. Since there are eight possible on–off combinations, there are eight different colors.

The second distinguishing feature of a color CRT is that it produces three electron beams, each of which scans only one color of the triads. Thus, one beam hits all the red circles but none of the blues or greens, and the same idea holds true for the other beams. A beam is prevented from hitting its "forbidden" circles by a component called a **shadow mask**, which is basically a perforated sheet placed strategically near the screen (figure 1.13). As the beams scan, they either hit the solid part of the mask, in which case no circles glow, or go through the holes. Everything is arranged so that when the beams do go through a hole, each ends up on a different circle of the triad, as shown in figure 1.14a (with angles and distances exaggerated). To appreciate the delicacy of this situation, consider figure 1.14b, in which the mask is slightly misaligned and the beams do not hit the triad.

Although many colors are theoretically possible, the number actually displayed is often limited. Recall that, in a monochrome system, one bit of the frame buffer stores information regarding whether a pixel is on or off. In a color system, one bit stores information regarding whether a circle is on or off, so three bits are needed for each triad. For the simplest eight-color system, the

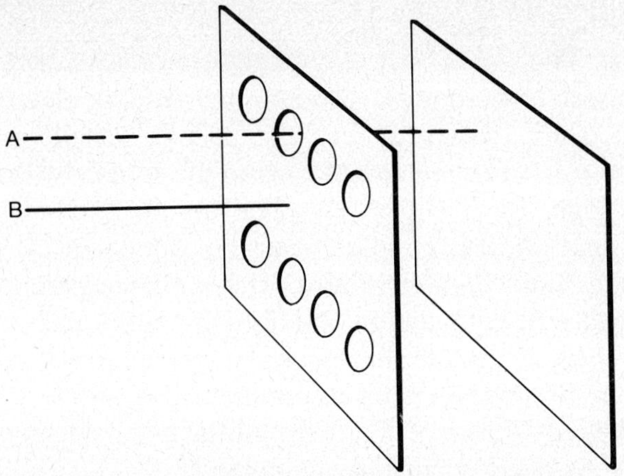

Figure 1.13 A shadow mask. Beam *A* goes through a hole; beam *B* is stopped.

frame buffer must be three times as large as that in a monochrome system of equivalent resolution. The only way to get more than eight colors is to vary the intensity of each beam so that more than one on state is possible. In that case, the frame buffer must be larger still to hold the extra information. If a manufacturer does not wish to devote so much memory to the frame buffer, the system will necessarily be restricted to a limited number of colors.

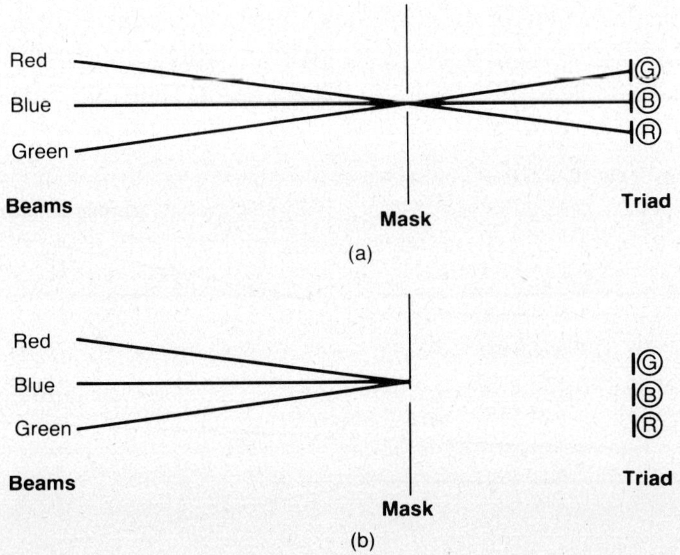

Figure 1.14 (a) A properly placed shadow mask. (b) An improperly placed shadow mask.

Although most color systems are raster scan displays, some vector scan color displays exist. The least costly way to get vector scan color is to coat the screen with two phosphors—one sensitive to high-energy electrons, the other to low-energy electrons. This produces two colors, usually red and green. Recall that the electrons are accelerated toward the screen by the anode; if the anode voltage is high, the electron energies are high. Hence, changes in electron energy, and therefore color, can be obtained by changing the accelerating voltage. Unfortunately, these voltage changes are relatively time-consuming, especially in comparison to changing bits in a frame buffer, for example. Hence, there is the familiar problem of inadequate refreshing time for complex images. Programmers try to minimize this problem by displaying, for example, all the red segments first, then all the green segments. Then only one voltage change is needed per refreshing cycle.

Direct View Storage Tubes (DVSTs)

The **direct view storage tube (DVST)** is a video display that does not need to be refreshed. Its operation can be understood with the aid of figure 1.15. Consider, first, the front of the tube. The inside surface of the glass, the **storage surface**, has a uniformly distributed negative charge but is non-conducting. (This is not a contradiction. It simply means that the negative charge on the surface cannot move about freely, as it would on a conductor.) Farther inside is a grid, which is positive with respect to the storage surface. At the rear of the tube are two **electron guns** (assemblies that produce electron beams). One of them creates a beam of electrons that is focused and deflected in the usual manner. This beam is called the **writing beam**. When electrons from the writing beam hit the storage surface, they shake loose some

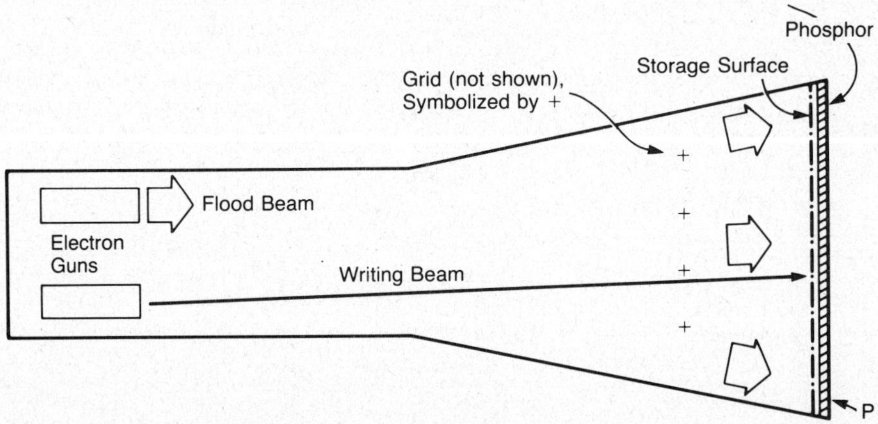

Figure 1.15 A direct view storage tube (DVST).

of the surface's electrons. These liberated electrons are attracted to the grid. As a result, the charge distribution on the storage surface becomes nonuniform; wherever the writing beam has written, the charge is less negative. Note that since the surface is nonconducting, charges on it cannot flow to restore uniformity. Hence, the effects of the writing beam are retained by the storage surface.

The actual image is brought to life by electrons from the second gun. This gun sends out a beam that covers the entire screen uniformly. The effect is similar to that of a floodlight; in fact, the beam is called the **flood beam**. Electrons in the flood beam are not so energetic as writing beam electrons. When they approach the storage surface, those incident on the strongly negative unwritten areas are repelled; those incident on the weakly negative written areas pass through to the phosphor, causing it to light. Then the pattern etched on the storage surface by the writing beam becomes visible on the screen. It is easy to see why there is no need to refresh the display in a DVST. Since the flood beam remains on continuously, the written areas are always displayed. The written areas, in turn, are maintained by the nonconducting nature of the storage surface. Of course, the picture is not permanent; it can be erased by a special procedure, as follows. The storage surface is connected briefly to a positive voltage. The entire surface then attracts electrons from the flood beam, which is the equivalent of writing onto the entire screen at once; hence, the original image literally disappears in a flash. At this point, the storage surface has fewer electrons than it had before the writing process began and it must be connected briefly to a negative voltage to replenish the electrons. The writing process can then begin anew.

The DVST was developed at a time when it was very expensive to produce memory and refreshing circuits, making it an attractive, low-cost display. Even today, however, the DVST is used to advantage. Since it does not have to be refreshed, it can display complicated, finely detailed images without any flicker. Of course, there is the obvious disadvantage of having to erase the entire screen when any change is desired. In addition, DVSTs have relatively poor contrast.

Printers

The **dot matrix printer** functions well as a graphics output device. Its operation can be best understood by examining figure 1.16. Figure 1.16a shows the relationship of the main parts, the **print head** and the **platen**, and, between them, the paper and the ribbon. Figure 1.16b shows an enlarged, head-on view of the front of the print head. It has a column of fine pins, each of which can be pushed against the paper by electromagnets in the head. As

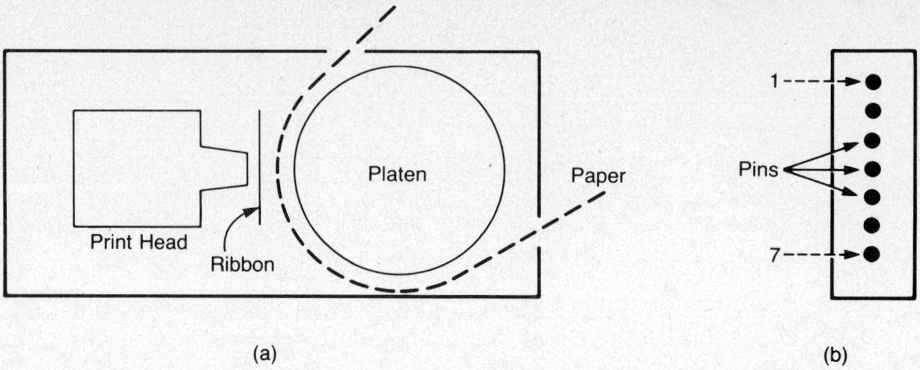

Figure 1.16 A dot matrix printer. (a) Main elements. (b) Print head (front view).

the print head moves across the paper, the pins are pushed out selectively, as illustrated in figure 1.17. All the pins (seven in this case) are pushed out to get the left-hand column of dots. Then the head moves slightly to the right, and pins 1, 4, and 7 are pushed. This second step is repeated three more times to get the complete character—an *E*.

For a dot matrix printer to produce a hard copy of a screen image, each pixel on the screen corresponds to a unique spot on the paper. As the print head moves across the paper, it puts a dot in the spots that correspond to lighted pixels. When the print head reaches the end of its travel, the platen advances the paper and the next row of pixels can be printed. In our example, the print head has seven pins; hence, one pass across the paper can take care of seven rows of pixels.

Plotters

A **plotter** is a device that draws a line between any two points simply by moving a pen from one point to the other. This can be done in several ways. In one type of plotter, the paper is held fixed on a flat bed while the pen moves freely in two perpendicular directions (figure 1.18). In another type, the pen is limited to moving in only one direction while the paper moves in the

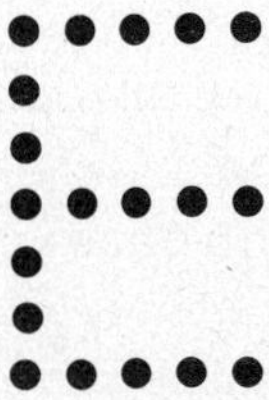

Figure 1.17 Creating an *E* with a dot matrix printer.

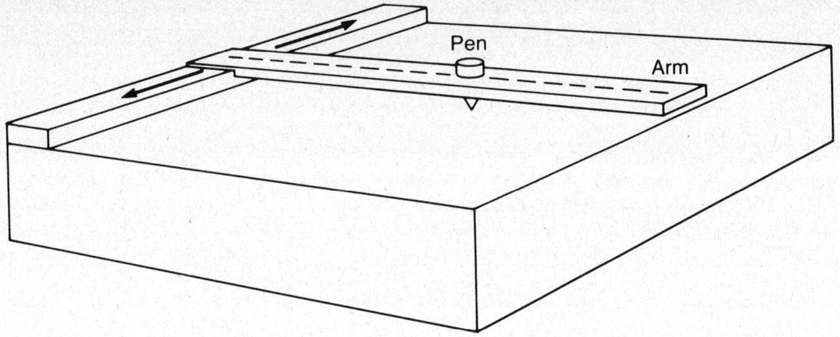

Figure 1.18 A plotter. The entire arm moves in the direction of the arrows; the pen moves simultaneously along the dashed line.

perpendicular direction (figure 1.19). In a variation of this plotter, the paper is wrapped around a drum, and as the drum turns, the pen moves back and forth in a line. Here, too, the pen moves perpendicular to the paper.

Users sometimes speak of a plotter's "intelligence." If the only commands a plotter can execute are simple pen-move commands, it is considered "dumb." If it has built-in commands to draw letters, numbers, and basic shapes, such as circles and ellipses, it is considered "intelligent." However, the built-in commands for these shapes are nothing more than prepackaged software routines that use simple pen-move commands. Hence, a dumb plotter, when interfaced with a clever programmer, can be made as capable as an intelligent plotter.

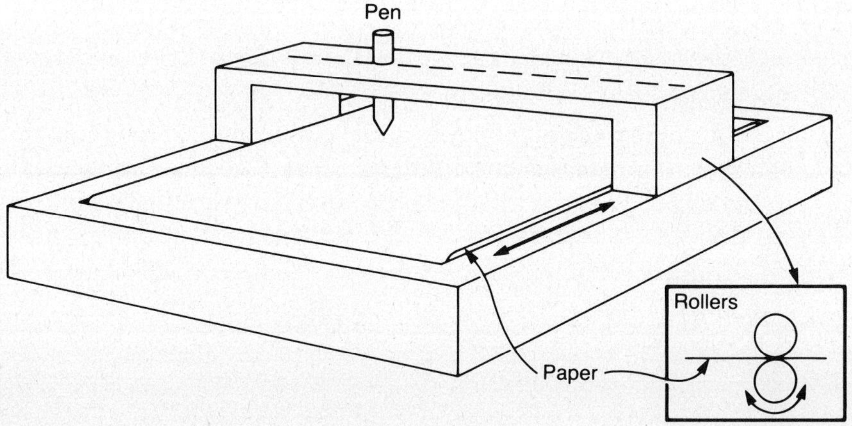

Figure 1.19 Another plotter. Rollers (see insert) move the paper in the direct of the arrows; the pen moves along the dashed line.

INPUT DEVICES

We are all familiar with that ubiquitous input device, the keyboard. Every computer has one, primarily for entering programs and data. There are other devices, however, that have advantages for graphics systems. The following sections will describe both the logical functions performed by input devices and their physical operation.

Logical Versus Physical Input Devices

Suppose we write a program that uses a sequence of ten numbers as data. We know that the outcome of the program will be the same whether we input the numbers from a set of cards, from a floppy disk, or from a keyboard. Thanks to the computer's operating system, the program "thinks" it is being fed ten numbers from a file, rather than from some piece of hardware. We call this a **logical file** because, from the point of view of the program's logic, the input behaves like a file. In a similar vein, we can speak of a **logical input device**, which is defined by the logical function it performs, rather than by its physical construction. Table 1.1 lists four categories of logical devices and their functions.

The physical device, of course, is the hardware itself. A given physical device is usually best suited for a particular logical function. For example, the keyboard is clearly a "natural" for the button function; every key performs a predefined operation. With appropriate software, however, a keyboard can emulate a pick. Unfortunately, the keyboard is clumsy in this role; as we shall see, a light pen is much better.

Examples of Physical Devices

The following devices are described in terms of their most natural logical functions.

A **game paddle** is simply a dial connected to a potentiometer. By turning the dial, the user selects a voltage from 0 to the supply voltage (see figure 1.20). This value is digitized by an analog-to-digital converter and made

TABLE 1.1 LOGICAL DEVICES AND THEIR FUNCTIONS

Device	Function
Button	Executes a predefined function
Valuator	Enters a scalar value into the computer
Locator	Enters position coordinates into the computer
Pick	Selects an area of the screen for processing

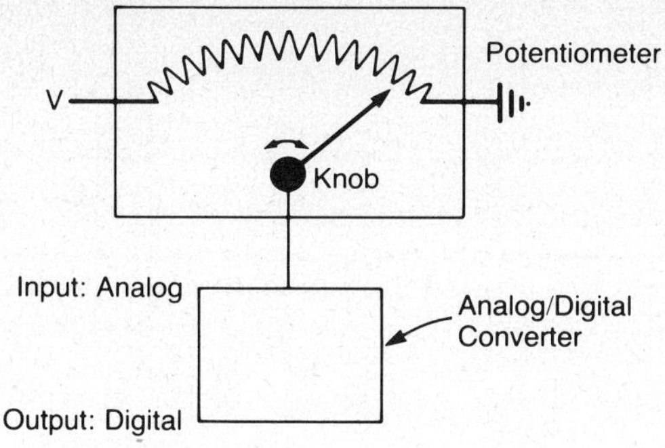

Figure 1.20 Game paddle. By turning a knob, the user selects a voltage between 0 and V. The signal is digitized by an analog-to-digital converter.

available to the computer as input. Clearly, a game paddle functions as a valuator.

A **joystick** is basically a rod connected to two potentiometers. As shown in figure 1.21, the rod pivots at A and can be pushed so that it leans varying amounts from the vertical in any direction. One potentiometer monitors the lean in the x-direction; the other monitors the lean in the y-direction. For every position of the rod, there is a unique combination of potentiometer values. Technically, each potentiometer functions as a valuator. However, the pair of values output by the joystick is easily transformed by the computer into x- and y-coordinates of a point. Hence, the joystick typically functions as a locator.

A **trackball** is a sphere about the size of a tennis ball that is mounted in a box, as shown in figure 1.22. Note that most of the ball lies within the confines of the box. It is operated by rolling the palm of one's hand over the part of the ball that sticks out. The ball's motion produces two series of electrical pulses—one for the x-component of the motion, another for the y-component of the motion. With the proper software, one can keep a running count of pulses for each direction, from the ball's initial position to its current position. This is translated by the computer into the coordinates of the current position. Hence, the trackball functions as a locator.

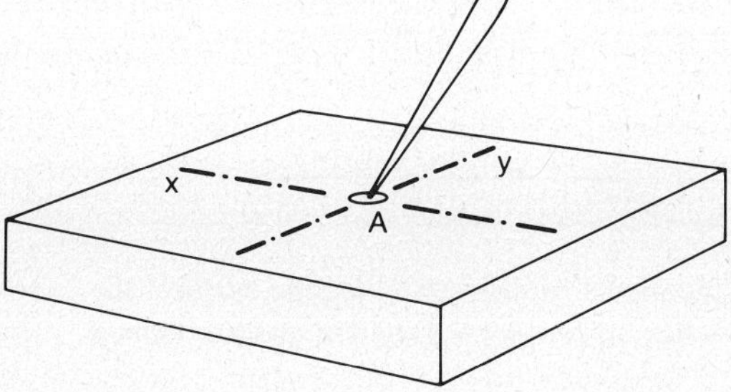

Figure 1.21 A joystick.

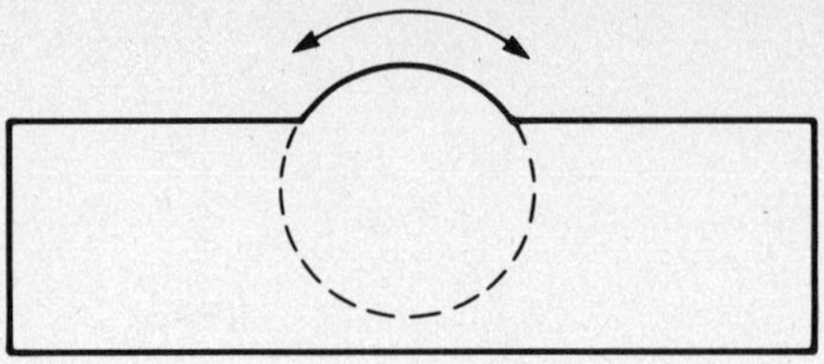

Figure 1.22 A trackball (cross section).

A **mouse** is a hand-held device like an upside-down trackball that is rolled along a surface (figure 1.23). Like the trackball, the mouse can function as a locator. It is especially convenient for executing a large change of coordinates in a small space. The user simply moves the mouse a short distance, lifts it up, brings it back to the original position, and repeats the motion as necessary. Software keeps track of the total displacement in both the x- and the y-directions. Often, a mouse has switches on the top of its housing that implement the logical button function; pressing a switch executes a predefined operation. If one of the predefined operations is the selection of part of the image for special treatment, then the mouse also functions as a pick. The mouse is considered unusually versatile and is gaining popularity as an input device.

A **light pen** is a penlike device that, when touched to the screen, reports which (lighted) pixel is underneath. Its operation is simple in principle. On moderately priced units, the part that touches the screen consists of a photoresistive cell (a component whose resistance changes with light intensity in a known way). In scanning the screen, the electron beam moves past one pixel after another. When the beam reaches the pixel being touched by the light pen, the photocell reports the momentary flash of light to the CPU. (Yes, the flash is momentary. Remember, a pixel that appears to be on is really flashing on and off, and is off most of the time.) The time that elapses from the beginning of the scan to the flash is unique for each pixel. Therefore, the computer can easily figure out which pixel is selected. In more expensive light

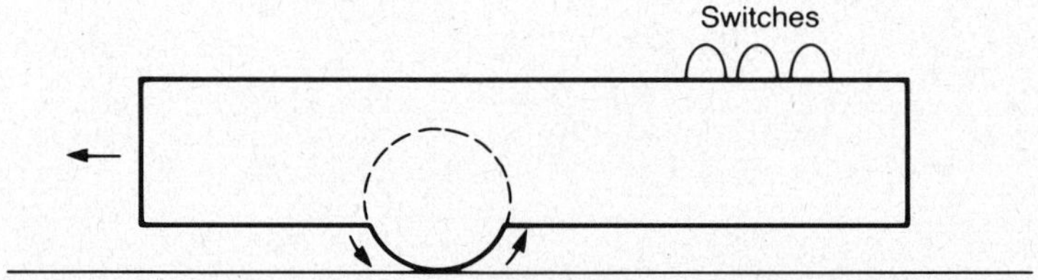

Figure 1.23 A mouse. As the mouse is dragged along the surface, the roller turns accordingly. Switches on top implement various predefined functions.

pen systems, the photocell is sensitive to the electron beam itself. This allows for greater precision in locating the pen.

A light pen functions either as a pick or a locator. In the pick mode, it selects the part of the image (for example, a chair in a floor plan) that includes the pixel. In the locator mode, it simply reports the *x*- and *y*-coordinates of the pixel.

A **graphics tablet**, also called a **digitizer**, can be thought of as an electronic sketchpad. It typically consists of a penlike rod that is electrically connected to a large board. Each pixel on the screen corresponds to a unique area on the board. When the pen is touched to the board, the corresponding pixel lights up.

As shown in figure 1.24, a fine mesh of wire is embedded in the digitizer board, with the intersection of two wires corresponding to a pixel. A special circuit determines which intersection is closest to the pen tip and informs the computer of the location. The computer can then figure out the screen coordinates and light the appropriate pixel. Many digitizers work on this basic idea, but there are wide variations in the way position is sensed.

A much simpler digitizer is shown in figure 1.25. It consists of two arms: an inner one connected to the board and pivoting at *A*, and an outer one connected to the inner one and pivoting at *B*. Physically, both pivots are potentiometers; as the arms move, the potentiometers turn. To use this digitizer, one simply places the tip of the arm system (*T*) at the desired point. Each point on the board corresponds to a unique set of θ's, and each set of θ's corresponds to a unique pair of potentiometer settings. The computer can interpret these settings as *x*- and *y*-coordinates and light the correct pixel on the screen. Note that there is no interaction between the board and the pen in this type of digitizer; there is no mesh of delicate wires and no special sensing circuitry. All of the work is done by the potentiometers. Consequently, this system is the least expensive of the digitizers. It is also the least accurate.

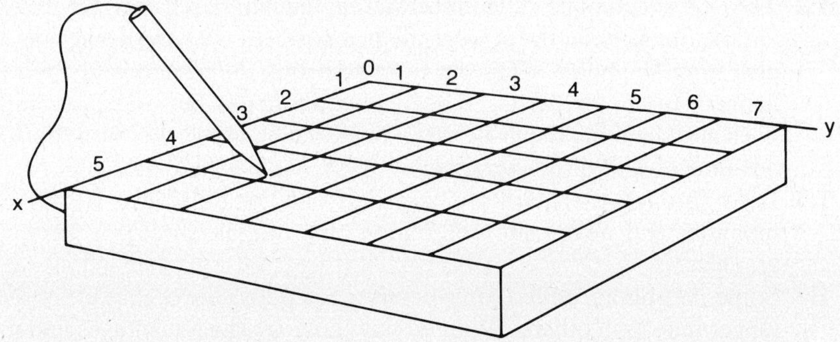

Figure 1.24 A simplified digitizer. In this hypothetical situation, the point (4.8, 2) is selected by the pen.

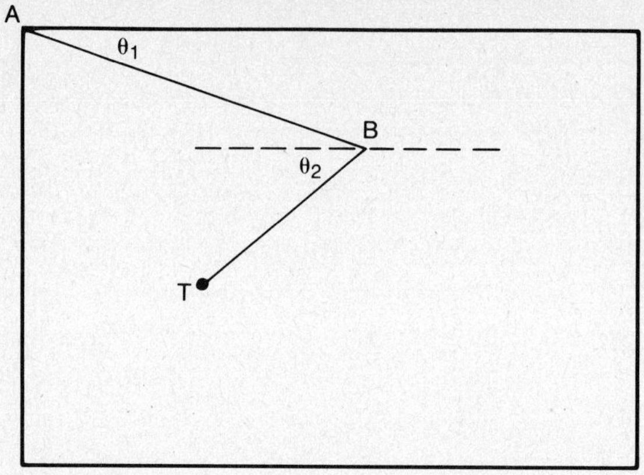

Figure 1.25 A potentiometer-based digitizer. Each position of point T corresponds to a unique pair (θ_1, θ_2).

PROBLEMS

1.1 The number of times per second that a beam can go across the screen and back is called the **horizontal scan frequency**. The number of times per second that it can scan an entire screen is called the **vertical scan frequency**. The number of scan lines displayed on the screen is simply the ratio of the two frequency rates:

Scan lines = horizontal scan rate/vertical scan rate

Find these two rates for the monitor on your system and determine the maximum number of scan lines the screen can show. Is this number consistent with the stated number of pixels in the vertical direction?

1.2 Through a technique called **interlacing**, the number of scan lines can be doubled. On the first scan of the screen, the beam moves over the usual scan lines. On the next scan, the beam starts out from a slightly different position, so that it moves *between* the original lines. The system alternates between scanning the original lines and scanning the in-between lines. Think about this system and describe its advantages and disadvantages.

1.3 Look through the literature and find out the difference between RGB color monitors and composite color monitors. Which would be better for detailed graphics?

1.4 Some phosphors, called **long-persistence phosphors**, stay lit for a considerably longer time than others. What do you think are the advantages and disadvantages of these phosphors?

REFERENCES

Foley, J. D., and Van Dam, A. *Fundamentals of Interactive Computer Graphics.* Reading, Mass.: Addison-Wesley, 1982, chapters 3 and 5.

Gabel, D. "Monitors: The Better to See Your Data With." *Personal Computing*, December 1982, 116–197.

Greenfield, S.E. *The Architecture of Microcomputers,* Vol. I. Boston: Little, Brown, 1983.

Williams, G. "A Graphics Primer." *Byte,* November 1982, 448–470.

Chapter 2

Essential Graphics Commands

When you have finished this chapter, you will have a nucleus of graphics commands suitable for the tasks in the remainder of the book.

Objectives

1. To introduce the various IBM text and graphics screens.
2. To understand relative and absolute plot instructions.
3. To understand some of the different drawing modes.
4. To understand how to put labels on the screen.

In the last chapter, we looked at the hardware aspects of computer graphics, and we learned that a graphics system builds an image out of fundamental pieces called pixels. The system itself is very primitive from a programmer's standpoint; all it can do is turn a pixel on or off. To understand just how primitive this is, consider that drawing a simple shape, such as a line, requires knowledge of every single pixel that must be lit. Since a system of even modest resolution has more than 50,000 pixels on its screen, this is a formidable task. Imagine what it would be like on a system with a million pixels!

We would like to avoid the responsibility of keeping track of all those pixels. Fortunately, most graphics systems are very obliging in this respect.

They operate with a standard high-level language, such as FORTRAN or Pascal, that has been enhanced with graphics-oriented procedures. For our purposes, we can think of these procedures as falling into one of two categories:

1. *Graphics output primitives*: These procedures are the building blocks from which a drawing is constructed. Depending on the system, they might be lines, circles, arcs, polygons, and so forth.
2. *Housekeeping procedures*: These procedures take care of miscellaneous needs, such as initializing the system, clearing the screen, choosing a color, and the like.

The graphics procedures we will use are a subset of a system called **Turtlegraphics**—a graphics package that comes with the IBM implementation of the UCSD p-System. Turtlegraphics is based on a clever idea introduced in the 1960s by Seymour Papert of MIT and was designed to teach mathematics to children. It features an imaginary creature the size of a dot that can crawl on a piece of paper and hold a pen. This creature, called a **turtle**, can execute two basic motions:

1. It can move in a straight line.
2. It can remain in place and change direction.

If the turtle drags the pen along the paper, it draws a straight line. If it holds the pen off the paper, it moves without leaving a mark. In Turtlegraphics, the only output primitive is the line segment.

The "paper" on which the turtle moves is, of course, the screen. We can think of the screen as a grid H units wide by V units high (figure 2.1). This grid forms a Cartesian coordinate system with a lower boundary of (0, 0) and an upper boundary of (H, V). As we shall see, there is some freedom in choosing the values of H and V. The turtle's coordinates are always integral values at or between these boundaries. Note that this coordinate system is not

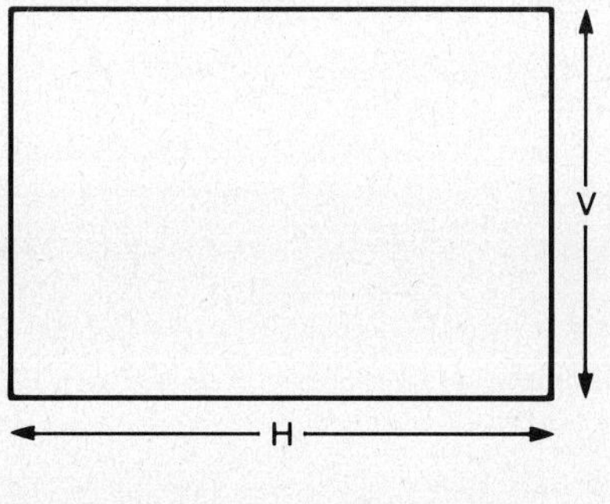

Figure 2.1 A graphics screen with a horizontal resolution H and a vertical resolution V.

arbitrarily chosen by the user; it is dictated by the hardware. Hence, it is called the **device coordinate system**. Other coordinate systems can be defined, as we shall see, but only for temporary use in solving a particular problem. Coordinate values in these other systems must be transformed into device coordinates. That is the only way the system can keep track of the turtle.

SCREENS

We have already discussed memory mapping, whereby a section of memory is reserved for the display. In a graphics system, at least two sections must be so reserved (figure 2.2). One section, the **text page**, is for the usual text material: prompts, error messages, program listings, and the like. The other section, the **graphics page**, is for the display of graphics images. (The terms *page* and *screen* are often used interchangeably.) Only one page can be displayed on the CRT at any given time. Hence, every system must have a way of switching between text and graphics pages. IBM supplies a procedure called `VideoMode` whose function is to choose between different possibilities. `VideoMode` has the following form:

```
VIDEOMODE (n:integer);
```

where the integer *n* selects either text or graphics, as follows:

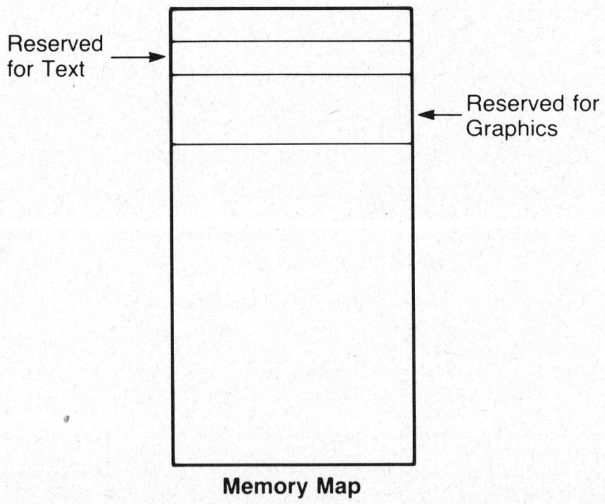

Figure 2.2 In a general-purpose microcomputer, two or more sections are reserved for screen output.

$n = 0$: 25 lines of 40 characters, monochrome, text

$n = 1$: 25 lines of 40 characters, color, text

$n = 2$: 25 lines of 80 characters, monochrome, text

$n = 3$: 25 lines of 80 characters, color, text

$n = 4$: $H = 320$, $V = 200$, color graphics

$n = 5$: $H = 320$, $V = 200$, monochrome graphics

$n = 6$: $H = 640$, $V = 200$, monochrome graphics

We will assume that no color set is available (they are expensive) and that we want the maximum resolution. Therefore, we will choose the 640 by 200 graphics mode ($n = 6$). This gives us a black background and white drawing (or green or amber, depending on CRT type).

CONTROLLING THE TURTLE

As we know, the turtle must be moved about to get an image on the screen. There are two fundamentally different types of move instructions: absolute and relative move commands. In an **absolute move command**, the turtle is moved (or turned) to a final position (or orientation) that is stated explicitly in the command. In a **relative move command**, it is the *change* from the turtle's current position (or orientation) that is explicitly stated in the command. When giving a relative move command, the user is obliged to keep track of where the turtle is and how it faces, since the statement contains no reminders about the turtle's absolute parameters.

Absolute Move Procedures

The absolute move command moves the turtle to any desired point on the screen. The Turtlegraphics procedure to do this, MOVETO, has the following form:

```
MOVETO(x,y:real);
```

where x and y are the coordinates of the turtle's destination. The turtle's direction is ignored by the MOVETO command and remains unchanged by it. Note that x and y are of type *real*. This is a convenience that allows the (usually real) results of calculations to be used as parameters in the procedure.

Example. MOVETO(75,100) moves the turtle to the point whose screen coordinates are $x = 75$ and $y = 100$ (see figure 2.3).

MOVETO is the most powerful of the moving procedures. Technically, it is the only move command a system needs, since it can be used by itself to create an entire drawing. Most systems have a procedure that is either the equivalent of MOVETO or very similar. Therefore, few readers should have problems implementing a command like this.

Turtlegraphics packages have three other move commands—one an absolute move command and the others relative move commands—that will be described here for the benefit of p-System users. Some of our routines allow for their *possible* use; in only one case do we make explicit use of them.

TURNTO(angle:real) causes the turtle to face in the direction specified by the argument *angle*. The convention for specifying the direction is shown in figure 2.4. Several aspects of turning should be noted. First, turning, in itself, is not visible on the screen; the function of turning the turtle is simply to prepare it to move in the desired direction when the relative move procedure (see next section) is invoked. Second, the new direction is independent of the old one. Finally, the turtle's position remains unchanged.

Example. TURNTO(340) turns the turtle so that it faces in the direction shown in figure 2.5. TURNTO(−20) has the same effect.

Relative Move Procedures

MOVE(distance:real) causes the turtle to move in the direction it faces. The argument *distance* is the number of device coordinate units the turtle is to move. The turtle's direction is unchanged by the MOVE procedure.

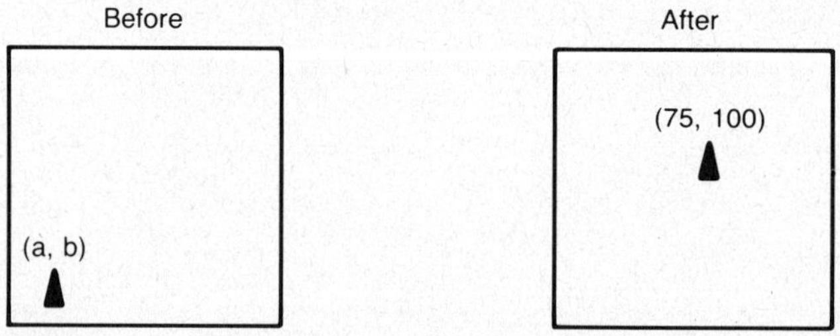

Figure 2.3 The MOVETO instruction. With MOVETO(75,100), the turtle's direction is unchanged. (*Note*: The triangle indicating the turtle's direction here is not visible on the screen.)

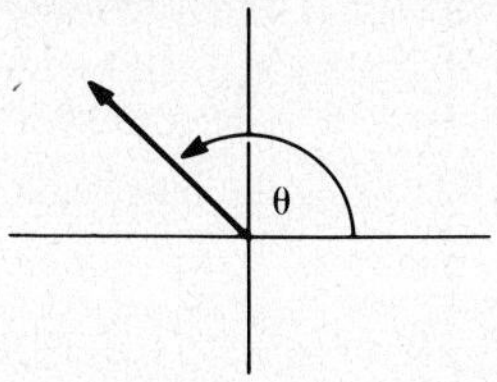

Figure 2.4 Angle convention.

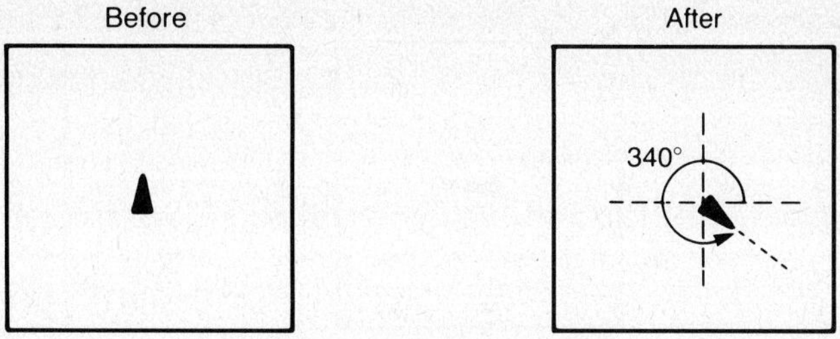

Figure 2.5 Execution of `TURNTO(340)`.

Example. `MOVE(70)` causes the turtle to move 70 units in its current direction (figure 2.6).

`TURN(degrees:real)` is used to change the direction in which the turtle faces. The argument *degrees* is the number of degrees turned from the current position. By convention, the turtle turns counterclockwise when *degrees* is positive, clockwise when *degrees* is negative. The turtle's position does not change with this procedure. As with `TURNTO`, nothing visible happens.

Example. `TURN(45)` turns the turtle 45 degrees counterclockwise from its current position (figure 2.7).

Example. `TURN(−20)` turns the turtle 20 degrees clockwise from its current position.

DRAWING MODES

As already noted, the turtle can draw or not draw as it moves, depending on what we desire. Turtlegraphics designers have also endowed the turtle with

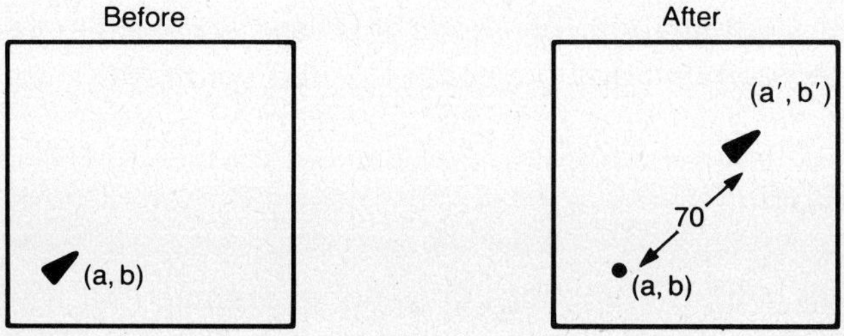

Figure 2.6 Execution of `MOVE(70)`.

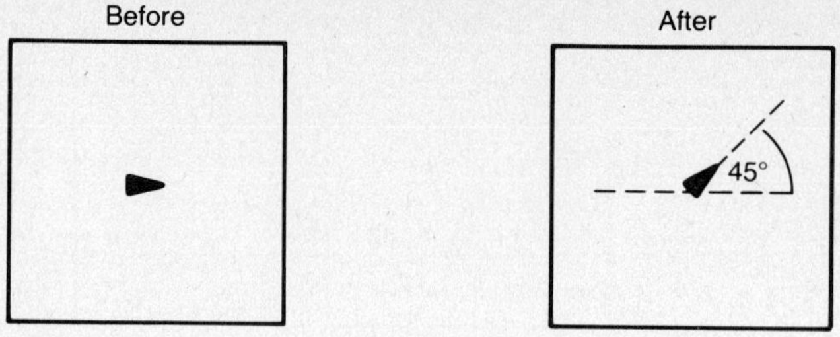

Figure 2.7 Execution of `TURN(45)`.

powers beyond those two. For our purposes, the only additional drawing feature we need is the ability to erase. The IBM p-System has two procedures that control the drawing mode: PENCOLOR, which sets the drawing color, and PENMODE, which basically determines what the turtle does with the pen. The formats of these procedures are as follows:

```
PENCOLOR(color:integer);
PENMODE(mode:integer);
```

The choices for the variable *color* depend on the selection made by VIDEOMODE. Since we have assumed the 640 by 200 monochrome mode, there is obviously no choice of color:

color = 0: pen draws black

color = 1: pen draws normal screen color (white, green, amber)

For the variable *mode*, three choices are of interest to us:

mode = 0: turtle moves without drawing

mode = 2: turtle draws according to PENCOLOR

mode = 4: turtle erases

Note that the combination of *mode* = 0 and *color* = 1 is functionally equivalent to the combination of *mode* = 2 and *color* = 0.

INITIALIZING GRAPHICS

Merely invoking graphics functions does not guarantee that we can go ahead and create graphics. Most systems require that some preliminary steps be taken. For example, p-System graphics routines are part of one or more groups of related routines called UNITS, which are stored on a disk in a file called SYSTEM.LIBRARY. If a programmer desires to use a routine from SYSTEM.LIBRARY, he or she must specify the UNIT where it is found. In the p-System, this is done with the USES declaration, as shown in the following example.

Example. The IBM-p-System has graphics routines in two UNITs, one called IBMSPECIAL, the other called TURTLEGRAPHICS. Hence, the start of a graphics program looks like this:

```
PROGRAM somename;

USES
    IBMSPECIAL, TURTLEGRAPHICS;
        (etc.)
```

LABELS

Any character or string of characters that we wish to display on a graphics screen is called a **label**. Since characters are normally sent to the text screen, the system must have a way of redirecting such information to the graphics screen.

The IBM PC writes labels without moving the turtle. It has a procedure called ALIGNCURSOR that positions a cursor at the starting point of the string. Then a call to the standard WRITE or WRITELN procedure writes the string to the graphics screen. Note the the cursor cannot be seen.

Example. Assuming that the variable *str* has the value "hello", the statements

```
ALIGNCURSOR(50,50);
WRITELN(str);
```

would put the label "hello" starting at the point (50, 50).

PROBLEMS

2.1. In some computers, one can read the contents of a specific byte of the memory. The system can be designed so that when a particular location is read, a certain system function is activated. When that location is read again, the function is deactivated. We refer to this arrangement as a **soft switch**. Suppose that a hypothetical computer has the following set of soft switches to control its pages:

Location	*Mode*
100	600 × 400
101	600 × 200
102	300 × 200
103	300 × 100
104	80-col. text
105	40-col. text

Suppose that the system has a function called `MEM(loc)` that switches *loc* one way or the other when invoked.

(a) Write a Pascal routine that is similar to `VIDEOMODE(n)` where *n* is an integer. Assume that the system gives an error message if an attempt is made to have more than one mode in effect at one time.

(b) What is the minimum amount of memory that the system must reserve for its graphics?

2.2. How would you implement the functions `TURN`, `TURNTO`, and `MOVE` on a system that has only the `MOVETO` command? Assume that the system has the trigonometric functions `SIN` and `COS`. Define any variables that you need, and state whether they should be global or local. How would you implement the above three functions on Turbo Pascal (Appendix C)?

2.3. For the graphics procedures of your system, find out about these small but important details:

(a) Are the arguments to procedures integers or reals?

(b) If `MOVETO` accepts reals, does it use `ROUND` or `TRUNC` to get rid of the decimal part of a device coordinate?

(c) After a graphics program runs, does the system automatically return to a text mode? If so, what can you do to delay that step (so that the image does not disppear from the screen immediately)?

(d) Can a cursor be seen on the screen in any of the graphics modes?

(e) What are the default values of the various procedures?

REFERENCES

Hume, J. N. P., and Holt, R. C. *UCSD Pascal: A Beginner's Guide to Programming Microcomputers*. Reston, Va.: Reston, 1982, chapter 13.

IBM User's Guide for the UCSD p-System. Boca Raton, Fla.: IBM Corporation, 1982, book 2, chapter 5.

Turbo Pascal Reference Manual Addendum. Scotts Valley, Calif.: Borland International, 1984, pp. 17–24.

Chapter 3

Graphs and Polygons

When you have finished this chapter, you will be able to use the graphics commands introduced in the preceding chapter to produce simple two-dimensional shapes.

Objectives

1. To understand the relationship between device and world coordinates.
2. To learn how to plot line and bar graphs.
3. To learn how to draw and fill polygons.

As you undoubtedly know, graphs of all sorts are used to reduce large quantities of data into easily understandable form. Line graphs can be used to plot real physical data (temperature, pressure, and so forth) or abstract quantities (projected population growth, future reliance on imported energy, and the like). Bar graphs are used when a given quantity (such as profit) must be broken down into categories (such as quarters). In this chapter, we use line and bar graphs as vehicles for introducing the IBM coordinate system and procedures for drawing simple shapes.

WORLD COORDINATES

The device coordinates that define the graphics screen are a poor representation of the real world for several reasons. First, device coordinate values can never be negative. Also, device coordinate *boundaries* rarely correspond to the maxima and minima found in real-world data. In fact, a particular real-world situation is best represented by a specific choice of coordinate values; no single choice can possibly be adequate for all situations.

A coordinate system that is appropriate for a given problem—referred to as a *world coordinate* system—is the system with which the computer graphics user deals most comfortably with a given problem. Unfortunately, computers are comfortable only with device coordinates. Therefore, our first order of business is the problem of mapping the world system to the device system.

CONVERTING TO DEVICE COORDINATES

Suppose that we are interested in plotting the rise and fall of the sea surface—the tides—over a 24-hour period. Suppose, further, that the water level is never more than 10 feet above or below normal. If we plot time along the x-axis and surface height deviations along the y-axis, the world x-axis will be 24 units long and the world y-axis will be 20 units long. Most likely, these are not the same as the device values. How can we make them correspond?

Consider figure 3.1a, which shows three points on a horizontal line across the screen. We are interested in the x-coordinate of each point in both the world and the device systems. (We'll deal with the y-coordinate later.) At the left boundary, the x-coordinate is 0 in the world system (time starts at 0 hours) and, of course, 0 in the device system. At the right boundary, the x-coordinate is 24 in the world system (time ends at 24 hours). Its value in the

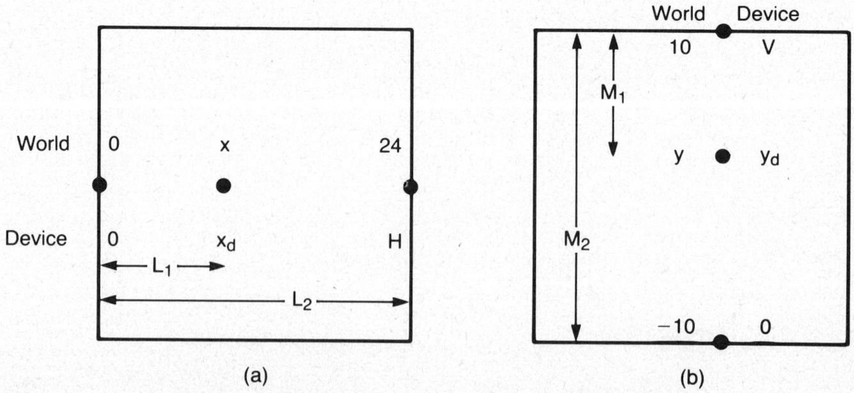

Figure 3.1 Geometry for tide problem derivations. (a) x-coordinate conversion. (b) y-coordinate conversion.

device system, however, is the horizontal resolution H. For all other points, we will denote the world x-value by x and the device x-value by x_d.

We would like to find an expression for x_d in terms of x. To do this, we will set up two expressions for the ratio L_1/L_2 (refer to the figure)—one in the device system and one in the world system. Since this ratio must be the same regardless of coordinate system, we can set the two expressions equal. This will lead to a conversion equation. Using the quantities indicated in figure 3.1a, we have

World system: $L_1 = x - 0$

$L_2 = 24 - 0$

Device system: $L_1 = x_d - 0$

$L_2 = H - 0$

Forming the ratio L_1/L_2 in each system and setting them equal yields:

$$(x - 0)/(24 - 0) = (x_d - 0)/(24 - 0)$$

Solving for x_d yields:

$$x_d = x \cdot H/24 \qquad (3.1)$$

For the y-coordinates, we follow the same procedure, but we use the parameters indicated in figure 3.1b. The lower screen boundary has a world y-coordinate of -10 and a device y-coordinate of 0. The upper boundary has a world y-coordinate of 10 and a device y-coordinate equal to the vertical resolution V. All other points have world y-coordinates denoted by y and device y-coordinates denoted by y_d. Referring to figure 3.1b, we have:

World system: $M_1 = y - 10$

$M_2 = 10 - (-10) = 20$

Device system: $M_1 = y_d - V$

$M_2 = V - 0$

Forming the ratio M_1/M_2 in both systems and setting them equal yields:

$$y_d = V(y + 10)/20 \qquad (3.2)$$

These equations enable us to do the conversions, but they have two inherent flaws: they are good only for this particular problem, and they use the entire screen for the graph, leaving no space for a border. Fortunately, IBM's implementation of the p-System has a procedure that takes care of these problems for us—the procedure DISPLAYSCALE. DISPLAYSCALE does the conversions for us when we specify the extremes of the x- and y-coordinates of the world system. The form of DISPLAYSCALE is as follows:

```
DISPLAYSCALE(xmin,ymin,xmax,ymax:real)
```

where the parameters are the minimum and maximum *x*- and *y*-coordinates of the world values.

Example. In the tide problem, we would write

```
DISPLAYSCALE(0,−10,24,10)
```

The point 0 hours and −10 feet is at the lower left of the screen; 24 hours and 10 feet is at the upper right.

What about borders around the graph? If we want them, we must pass values to *xmax* and *ymax* that are greater than the actual maxima in the world data (and *xmin* and *ymin* that are smaller than the actual world minima).

Examples. In the tide problem, we could have written

```
DISPLAYSCALE(−4,−15,28,15)
```

Then the lower left of the screen would theoretically be the point −4 hours and −15 feet. Since the smallest world values are 0 hours and −10 feet, that point would be plotted upward and to the right of the corner. Similarly, the largest world values, 24 hours and 10 feet, would be plotted downward and to the left of the upper right of the screen. Figure 3.2 illustrates this plotting.

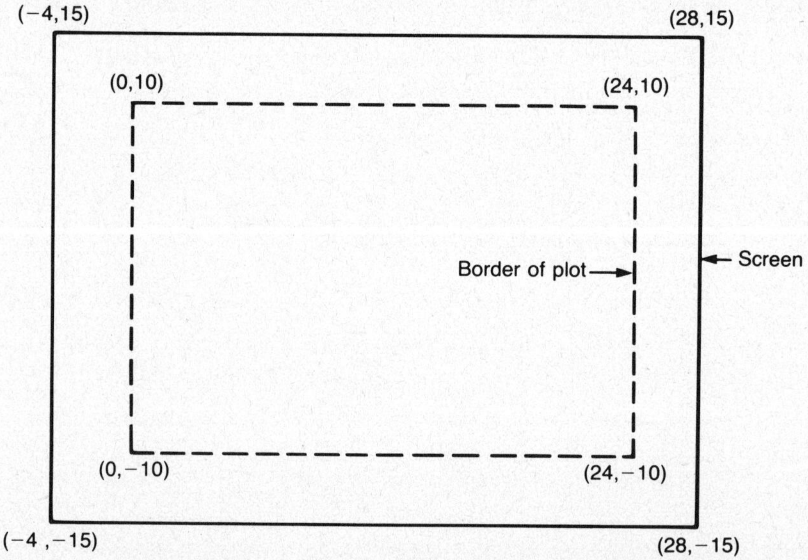

Figure 3.2 Leaving borders on a screen. If we choose xmin = −4, ymin = −15, xmax = 28, and ymax = 15, then the actual plot does not extend beyond the dashed lines.

From this point on, we will refer to the *xmin, xmax, ymin,* and *ymax* that we pass to DISPLAYSCALE as the **scaling parameters**. They can be considered arbitrary in the sense that we can choose them as we please. However, we must be aware of the actual values in the data so that our choice is a wise one.

CREATING LINE GRAPHS

Generating the Plot

Let us write a short program to illustrate the ideas we have discussed. We will leave the task of plotting a set of data points for a later exercise. Instead, we will plot the following equation:

$$y = 2x - 5$$

and let the program generate the points. This is a straight line that slopes upward to the right; we arbitrarily choose to plot it from $x = -4$ to $x = 8$. Hence, $xmin = -4$ and $xmax = 8$. From the equation, we can figure out that $ymin = -13$ and $ymax = 11$. Note that this leaves no border around the graph.

Program 3.1: Graph of $y = 2x - 5$

```
PROGRAM GRAPHLINE
USES TURTLEGRAPHICS, IBMSPECIAL:
VAR x,y:REAL;

BEGIN
  VIDEOMODE(6);
  DISPLAYSCALE(-4,-13,8,11);
  PENMODE(1);
  PENCOLOR(0);
  x:= -4;
  WHILE x < 9 DO
    BEGIN
      y:= 2*x - 5;
      MOVETO(x,y);
      PENCOLOR(1);
      x:= x + 1
    END;
  READLN;
  VIDEOMODE(2)
END.
```

Here is how the program works: After the first *x*-value, $x = -4$, is chosen, the program enters a loop. First, the *y*-value that corresponds to

$x = -4$ is calculated. The turtle is moved (without drawing) to (x, y). Then the x value is incremented by one unit. Nothing has been plotted yet; the turtle has simply been placed at the first point on the line.

The program then executes the second pass of the loop. A new y-coordinate is calculated for the newly incremented x. Now, however, PENCOLOR is 1, so when the turtle moves to the new point, it draws a line. After this, the x-value is incremented and the loop repeats. So long as the value of x is less than or equal to 8, the steps in this loop repeat. This is how the line gets drawn.

Note the READLN statement near the end of the program; this provides a pause that gives us as much time as we want to look at the drawing. Note, too, that we must switch back to the text mode, VIDEOMODE(2), before the program ends. Otherwise, we will not be able to see the cursor.

Figure 3.3 shows several possible results of the foregoing graph program. In figure 3.3a, we see the graph for DISPLAYSCALE(−4,−13,8,11). To get figure 3.3b, we ran the program with DISPLAYSCALE(−4, −15,8,13). This gave us top and bottom borders, since the choice of *ymax* was larger (and *ymin* was smaller) than the values in the data. To get figure 3.3c, we ran the program with DISPLAYSCALE(−6,−15,10,13). Note that *xmax* and *ymax* are larger (and *xmin* and *ymin* are smaller) than the values in the data; thus, there is a border on all sides.

Although the program just given is for a very simple equation, complex equations would be done similarly. The program line

```
y:= 2*x - 5
```

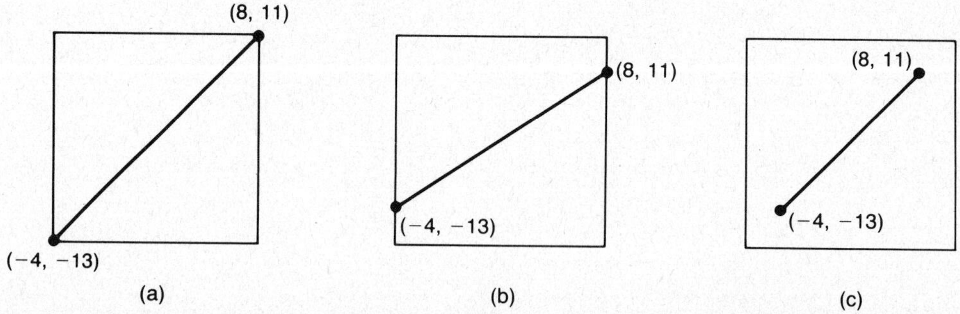

Figure 3.3 Plot of $y = 2x - 5$ under three different conditions. (a) $xmin = -4$, $xmax = 8$, $ymax = 11$, $ymin = -13$. (b) $xmin = -4$, $xmax = 8$, $ymax = 13$, $ymin = -15$. (c) $xmin = -6$, $xmax = 10$, $ymax = 13$, $ymin = -15$.

would change to reflect the different function; also, different parameters would be used.

A final note: From this point on, all illustrative routines will consist of only relevant procedures, not entire programs. This will save us the trouble of listing code that is part of every program such as VIDEOMODE, DISPLAYSCALE, and the like. Also, procedure headings will almost always be written without parameter lists. In other words, decisions about global variables and parameter passing will be entirely up to you when you write your programs.

Drawing Axes

The plots created in the preceding section look rather bare; they lack the two coordinate axes that serve as a frame of reference: the lines $x = 0$ (y-axis) and $y = 0$ (x-axis). Note that these are world values; one must avoid the mistake of simply plotting $x_d = 0$ and $y_d = 0$, because such a choice would always put the axes at the left and bottom of the screen, whether or not they belong there. The correct placement of the axes is a function of the scaling parameters. We would expect, for example, that if $xmin = -xmax$, the y-axis would be centered between left and right. Program 3.2 gives a simple procedure to draw axes. The comments in the program should be sufficient to explain its simple action.

Program 3.2: Construction of Axes

```
PROCEDURE AXES;

BEGIN
  PENMODE(1);
  PENCOLOR(0);        {turn pen off}
  MOVETO(xmin,0);         {move to left border}
  PENCOLOR(1);        {turn pen on}
  MOVETO(xmax,0);         {draw line to right border}
  PENCOLOR(0);        {turn pen off}
  MOVETO(0,ymin);         {move to bottom}
  PENCOLOR(1);        {turn pen on}
  MOVETO(0,ymax);         {draw line to top}
  PENCOLOR(0)
END;
```

PLOTTING SIMPLE SHAPES: THE BAR GRAPH

The plotting we do in this text involves various shapes. In this section, we will start with an easy shape—a rectangle—and use it to plot a bar graph.

Consider a typical bar graph, as illustrated in figure 3.4. It is constructed so that for every category of data, there is a bar that extends above or below a horizontal axis. This extension, which we refer to as the height of the bar, is proportional to the magnitude of the quantity the bar represents. There are a number of ways to plot a bar graph on the screen. We have chosen one that makes use of the fact that a bar graph is basically a collection of rectangles. The heart of our arrangement is a procedure (to be outlined shortly) that can draw a rectangle anyplace on the screen with any specified height and width. The bar graph itself is drawn by a main program that makes repeated calls to this procedure, passing an appropriate set of parameters to it with each call.

What are these parameters and how do we find them? The first parameter is the height. For simplicity, we will assume that we know the height of each category. Then we can input the heights directly from the keyboard and store them in an array.

The second parameter is the width. This parameter depends essentially on the total number of categories (bars). Consider that each bar in figure 3.5 is surrounded by a space. We can simplify matters by letting this space be equal to the width of a bar. Since there are n bars, there $n + 1$ spaces. The total width of the graph is then

$$\text{Screen width} = nW + (n + 1)W$$
$$= (2n + 1)W$$

If we want the graph to take up some fraction $f(0 < f \leq 1)$ of the total width, then we can write:

$$(2n + 1)W = fH$$

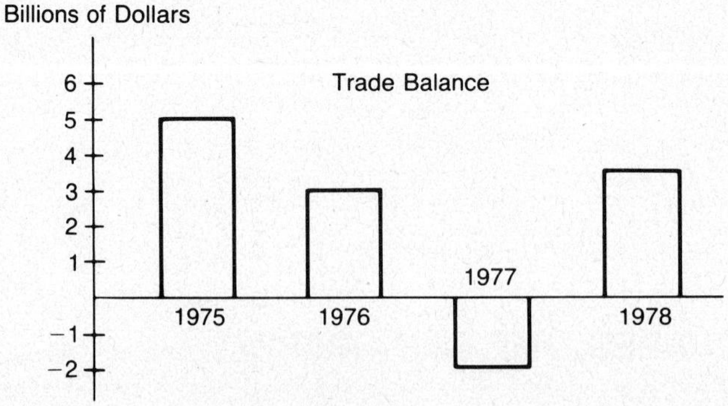

Figure 3.4 A typical bar graph.

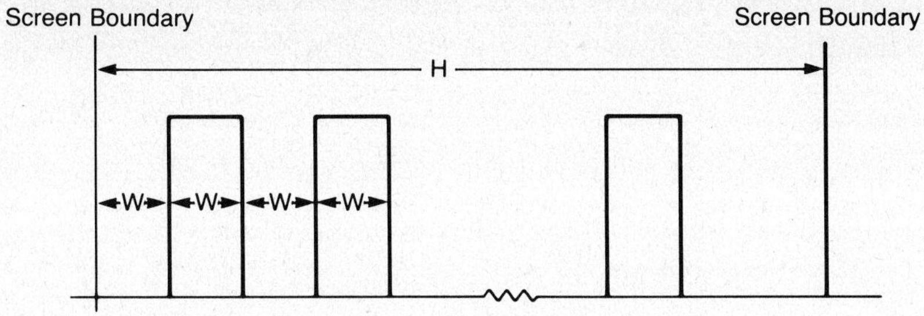

Figure 3.5 Geometry for bar graph derivation.

Solving this for the width, W, yields:

$$W = fH/(2n + 1)$$

Note that the width is given in device coordinates, while the height is given in world coordinates.

Finally, we must tell the procedure where the bar should be located. For this, all we need are the coordinates of one vertex. We will choose the one located at the left of the bar on the horizontal axis and call it the *initial vertex.* Its y-coordinate, which is the same for all bars, will be called y_0. Its x-coordinate depends on which bar we consider. The explicit expressions for the first four bars are as follows:

#1: $x = W$

#2: $x = 3W$

#3: $x = 5W$

#4: $x = 7W$

Clearly, the general expression for the x-coordinate of the initial vertex of the kth bar is

$$x = (2k - 1)W$$

Program 3.3: Procedure to Draw a Bar Graph Rectangle

Assumptions. y_0 = y-coordinate of initial vertex; $y[k]$ = height of k-th bar

```
PROCEDURE DRAWBAR;
BEGIN
  PENMODE(1);
  PENCOLOR(0);
  MOVETO(x,y0);
```

```
  PENCOLOR(1);
  MOVETO(x,y[k]);
  MOVETO(x + w,y[k]);
  MOVETO(x + w,y0)
END;
```

Program 3.4: Using DRAWBAR in a Program

Assumption. n = number of bars.

```
PROCEDURE BARGRAPH;
VAR k:INTEGER;

BEGIN
  FOR k := 1 to n DO
    BEGIN
      x := (2*k - 1)*width;          {calculate x-coordinate of}
      DRAWBAR                              {initial vertex}
    END                                {then call DRAWBAR}
END;
```

POLYGONS

A polygon is simply a many-sided, closed figure. Polygons of many shapes are used in computer graphics problems. For the components in a floor plan, for example, an architect would use a variety of polygons. Similarly, the designer of a microprocessor would use polygons, mostly rectangles, to represent the different sections. The rectangles that we just considered are special cases of polygons with rather desirable features: their internal angles are all 90 degrees, and each side is parallel to one of the two axes. This makes them easy to draw, both in outline and in solid form. Most polygons don't have these characteristics, however. Therefore, this section is devoted to learning how to deal with an arbitrary, n-sided polygon.

It is useful to understand the mathematical difference between a convex polygon and a concave polygon. Figure 3.6 illustrates both types. First, consider the convex polygon in figure 3.6a. Draw two points inside the figure and connect them with a line. No matter which two inside points you use, the line connecting them lies entirely inside the figure. For the concave polygon in figure 3.6b, it is clearly possible to find two points inside the figure such that a line connecting them lies partially outside the figure.

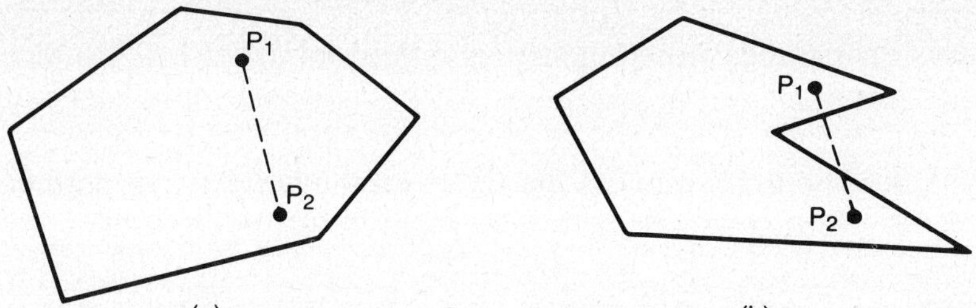

(a) (b)

Figure 3.6 Polygons. (a) Convex polygon. (b) Concave polygon. Note that lines joining two inside points of a concave polygon are not always completely inside the figure.

Drawing a Polygon

Let us first consider the simplest possible case, the regular polygon, in which all sides are equal and all internal angles are equal. The formula for the internal angle is

$$\theta = 180 \cdot (n - 2)/n$$

A regular pentagon, for example, has interior angles of 108 degrees. We will illustrate this simple case with relative move commands.

Program 3.5: Drawing a Regular Polygon with Relative Move Commands

Assumption. Side, Angle are known beforehand.

```
PROCEDURE POLY1;
  VAR j:integer;

BEGIN
  FOR j:= 1 to numsides DO
  BEGIN
    MOVE(side);
    TURN(angle)
  END
END;
```

We have assumed that the turtle has the desired location and orientation prior to the procedure call. If the polygon were irregular, side and angle information would have to be provided for each of the *n* sides and angles. We will draw irregular polygons by using the MOVETO procedure; this requires that we have the vertices stored in an array. We will use the following convention for this array:

1. The first vertex is the one with the smallest x-coordinate.
2. Subsequent vertices are stored in clockwise order.

Program 3.6: Drawing a Polygon with the Absolute Move Command

Assumption. x, y: array [0..numsides − 1] of real

```
PROCEDURE POLY2;
  VAR j:integer;

BEGIN
  PENMODE(1);
  PENCOLOR(0);
  MOVETO(x[0],y[0]);
  PENCOLOR(1);
  FOR j:= 1 to numsides-1 DO
    MOVETO(x[j],y[j]);
  MOVETO(x[0],y[0])
END;
```

Note that the coordinates of the first vertex are labeled (x[0], y[0]), not (x[1], y[1]). This will be useful later on.

Filling the Polygon

In our discussion of the bar graph, we initially drew the bars as outlines. If you do problem 3.4, you will see that it takes only a slight modification of the procedure to redraw them as filled (solid) rectangles. The easy transition from outline to filled rectangle is made possible by the fact that all sides are parallel to one or the other coordinate axes.

A quick glance at figure 3.6 will show that we have no such luck in the case of an irregular polygon. In fact, filling an irregular polygon requires a fair amount of work. The general idea, however, is not difficult. The interior of any polygon is made up of sections of scan lines that lie within the polygon boundaries (figure 3.7). In a filled polygon, the pixels that compose those sections are all lit. We can determine what those sections are if we know where each scan line intersects the polygon boundaries. Once we know the intersection points, we can issue plot instructions to the turtle. In summary, a general filling procedure should do the following:

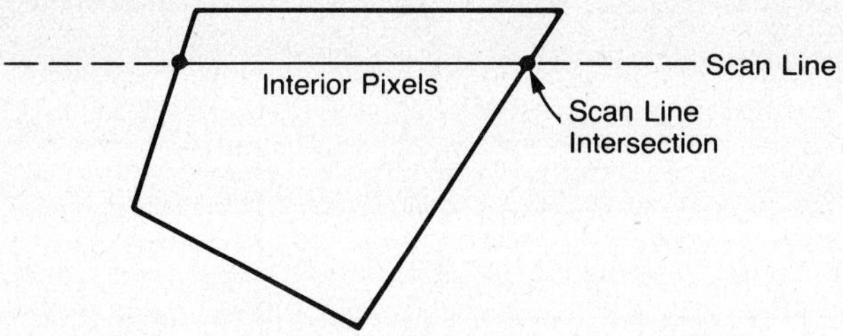

Figure 3.7 Intersection of scan line with polygon.

1. Search the y-coordinates of the vertices to find the largest and smallest values.
2. For every scan line between those values, determine the points of intersection with the polygon.
3. Light the interior pixels by moving the turtle between appropriate intersection points.

We will write a procedure that does the last two, leaving the search routine for a later exercise.

Qualitative Considerations Figure 3.8 shows a rather bizarre-looking polygon with several intersecting scan lines. These lines were chosen to illustrate all possible ways a scan line can intersect a polygon. Any procedure that we write must be able to handle all these cases.

Case 1. Line L_1 intersects the polygon only once, at its lowest vertex. Since no pixel on this scan line, other than the vertex, should be lit, our procedure should ignore this intersection. The vertex, of course, is already lit.

Case 2. Line L_2 intersects at two points, one of which is a vertex. Clearly, all the pixels between B_1 and B_2 should be lit. Hence, the intersection with this vertex cannot be ignored. Our procedure must be able to determine when an intersection with a vertex can and cannot be ignored.

Case 3. Line L_3 intersects at three points. Since all pixels between C_1 and C_3 should be lit, our procedure should ignore the intersection at C_2.

Case 4. Line L_4 coincides completely with side S_3, which is horizontal. Since every pixel between D_1 and D_2 should be lit, our procedure can act as if side S_3 does not exist. Also, the pixels between D_2 and D_3 should not be lit, while those between D_3 and D_4 should be lit.

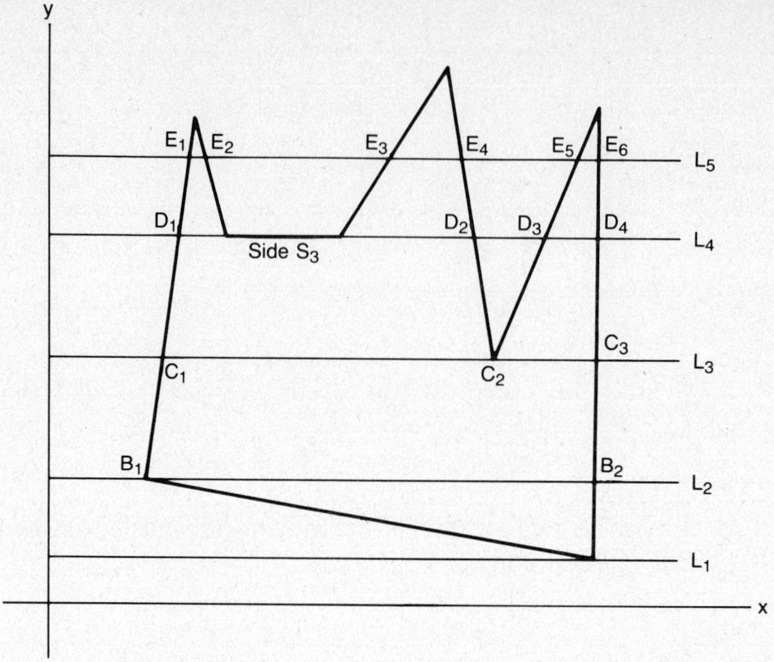

Figure 3.8 Different types of intersections of scan lines with polygon sides.

Case 5. Line L_5 intersects at six points, none of which should be ignored. The pixels between E_1 and E_2, E_3 and E_4, and E_5 and E_6 should all be lit.

Programming Considerations The first step in our algorithm should be a check for intersections. We do this by testing a scan line against each side. We compare the y-value of the scan line (*yscan*) to the y-coordinates of the endpoints of a side:

1. If the y-coordinates of the endpoints are both greater (or both smaller) than *yscan* (figure 3.9a,b), there is no intersection.
2. If the y-coordinate of one endpoint equals *yscan* (figure 3.9c), the intersection is at a vertex.
3. If the y-coordinates of both endpoints equal *yscan* (figure 3.9d), the side is horizontal.
4. If one y-coordinate is less than *yscan* and the other is greater than *yscan* (figure 3.9e), the scan line intersects that side.

Having determined the type of intersection, we must take further action:

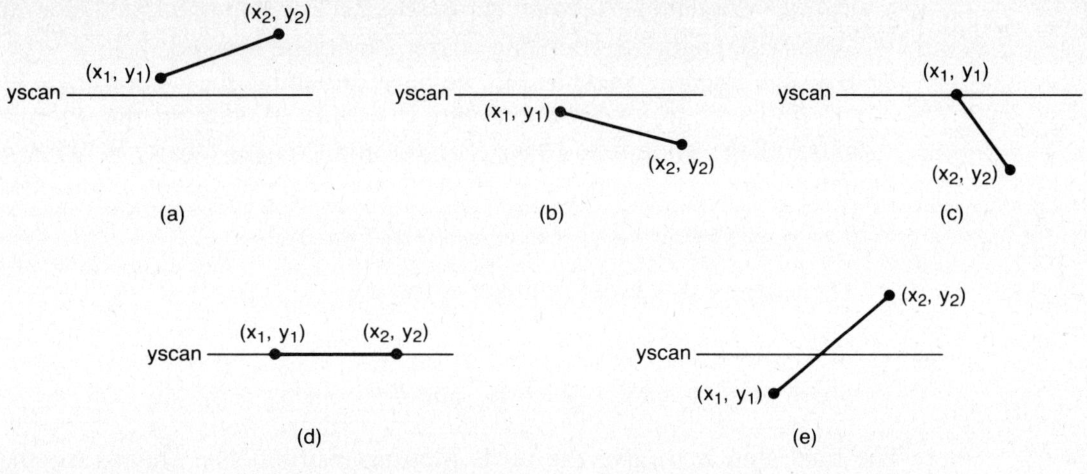

Figure 3.9 Tests for possible intersections. (a) $y_1, y_2 > yscan$: no intersection. (b) $(y_1, y_2) < yscan$: no intersection. (c) $y_1 = yscan$: intersection at vertex. (d) $y_1 = y_2 = yscan$: horizontal segment. (e) $y_1 < yscan < y_2$: intersection between segment endpoints.

1. If the intersected side is horizontal, we simply ignore it and proceed to the examination of the next side.
2. If the intersection is a vertex, we check the y-coordinates of the vertices just before and just after the one in question. If those coordinates are both greater than (or both less than) *yscan* (figure 3.10a,b), the two sides involved lie on the same side of the scan line.

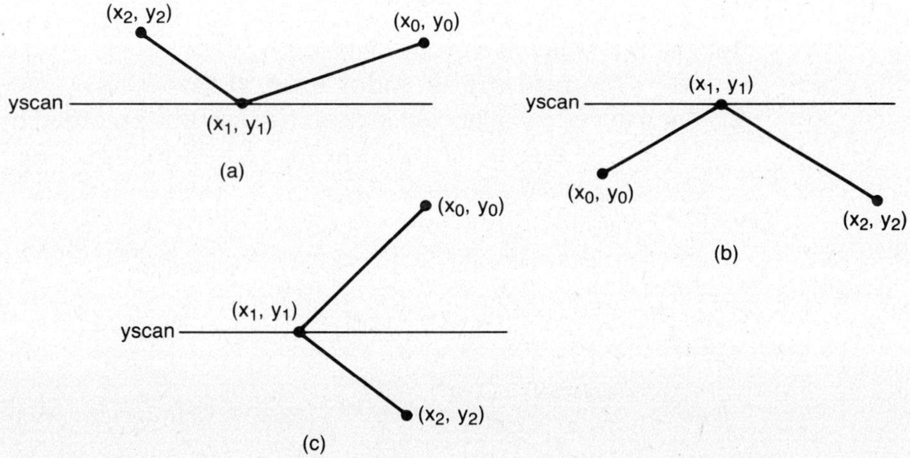

Figure 3.10 Vertex intersection tests. (a) $y_0, y_2 > y_1$: ignore intersection. (b) $(y_0, y_2) < y_1$: ignore intersection. (c) y_1 between y_0 and y_2: do *not* ignore intersection.

Hence, the vertex is like C_2 of figure 3.8 and can be ignored. Otherwise (figure 3.10c), the vertex cannot be ignored.

3. If a scan line intersects a side, we must determine the x-coordinate of the intersection (the y-coordinate $= yscan$). Assuming the coordinates of the endpoints to be (x_0, y_0) and (x_1, y_1) (figure 3.11), we have:

$$y - y_0 = (xint - x_0) \cdot (y_1 - y_0)/(x_1 - x_0)$$

Then we let $y = yscan$ and solve for x:

$$xint = (yscan - b)/m$$

where $m = (y_1 - y_0)/(x_1 - x_0)$ and $b = -m \cdot x_0 + y_0$.

The final step is to give the turtle plotting instructions. Thanks to our scheme of eliminating certain intersections, the total number of intersections is always even. This is very important; the actual fill command is a plot instruction that causes the turtle to draw from an odd-numbered intersection to an even-numbered one, then simply move without drawing from even to odd. Study figure 3.8 carefully to convince yourself of this even-odd arrangement.

A note about sides and vertices is necessary here. We need to be able to refer to a side or vertex as *previous* or *following*. Suppose that we label the sides with the integer n. Then the following side is $n + 1$, and the previous side is $n - 1$. This scheme breaks down, however, when we are dealing with the last side or the first side. Side 4 of a quadrilateral, for example, is preceded by side $4 - 1 = 3$, but it is not followed by side $4 + 1$! We therefore use the following labeling scheme:

1. The nth side has vertices labeled `(n - 1) mod sides` and `n mod sides`.
2. The kth vertex is labeled `k mod sides`. It is preceded by one labeled `(k - 1 + sides) mod sides` and is followed by one labeled `(k + 1) mod sides`.

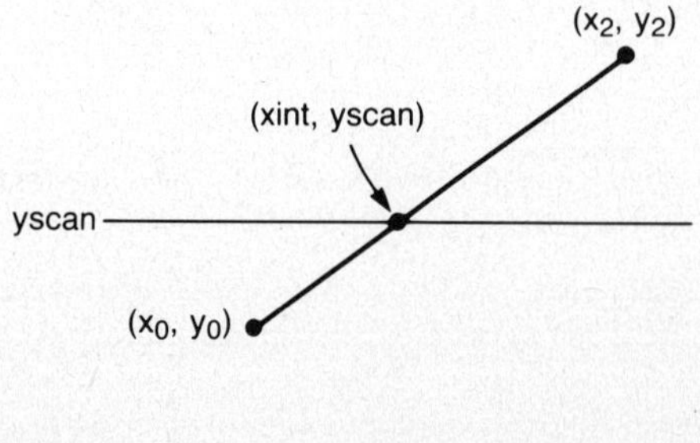

Figure 3.11 Geometry for determining the x-coordinate of an intersection.

This scheme assumes that you follow the conventions for entering the vertices in the array. (Problem 3.9 asks you to verify the labeling scheme.)

Program 3.7: Filling an Arbitrary Polygon

Assumptions. Coordinates of vertices are arrays *x* and *y*; highest (top) and lowest (bottom) scan lines are known before procedure is called

```
PROCEDURE FILL;

BEGIN {proc}
FOR yscan := bottom to top DO
BEGIN {1}
j := 0;      {counts intersections}
FOR n := 1 to sides DO                {run routine for each side}
  BEGIN {2}
  y0 := y[(n-1) mod sides];           {y0, y1 are the y-coordinates}
  y1 := y[n mod sides];               {of the endpoints of a side}
  IF y0 < > y1                        {make sure side not horizontal}
  THEN                                    {else get next side}
    BEGIN {3}
    x0 := x[(n-1) mod sides];         {x0, x1 are x-coordinates of}
    x1 := x[n mod sides];             {the endpoints of the side}
    IF (yscan = y0) OR                {is intersection a vertex?}
      (yscan = y1)
    THEN
     BEGIN {4}
     IF yscan = y0                    {yes? then find y-coordinates}
     THEN k := n-1                    {of the surrounding vertices,}
     ELSE k := n;
     pt1 := y[(k - 1 + sides)         {namely, pt1 and pt2}
       mod sides];
     pt2 := y[(k + 1) mod sides];
     IF ((pt1 < yscan) AND            {yes? then vertex is}
       (pt2 > yscan)) OR
        ((pt1 > yscan) AND            {not ignorable}
       (pt2 < yscan))
     THEN
     BEGIN {5}
     j := j + 1;                      {increment the vertex counter}
     xint[j] := x[k mod sides]        {get x-coordinate of the}
     END {5}                          {intersection}
     END {4}
    ELSE
    IF ((yscan > y0) AND (yscan < y1)) OR {if intersection is not}
    ((yscan < y0) AND (yscan > y1))       {at a vertex}
```

```
    THEN
    BEGIN {6}
    j:=j + 1;
    IF x0 = x1                        {is the side vertical? get}
    THEN xint[j] := x0                {x-coordinate of intersection}
    ELSE
     BEGIN {7}                        {side not vertical?}
     m := (y1 - y0)/(x1 - x0);         {use formulas for the}
     b := -m*x0 + y0;                 {intersection}
     xint[j] := (yscan - b)/m
     END {7}
    END {6}
  END {3}
END; {2}
k := 2;
FOR i := 2 to j DO
  BEGIN {8}
  IF xint[i-1] < xint[i]
  THEN
    BEGIN {9}
    xint[k] := xint[i];
    k := k + 1
    END {9}
  END; {8}
j := 1;
WHILE j < k - 1 DO
  BEGIN {10}
  PENMODE(1);
  PENCOLOR(0);
  MOVETO(xint[j],yscan);
  PENCOLOR(1);
  MOVETO(xint[j+1],yscan );
  j := j + 2
  END {10}
END {1}
END; {proc}
```

The comments in the listing should provide most of the help needed to understand the part that determines the intersections. The sections labeled BEGIN {8} and BEGIN {9} eliminate the apparent duplication of intersections that arises when a scan line intersects a nonignorable vertex. Since the program checks each side against the scan line, it counts such an intersection twice. The last part of the program plots from an odd intersection to an even intersection.

PROBLEMS

3.1. In the following table, we have listed tidal data for a particular location. The data consist of hourly measurements of the number of meters the water surface rises or falls above a particular level.

Hour	*Distance*	*Hour*	*Distance*	*Hour*	*Distance*
1	1.00	9	2.40	17	−3.50
2	1.35	10	2.90	18	−4.90
3	1.65	11	3.15	19	−5.00
4	1.65	12	3.15	20	−4.65
5	1.65	13	2.00	21	−3.70
6	1.65	14	0.95	22	−2.25
7	1.80	15	−0.20	23	−0.45
8	2.00	16	−2.00	24	0.50

(a) Take two different graphs of the foregoing data, each with a different choice of scaling parameters. Label the axes appropriately, put a title on the graph, and label the area around 19 hours "low tide."
(b) Assume that you have the 24 distances on a disk, not in a table. Write a short routine that searches the values and determines the maximum and minimum. Then establish a formula that picks reasonable values for the scaling parameters based on the foregoing determination.
(c) Is the average of all the distances equal to zero? Find out by plotting a horizontal line at the average value.

3.2. The most general form of a sine curve is given by the formula

$$y = A \sin(Bx + C)$$

Suppose that you wish to demonstrate the effect of each of the three parameters, A, B, and C. (A is the amplitude, B is the frequency, and C is the phase.) Write a program that allows two plots to appear on the screen at the same time. Each plot should have equal values for two of the parameters but different values for the remaining one. Three possibilities are as follows:

Case 1: $A = 1$, $B = 1$, $C = 0$ or 0.79

Case 2: $B = 1$, $C = 0$, $A = 1$ or 2

Case 3: $A = 1$, $C = 0$, $B = 1$ or 3

Keep in mind that the value of x must be in radians. Also, when the program has finished, the user should have the option of trying the program again with different combinations.

3.3 Write a program to draw a bar chart from the following data. Label each bar with a two-letter abbreviation for the month. Then put a title on the chart and label the vertical axis with appropriate values.

Month	*Profits*	*Month*	*Profits*
1	5200	7	4600
2	6700	8	6000
3	4500	9	9200
4	−3000	10	9100
5	−6000	11	9000
6	−3100	12	7800

3.4 Modify procedure DRAWBAR so that it fills the rectangles as it draws them. Rework the problem 3.3 so that bars with positive values are filled.

3.5. Rederive the formula for the width of a bar without the assumption that the space between the bars is the same as the width. What is the general formula for the x_d-coordinate of the initial vertex in this case?

3.6. Write a DRAWBAR procedure using MOVE and TURN instructions.

3.7. Write the complete polygon drawing and filling program. Use procedure POLY to draw the figure and the procedure FILL to fill it. Design the program so that the empty figure is displayed for a short while, then filled as you watch. Test the program on a polygon like that shown in figure 3.8 (but use coordinates appropriate to your system).

3.8. What would happen to our scheme for labeling sides and vertices in FILL if we labeled the coordinates of the first vertex ($x[1]$, $y[1]$) instead of ($x[0]$, $y[0]$)? Why should the vertex with the smallest x-coordinate be the first one?

3.9. Verify the vertex labeling scheme that uses the mod function.

3.10. The path of a planet around the sun is technically an ellipse with the sun at one focus, but a circle is a reasonable approximation in most cases. For the planets in the following table, plot a diagram showing the relative size of the orbits. Label the sun, and place the name of each planet near its path.

Planet	*Distance from Sun (millions of km)*
Mercury	58
Venus	108
Earth	150
Mars	228

3.11. When a shell is fired from a cannon, its path (ignoring air resistance) has the shape of a parabola (see figure 3.12). The most convenient form of this curve for our needs is

$$y = [\tan(A)]x - 4.9x^2/[V\cos(A)]^2$$

where V = velocity at firing time (in meters per second) and A = angle of inclination of the gun. Using an initial velocity of 250 m/s, plot the parabola for

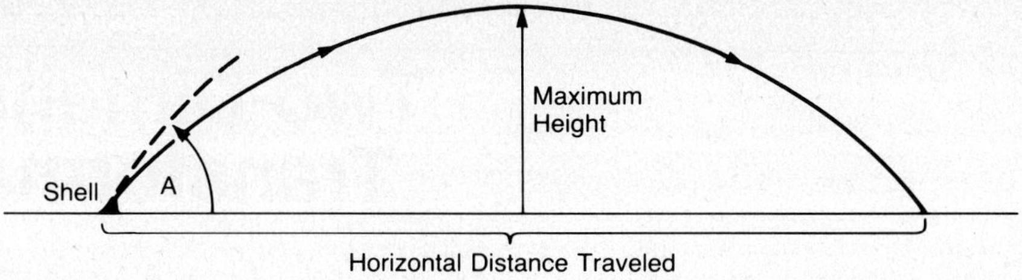

Figure 3.12 Parabola for problem 3.11.

various angles, being sure to include several values above and below 45 degrees. You will need the following data to make this plot:

Maximum height $= V^2 \sin(A)/17.6$

Maximum horizontal distance $= V^2 \cos(A)\sin(A)/4.9$

REFERENCES

Harrington, S. *Computer Graphics: A Programming Approach.* New York: McGraw-Hill, 1983, chapter 3.

Hearn, D., and Baker, M. P. *Microcomputer Graphics.* Englewood Cliffs, N.J.: Prentice-Hall, 1983, chapter 4.

Pavlidis, T. "Filling Algorithms for Raster Graphics." *Computer Graphics and Image Processing 10*, June 1979, 126–141.

Chapter 4

Two-Dimensional Transformations

When you have finished this chapter, you will be able to make calculated changes to the basic polygon shapes introduced in the preceding chapter.

Objectives

1. To introduce the concept of the centroid.
2. To understand several different transformations: translation, scaling, shearing, rotation, and reflection.
3. To understand the role of homogeneous coordinates.
4. To introduce the idea of interactive graphics.
5. To understand the ideas involved in animation.

By now, you should realize that an array of numbers is the raw material a computer needs to create an image. The numbers are passed to the system's graphics functions as arguments. A great advantage of a computer-generated image is that the array that defines it can be altered quickly and easily by the computer. Thus, an image can be transformed into a new one by a relatively simple mathematical operation, known as a **transformation**. Certain computer graphics problems make extensive use of transformations. For example, an engineer who was simulating the deformation of a steel beam would find transformations very useful. Also, a computer-assisted tutorial showing a particular chemistry lab procedure would make use of transformations. In this chapter, we shall discuss the geometric and mathematical aspects of transformations.

THE CENTROID

Before getting into the details of transformations, we should understand the concept of a **centroid**. The word itself suggests the notion of center—but center of what? For a circle or a regular polygon, we think of the center as a point that is equidistant from other points. For an irregular polygon, however, we cannot find a point with that characteristic, so we must appeal to our physical intuition for help. Suppose that we have a uniform plate in the shape of an irregular polygon and that we wish to attach a string to a point on the plate so that the plate can hang parallel to the ground. Only one point will do—the centroid.

Why are we interested in the centroid? At this time, we can give only a general answer: the centroid is a valuable reference point. Of more immediate practical concern is how we find the centroid, and this turns out to be easy: the *x*- and *y*-coordinates of a centroid are the average of the *x*- and *y*-coordinates, respectively, of the vertices.

Example. A polygon has vertices of (2, 1), (8, 1), (10, 4), and (4, 6). Its centroid has the following coordinates:

$x_c = (2 + 4 + 8 + 10)/4 = 6$

$y_c = (1 + 6 + 4 + 1)/4 = 3$

This calculation is plotted in figure 4.1.

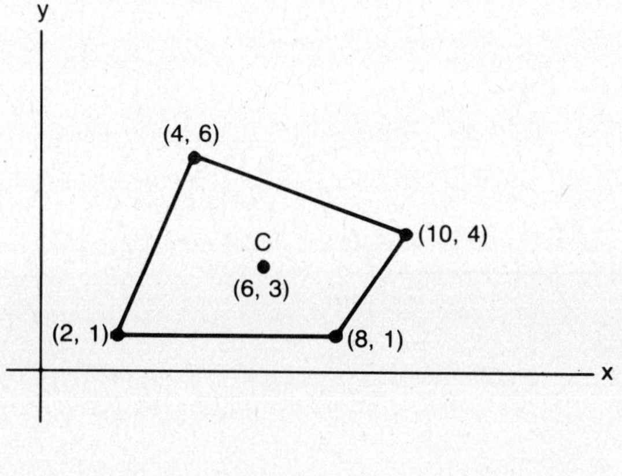

Figure 4.1 Centroid calculation.

TRANSLATION

A **translation** has the sole effect of changing the *location* of a figure; the figure's size, shape, and orientation remain the same. As a result of a translation, the x-coordinate of each vertex changes by a fixed amount t_x; similarly, each y-coordinate changes by a fixed amount t_y. This can all be summarized by the following equations:

$$x' = x + t_x$$
$$y' = y + t_y$$

Example. Where would the vertices of the polygon in figure 4.1 be located if it were translated so that its centroid ends up at (12, 5)? We can easily see that the amount of x translation is 6, while the amount of y translation is 2. The new coordinates are as follows:

$$x' = 2 + 6 = 8, \quad y' = 1 + 2 = 3$$
$$x' = 8 + 6 = 14, \quad y' = 1 + 2 = 3$$
$$x' = 10 + 6 = 16, \quad y' = 4 + 2 = 6$$
$$x' = 4 + 6 = 10, \quad y' = 6 + 2 = 8$$

The result is plotted in figure 4.2.

A translation procedure is listed in program 4.1. The coordinates of the polygon are passed to it as the arrays x and y. The transformed coordinates are passed back to the program as *xnew* and *ynew*. This is a very simple procedure whose form can serve as a model for all future transformations, only the equations for *xnew* and *ynew* will change. Note that this procedure is called only once for the polygon; also, it does not plot the new polygon!

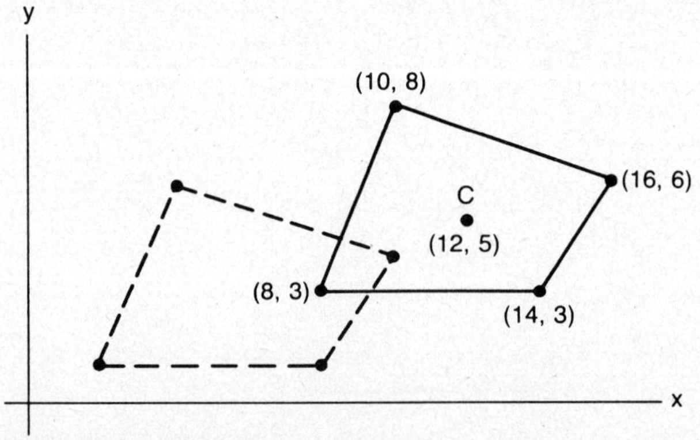

Figure 4.2 Translation.

Program 4.1: Translation Procedure

Assumptions. t_x and t_y are amounts of x and y translation; x and y are arrays of original coordinates; *xnew* and *ynew* are arrays of translated coordinates; s is number of sides.

```
PROCEDURE TRANSLATE;
VAR n:integer;

BEGIN
  FOR n:= 0 to s-1
    BEGIN
      xnew[n]:= x[n] + tx;
      ynew[n]:= y[n] + ty
    END
END;
```

SCALING

Suppose that we have a square, as shown in figure 4.3, and we double each x-coordinate. What happens? As we can see, we end up with a rectangle that is twice as wide as the square. Had we doubled only the y-coordinates, we would have ended up with a rectangle twice as high as the square. In general, we can stretch a polygon by a factor S_x in the horizontal direction if we multiply each x-coordinate by S_x. Similarly, we can stretch it by a factor S_y in the vertical direction if we multiply each y-coordinate by S_y. This process, called **scaling**, is represented by the following equations:

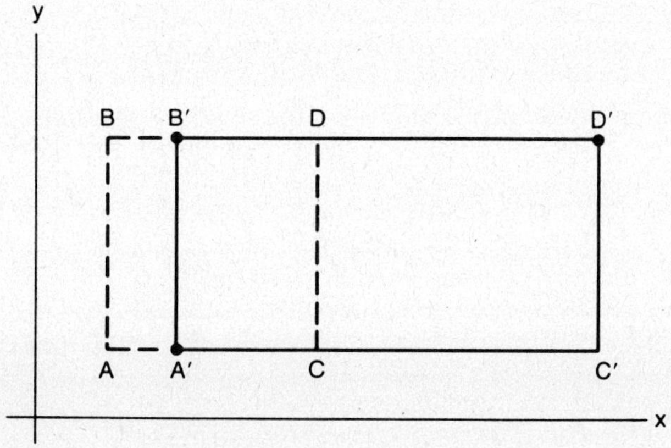

Figure 4.3 Scaling in the x-direction. Primed vertices represent new figure.

$x' = x \cdot S_x$

$y' = y \cdot S_y$

Note that the original polygon can maintain its original proportions only if $S_x = S_y$. Otherwise, it becomes distorted. The internal angles remain unchanged, however, regardless of the choice of S_x and S_y.

SHEARING

We have seen that the translation operation leaves the shape of a figure unchanged. If $S_x = S_y$, the same can be said of the scaling operation. Even if $S_x \neq S_y$, the worst that can happen in the way of distortion is that an image becomes elongated in one direction; the internal angles don't change.

It is not always desirable to maintain the shape in this way. There is one transformation, called **shear**, that distorts the shape of a figure in a fairly simple, predictable way. In this transformation, the change in the *x*-coordinate of a point depends *only* on the *y*-coordinate of that point. Similarly, the change in the *y*-coordinate of a point depends *only* on its *x*-coordinate. This can be formally expressed as follows:

Change in *x*-coordinate $= x' - x = ay$

Change in *y*-coordinate $= y' - y = bx$

where the factors a and b are constants of proportionality that indicate the linear dependence of the change on the *x*- and *y*-coordinates. From this definition, we can easily write the equations for the shear transformation:

$x' = x + ay$

$y' = y + bx$

Example. Assume that we have a box with vertices (2, 1), (8, 1), (8, 7), and (2, 7). The box is subject to a shear in the *x*-direction only, with $a = 0.4$. What does the transformed box look like? We calculate the new *x*-coordinates according to the following equations:

Old Coordinates	*New* x-*Coordinate*
(2, 1)	$x' = 2 + 0.4(1) = 2.4$
(8, 1)	$x' = 8 + 0.4(1) = 8.4$
(8, 7)	$x' = 8 + 0.4(7) = 10.8$
(2, 7)	$x' = 2 + 0.4(7) = 4.8$

Figure 4.4 shows the results. Note that the bottom two points were shifted by an equal amount, 0.4. The top two were also shifted by an equal amount, 2.8, but more than the bottom points. The *y*-coordinates are, of course, the same.

Although it may seem strange to subject an image to this kind of distortion, there are actually many examples of shear in nature. For example, horizontal wind speed (an *x*-coordinate) often depends on the height above ground (a *y*-coordinate). Thus, if we were modeling the shape of a cloud under the influence of an air current that varies with height, we would need the shear transformation.

A TEMPORARY COORDINATE SYSTEM

In each of the foregoing transformations, the centroid of the figure moved from its original position. This is desirable (and unavoidable) in the case of translation. For other transformations, however, we often want the centroid to remain fixed. How can this be arranged? A little thought will show that only the point with coordinate values of $x = 0$ and $y = 0$ has the potential of being unaffected by a transformation. In the device system, this point is normally at the lower left corner of the screen. The problem is that no centroid can be located there (why?). We can get around this problem by temporarily leaving the device system and switching to a system whose origin is the centroid itself. This guarantees a centroid that is initially at (0, 0). Any transformation that leaves the (0, 0) point unchanged will not affect the centroid in this system.

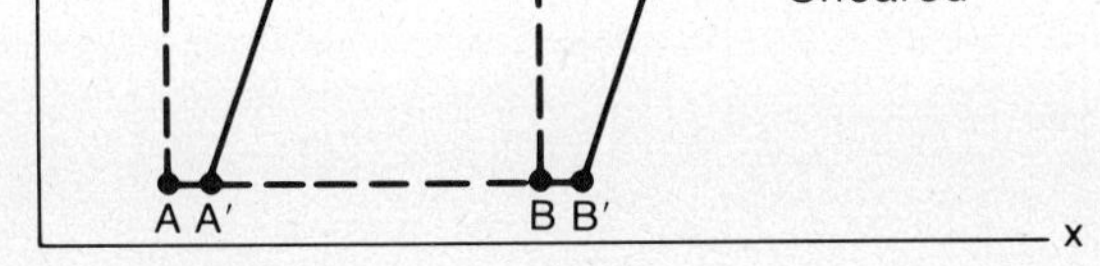

Figure 4.4 Shear in the *x*-direction.

Example. If the origin were at the centroid, the 6 by 6 square of the preceding example would look like the inside square in figure 4.5. Let us scale everything by a factor of 2:

Unscaled Coordinates	*Scaled Coordinates*
(−3, −3)	(−6, −6)
(3, −3)	(6, −6)
(3, 3)	(6, 6)
(−3, 3)	(−6, 6)

In figure 4.5, we can see that the square is twice as large in both dimensions, but the centroid has not moved.

Although we have solved the problem of keeping the centroid fixed, we have introduced another problem. Some of the vertices have negative coordinates, and we know that the graphics functions cannot handle them. Therefore, after performing the transformation, we must switch from the new system back to the device system so that we can do the actual plotting. Since the new system is only temporarily useful, we will refer to it from now on as the **temporary system**. Figure 4.6 summarizes the use of a temporary system.

How do we find the coordinates of the vertices in the temporary system? We can answer this question with the aid of figure 4.7. A point (x, y) in the device system is $x - x_c$ units from the temporary system y-axis, y''. Note that

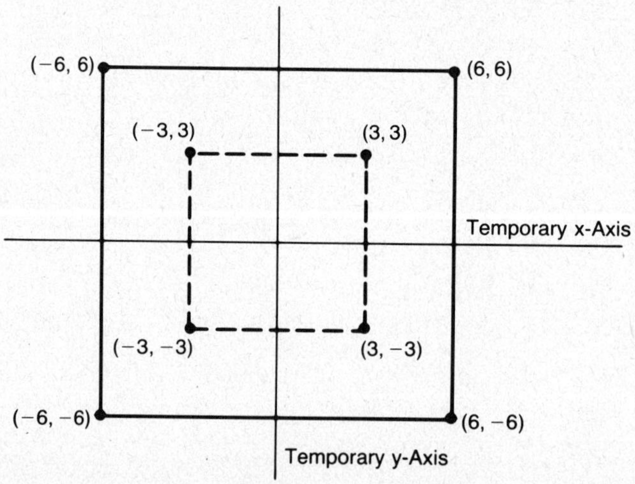

Figure 4.5 Scaling a figure whose centroid is at origin (and remains there).

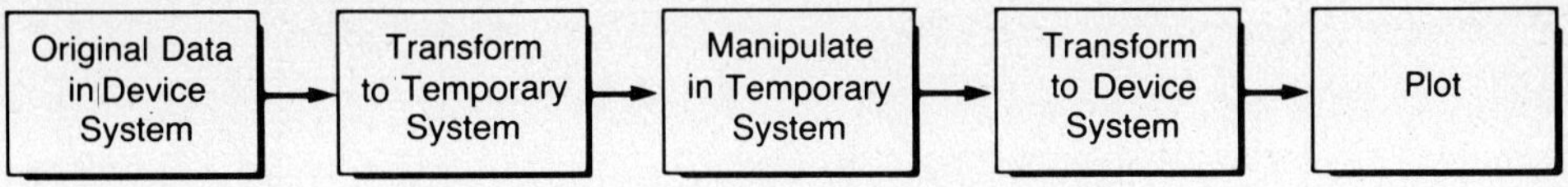

Figure 4.6 Steps in transforming to and from a temporary system.

this is just the definition of an x-coordinate. Similarly, the point is $y - y_c$ units from the temporary system x-axis, x''. Thus, we have:

$$x'' = x - x_c$$

$$y'' = y - y_c$$

which are the equations we would get if we translated the centroid of the object to the origin of the device system. We cannot do that, however, so we essentially bring the origin to the centroid.

Although we often locate the temporary system's origin at the centroid, we can really put it anywhere we please. We can still use the foregoing equations; we just use the device coordinates of the temporary system's origin in place of x_c and y_c.

Example. A triangle with vertices (3, 2), (11, 5), and (10, 11) is placed on the screen as shown in figure 4.8a. What are its coordinates in a temporary system located at the centroid? First, we figure out the coordinates of the centroid:

$$x_c = (3 + 11 + 10)/3 = 24/3 = 8$$

$$y_c = (2 + 5 + 11)/3 = 18/3 = 6$$

Then we subtract these coordinates from the coordinates of each vertex:

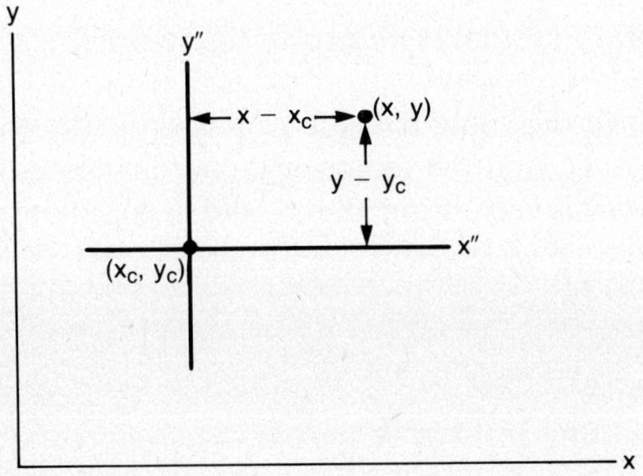

Figure 4.7 Temporary versus screen coordinate system.

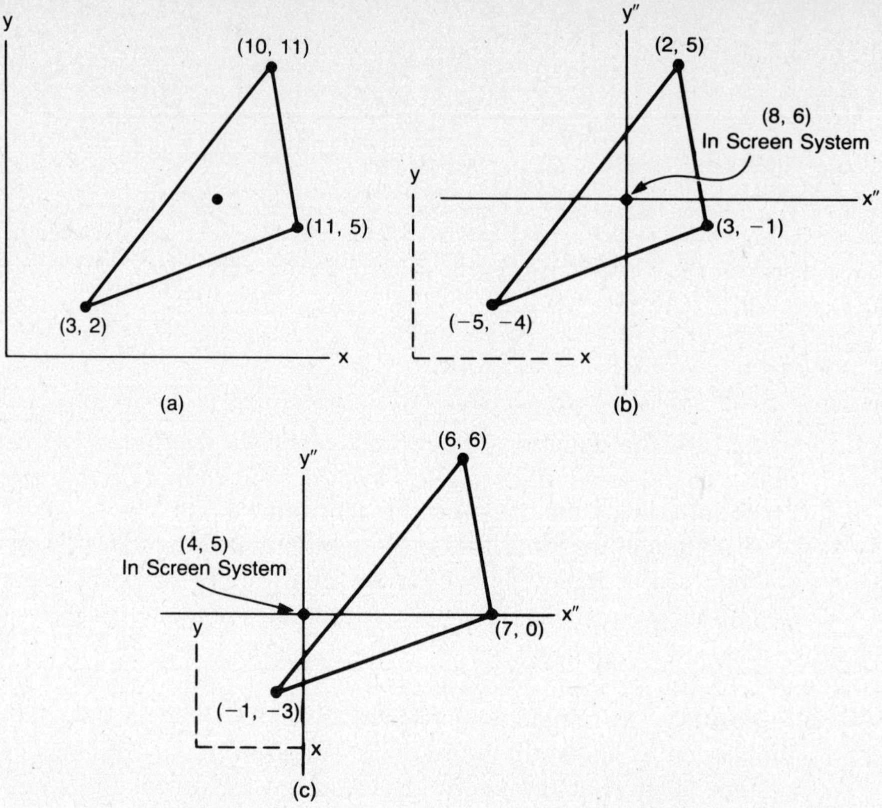

Figure 4.8 (a) A triangle in the screen system. (b) The same triangle in a system whose origin is the centroid. (c) The same triangle in a system whose origin is (4, 5).

(3, 2): $x'' = 3 - 8 = -5, \quad y'' = 2 - 6 = -4$
(11, 5): $x'' = 11 - 8 = 3, \quad y'' = 5 - 6 = -1$
(10, 11): $x'' = 10 - 8 = 2, \quad y'' = 11 - 6 = 5$

The same triangle in the temporary system is shown in figure 4.8b.

Example. Now we wish to move the same triangle to a coordinate system whose origin is located at (4, 5). To find the temporary coordinates of each vertex, we subtract 4 and 5, respectively, from the *x*- and *y*-coordinates of each vertex:

(3, 2): $x'' = 3 - 4 = -1, \quad y'' = 2 - 5 = -3$
(11, 5): $x'' = 11 - 4 = 7, \quad y'' = 5 - 5 = 0$
(10, 11): $x'' = 10 - 4 = 6, \quad y'' = 11 - 5 = 6$

The result is shown in figure 4.8c.

ROTATION

A **rotation** changes the orientation of a figure but leaves its size and shape intact. For a rotation about Q, every point on the figure moves through a circular arc centered at Q. In this section, we shall derive relatively simple equations for rotation when Q is the origin. Then we will see how to deal with rotations about other points.

Consider a point P whose initial coordinates are (x, y) (see figure 4.9). The line L connecting P to the origin initially makes an angle A with the x-axis. If we rotate P about the origin through an angle B, L ends up making an angle $A + B$ with the x-axis; the new coordinates of point P' are (x', y'). We wish to find x' and y' in terms of x, y, and B. To start, let us analyze the triangle with the vertex (x', y'). Using the definition of sine and cosine for a right triangle, we have:

$$x' = L\cos(A + B)$$
$$y' = L\sin(A + B)$$

These can be expanded using trigonometric identities (see appendix A):

$$x' = L\cos(A)\cos(B) - L\sin(A)\sin(B)$$
$$y' = L\cos(A)\sin(B) + L\sin(A)\cos(B)$$

Now look at the triangle with the vertex (x, y). Using the definitions of sine and cosine once again, we have:

$$x = L\cos(A)$$
$$y = L\sin(A)$$

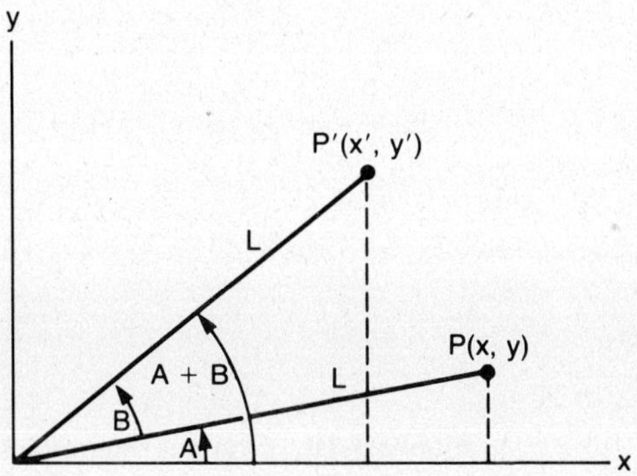

Figure 4.9 Geometry for rotation derivation.

Substituting these into the previous two equations, we get:

$$x' = x\cos(B) - y\sin(B)$$
$$y' = x\sin(B) + y\cos(B)$$

Note that although each new coordinate depends on both x and y, the dependence is not the simple linear one that characterizes shear. This transformation does not affect any of the internal angles.

As noted, the foregoing derivation is for a rotation about the origin. What if we desire to rotate P about a point Q that is not the origin? In that case, we simply construct a temporary coordinate system whose origin is located at Q. Then we can use the foregoing equations with the temporary values x'' and y'' in place of x and y. After the rotation, we can convert back to the device system.

Example. Suppose that we wish to rotate the square in figure 4.10 about the centroid by an angle of 45 degrees. What are the new coordinates? First, we find the centroid:

$$x_c = (5 + 5 + 9 + 9)/4 = 28/4 = 7$$
$$y_c = (3 + 3 + 7 + 7)/4 = 20/4 = 5$$

Second, we find the vertices in the temporary system:

A: $x'' = 5 - 7 = -2, \quad y'' = 3 - 5 = -2$

B: $x'' = 9 - 7 = 2, \quad y'' = 3 - 5 = -2$

C: $x'' = 9 - 7 = 2, \quad y'' = 7 - 5 = 2$

D: $x'' = 5 - 7 = -2, \quad y'' = 7 - 5 = 2$

Third, we substitute the temporary coordinates of each vertex into the rotation equations:

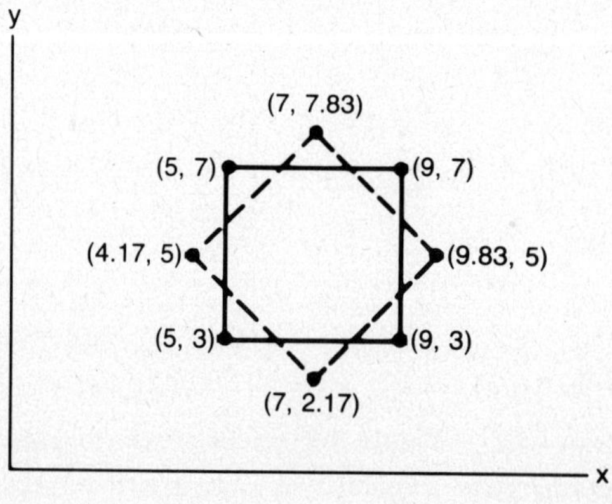

Figure 4.10 Original square (solid lines) and rotated square (dashed lines).

A: $x' = (-2)\cos(45) - (-2)\sin(45) = 0$

$y' = (-2)\sin(45) + (-2)\cos(45) = -2.83$

B: $x' = (2)\cos(45) - (-2)\sin(45) = 2.83$

$y' = (2)\sin(45) + (-2)\cos(45) = 0$

C: $x' = (2)\cos(45) - (2)\sin(45) = 0$

$y' = (2)\sin(45) + (2)\cos(45) = 2.83$

D: $x' = (-2)\cos(45) - (2)\sin(45) = -2.83$

$y' = (-2)\sin(45) + (2)\cos(45) = 0$

Fourth, we convert back to device coordinates by adding the coordinates of the centroid:

A: $x = 0 + 7 = 7$

$y = -2.83 + 5 = 2.17$

B: $x = 2.83 + 7 = 9.83$

$y = 0 + 5 = 5$

C: $x = 0 + 7 = 7$

$y = 2.83 + 5 = 7.83$

D: $x = -2.83 + 7 = 4.17$

$y = 0 + 5 = 5$

The plot of these points is also shown in figure 4.10.

REFLECTIONS

Intuitively, we know what a reflection is. We look in a mirror and see that for a given point on our body, there appears to be a point an equal distance on the other side of the glass. In computer graphics, where we are restricted to a two-dimensional screen, we speak of a figure as being reflected in a line or a point. In figure 4.11, the reflection of point *P* in line *L* is obtained by moving from *P* perpendicular to the line, then continuing in the same direction an equal distance on the other side. For reflection in a point *Q*, we move from *P* to *Q*, then continue in the same direction for an equal distance.

In this section, we will look at these types of reflections, but we will restrict our lines to vertical, horizontal, and 45-degree examples. As it turns out, the easiest reflections to calculate are those in the axes and the origin. These are the equations we shall derive. They can be applied to other cases as follows:

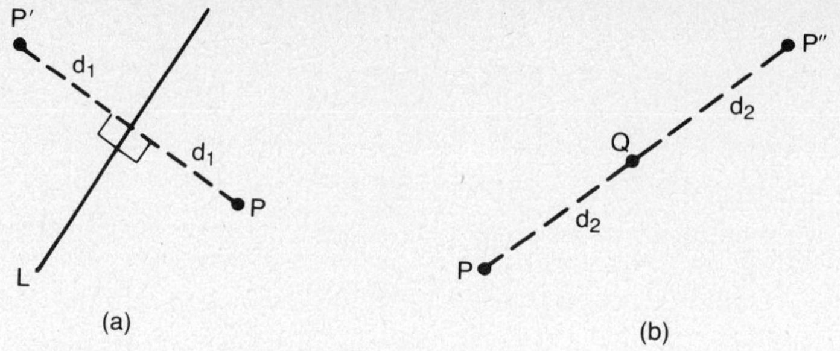

Figure 4.11 Reflections. (a) Reflection of point P in a line L. (b) Reflection of point P in a point Q.

1. For a reflection in a horizontal (or vertical) line, we will convert to a temporary system whose x-axis (or y-axis) coincides with the line. We will calculate the reflection in the temporary x-axis (or y-axis), then convert back to the device system.
2. For a reflection in a 45-degree line, we locate the temporary system so that the line goes through the temporary origin. After reflection, we convert back to the device system.
3. For reflection in a point, the temporary system should be located so that its origin is at the point.

Now let us derive the equations. In figure 4.12, we see a point P and three of its reflections. Assume that its coordinates are (A, B). It is reflected in the x-axis at P_x. By definition, the line joining these two points is vertical, so they must have the same x-coordinate. Since they are equidistant from the x-axis and on opposite sides of it, they must have equal but opposite y-

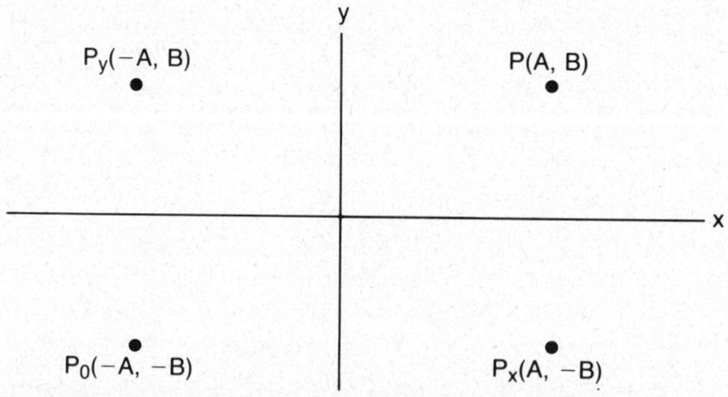

Figure 4.12 Original point P and its reflections: in the x-axis—P_x; in the y-axis—P_y; in the origin—P_0 (equivalent to P_x, then P_y).

coordinates. Hence, the coordinates of P_x are $(A, -B)$. The equations for a reflection in the x-axis are therefore

$$x' = x$$
$$y' = -y$$

Similarly, P_y lies on the same horizontal line as P; it must have the same y-coordinate. Since it is equidistant from the y-axis and on the opposite side, it must have an equal and opposite x-coordinate. Hence, the coordinates of P_y are $(-A, B)$. The equations for a reflection in the y-axis are therefore

$$x' = -x$$
$$y' = y$$

Reflection in the origin is like a reflection in the x-axis, then a reflection in the y-axis. We can see that P_0 must have the same y-coordinate as P_x and the same x-coordinate as p_y. Hence, its coordinates are $(-A, -B)$. For a reflection in the origin, we therefore have

$$x' = -x$$
$$y' = -y$$

For reflection in a 45-degree line, we have to do some work. The two most important cases are reflections in $y = x$ and in $y = -x$. Let us consider the former. In figure 4.13, H is the original point, with coordinates (A, B), and J is the reflected point whose coordinates we have to find. From the definition of reflection, $KH = KJ$, and they are both perpendicular to the line $y = x$. In the figure, there are two more points, I and G. These have been marked off on the line $y = x$ such that $KI = KG = KJ = KH$. The points G, H, I, and J are thus the vertices of a square whose sides are parallel to the axes. Now we can

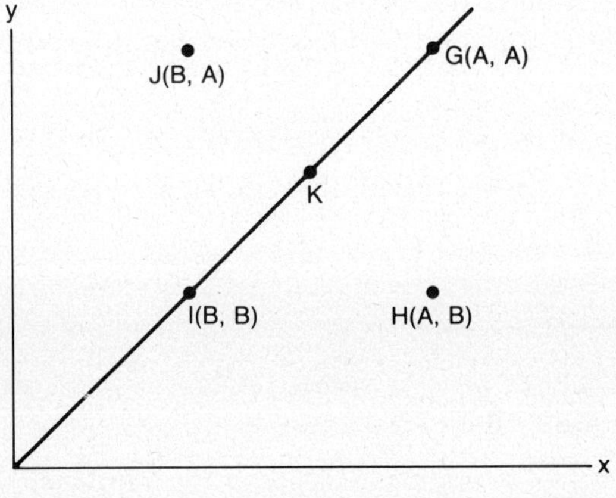

Figure 4.13 Reflection of H in a 45-degree line. The reflected point is J. (Refer to text for other points.)

determine the coordinates of all the vertices in terms of A and B. First, I has the same y-coordinate as H—namely, B. I is also on the line $y = x$, so its y-coordinate equals its x-coordinate. Hence, the coordinates of I are (B, B). Similarly, G has the same x-coordinate as H; since it, too, lies on $y = x$, its x-coordinate must equal its y-coordinate. The coordinates of G, therefore, are (A, A). Finally, J must have the same y-coordinate as G and the same x-coordinate as I. Hence, its coordinates are (B, A). Therefore, the x- and y-coordinates of H and its reflection, J, are simply reversed. We can write the transformation equations as follows:

$$x' = y$$

$$y' = x$$

Using similar reasoning, we can show that a reflection in $y = -x$ has the following equations:

$$y' = -x$$

$$x' = -y$$

Example. What does the triangle in figure 4.14 look like when it is reflected in the line $x = 7$? First, we create a temporary system whose y-axis is coincident with $x = 7$. The most convenient way to do this is to locate its origin at (7, 0). The coordinates in the temporary system can then be obtained by subtracting 7 from the x-value and 0 from the y-value of each vertex:

A: $x'' = 8 - 7 = 1, \qquad y'' = 5 - 0 = 5$

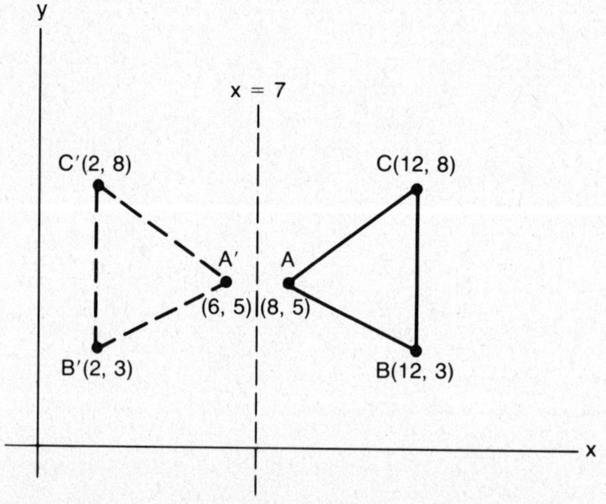

Figure 4.14 Reflection of ABC in the line $x = 7$.

B: $x'' = 12 - 7 = 5, \quad y'' = 3 - 0 = 3$

C: $x'' = 12 - 7 = 5, \quad y'' = 8 - 0 = 8$

Second, we perform the reflection $x' = -x''$, $y' = y''$:

A: $x' = -1, \quad y' = 5$

B: $x' = -5, \quad y' = 3$

C: $x' = -5, \quad y' = 8$

Third, we convert back to the device system by adding 7 to each x'-coordinate and 0 to each y'-coordinate:

A: $x = -1 + 7 = 6, \quad y = 5$

B: $x = -5 + 7 = 2, \quad y = 3$

C: $x = -5 + 7 = 2, \quad y = 8$

The plot of the reflected figure is shown with the original in figure 4.14.

Example. What would the same triangle look like if it were reflected in the point (7, 5)? We locate our temporary system at (7, 5), then recalculate the vertices:

A: $x'' = 8 - 7 = 1, \quad y'' = 5 - 5 = 0$

B: $x'' = 12 - 7 = 5, \quad y'' = 3 - 5 = -2$

C: $x'' = 12 - 7 = 5, \quad y'' = 8 - 5 = 3$

Then we reflect using $x' = -x''$, $y' = -y''$:

A: $x' = -1, \quad y' = 0$

B: $x' = -5, \quad y' = 2$

C: $x' = -5, \quad y' = -3$

Finally, we add the coordinates of the temporary origin:

A: $x = -1 + 7 = 6, \quad y = 0 + 5 = 5$

B: $x = -5 + 7 = 2, \quad y = 2 + 5 = 7$

C: $x = -5 + 7 = 2, \quad y = -3 + 5 = 2$

The plot of the original and reflected triangles is shown in figure 4.15.

Example. Reflect the same triangle in the line $y = x - 12$. (Note that this line makes a 45-degree angle with the x-axis.) We must locate the temporary system so that this line passes through its origin. A good choice is the point

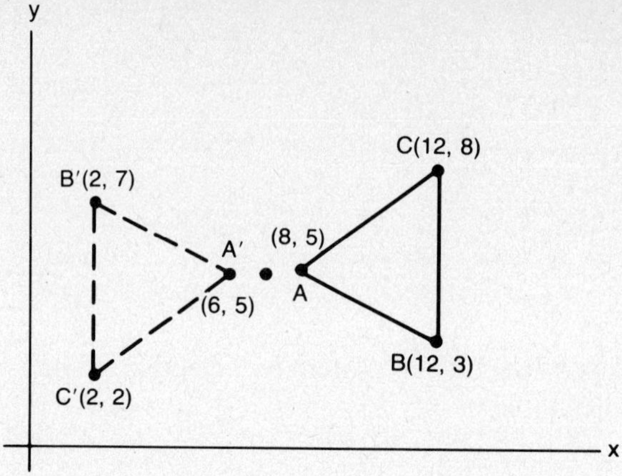

Figure 4.15 Reflection of ABC in the point (7, 5). Note the slight difference between this figure and figure 4.14.

where the line crosses the x-axis, in this case (12, 0). The temporary coordinates are

A: $x'' = 8 - 12 = -4, \quad y'' = 5$
B: $x'' = 12 - 12 = 0, \quad y'' = 3$
C: $x'' = 12 - 12 = 0, \quad y'' = 8$

For this reflection, $x' = y''$ and $y' = x''$, yielding

A: $x' = 5, \quad y' = -4$
B: $x' = 3, \quad y' = 0$
C: $x' = 8, \quad y' = 0$

Adding back the coordinates of the temporary origin, we obtain:

A: $x = 5 + 12 = 17, \quad y = -4$
B: $x = 3 + 12 = 15, \quad y = 0$
C: $x = 8 + 12 = 20, \quad y = 0$

The plot of the original and reflected images is shown in figure 4.16.

MATRICES AND HOMOGENEOUS COORDINATES

There is a very neat, compact way to represent all the transformations we have studied. It involves matrices, but in a somewhat unusual way. Consider the case of a rotation through an angle B:

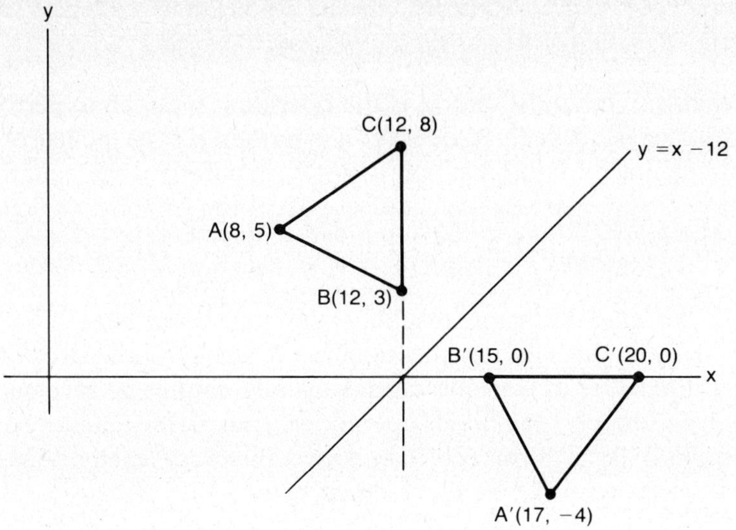

Figure 4.16 Reflection of *ABC* in the line $y = x - 12$.

$$x' = x \cos(B) - y \sin(B)$$
$$y' = x \sin(B) + y \cos(B)$$

If we think of the coordinates of a point as a one-column matrix and obey the rules of matrix multiplication, then the foregoing set of equations can be written as

$$\begin{pmatrix} x' \\ y' \end{pmatrix} = \begin{pmatrix} \cos(B) & -\sin(B) \\ \sin(B) & \cos(B) \end{pmatrix} \begin{pmatrix} x \\ y \end{pmatrix}$$

Similarly, the shear equations:

$$x' = x + ay$$
$$y' = y + bx$$

can be rewritten as

$$\begin{pmatrix} x' \\ y' \end{pmatrix} = \begin{pmatrix} 1 + a \\ b + 1 \end{pmatrix} \begin{pmatrix} x \\ y \end{pmatrix}$$

These two examples demonstrate that a transformation can be written as a matrix multiplication. Performing more than one transformation is simply a matter of setting up a matrix multiplication with more than one matrix. For example, to perform a rotation, then a shear, we set up the matrix equations as follows:

$$\begin{pmatrix} x' \\ y' \end{pmatrix} = \begin{pmatrix} 1 + a \\ b + 1 \end{pmatrix} \begin{pmatrix} \cos(B) & -\sin(B) \\ \sin(B) & \cos(B) \end{pmatrix} \begin{pmatrix} x \\ y \end{pmatrix}$$

Note that the rightmost matrix is the operation we wish to perform first. The matrix for each succeeding operation is written just to the left of the previous one. Since matrix multiplication is not commutative, the equations

$$\begin{pmatrix} x' \\ y' \end{pmatrix} = \begin{pmatrix} \cos(B) & -\sin(B) \\ \sin(B) & \cos(B) \end{pmatrix} \begin{pmatrix} 1 + a \\ b + 1 \end{pmatrix} \begin{pmatrix} x \\ y \end{pmatrix}$$

do not produce the same result as the preceding ones. Thus, a rotation followed by a shear is not the same as a shear followed by a rotation. In general, the order of transformations usually cannot be reversed.

Unfortunately, one of our operations, translation, cannot be expressed in the simple 2 by 2 form. We can prove this very easily. Assume that the translation process can be represented by

$$\begin{pmatrix} x' \\ y' \end{pmatrix} = \begin{pmatrix} A & B \\ C & D \end{pmatrix} \begin{pmatrix} x \\ y \end{pmatrix}$$

where we have to solve for A, B, C, and D. This is equivalent to:

$$x' = Ax + By$$
$$y' = Cx + Dy$$

For translation, there is no y dependence in the x' equation; B must be 0. Similarly, there is no x dependence in the y' equation; C must be 0. Hence, the best we can do for a solution is

$$\begin{pmatrix} A & 0 \\ 0 & D \end{pmatrix}$$

Unfortunately, this has the form of a scaling matrix, so it could not possibly be translation. We must conclude that there is no way to represent translation using a 2 by 2 matrix.

All is not lost, however. There is a clever way to write the translation operation in matrix form. It involves a system called **homogeneous coordinates**. In this system, a point in a plane has three coordinates, not two. Two of these coordinates are just x and y; the third is completely meaningless and is always equal to 1. Since this probably seems strange, let us investigate how this system works for those transformations that were adequately represented by 2 by 2 matrices.

In homogeneous coordinates, a column matrix representing a point looks like this:

$$\begin{pmatrix} x \\ y \\ 1 \end{pmatrix}$$

This has an important implication for the transformation matrix: it must be a 3 by 3 matrix to satisfy the rules of matrix multiplication. Fortunately, we can easily modify the previous 2 by 2 matrices to meet this requirement. We simply pad them out with both a row and a column that have no effect on their function. Using shear as an example, we have:

$$\begin{pmatrix} 1 & a & 0 \\ b & 1 & 0 \\ 0 & 0 & 1 \end{pmatrix}$$

We can see the effect of the new row and column by writing out the complete 3 by 3 shear transformation:

$$\begin{pmatrix} x' \\ y' \\ 1 \end{pmatrix} = \begin{pmatrix} 1 & a & 0 \\ b & 1 & 0 \\ 0 & 0 & 1 \end{pmatrix} \begin{pmatrix} x \\ y \\ 1 \end{pmatrix}$$

and expanding to get the equations

$$x' = x + ay$$

$$y' = bx + y$$

$$1 = 1$$

Clearly, the only effect of solving the shear problem in homogeneous coordinates is that a trivial equation, $1 = 1$, is added to the solution. Since the first two equations correctly represent shear, we can ignore the third. In general, any transformation that we were able to represent in 2 by 2 form as

$$\begin{pmatrix} T_1 & T_2 \\ T_3 & T_4 \end{pmatrix}$$

can be represented as

$$\begin{pmatrix} T_1 & T_2 & 0 \\ T_3 & T_4 & 0 \\ 0 & 0 & 1 \end{pmatrix}$$

Now we can attend to the problem that prompted this whole discussion: the translation matrix. It can be written as follows:

$$\begin{pmatrix} 1 & 0 & t_x \\ 0 & 1 & t_y \\ 0 & 0 & 1 \end{pmatrix}$$

This has a form somewhat different from the other transformations. Since it could not be represented by a 2 by 2 matrix, we should not be surprised that the third column does not contain trivial information. The transformation equations in matrix form are:

$$\begin{pmatrix} x' \\ y' \\ 1 \end{pmatrix} = \begin{pmatrix} 1 & 0 & t_x \\ 0 & 1 & t_y \\ 0 & 0 & 1 \end{pmatrix} \begin{pmatrix} x \\ y \\ 1 \end{pmatrix}$$

We leave it to you to verify that this produces the original translation equations.

INTERACTIVE GRAPHICS

Figure 4.17a shows a flowchart for a simple translation problem. After reading the coordinates of the vertices of a polygon, we draw the figure, change the vertices by the desired amounts, erase the old figure, and draw the new one. What if we are displeased by the results of the change? We could run the program again with a different translation, but we would have to reenter the coordinates of all the vertices. Clearly, we wish to avoid the latter task. Figure 4.17b shows the flowchart for a modified version of the program. After the coordinates are entered and the first drawing is made, the program allows the user to take one of two paths: redraw or quit. We refer to this program as **interactive** because it allows the user to respond to the program's output.

In a real-world computer graphics system, user responses could come from any of the input devices described in chapter 1, depending on the situation. In this book, we have assumed only a minimal system that is normally programmed to accept input from the keyboard. From the example shown in figure 4.17, we can see that a loop with a READ or READLN statement is essentially all we need to make an otherwise ordinary program interactive. We therefore encourage you to make your programs interactive wherever possible.

ANIMATION

In this section, we shall take a brief look at animation. Basically, animation is achieved by repeated application of the transformation procedures discussed

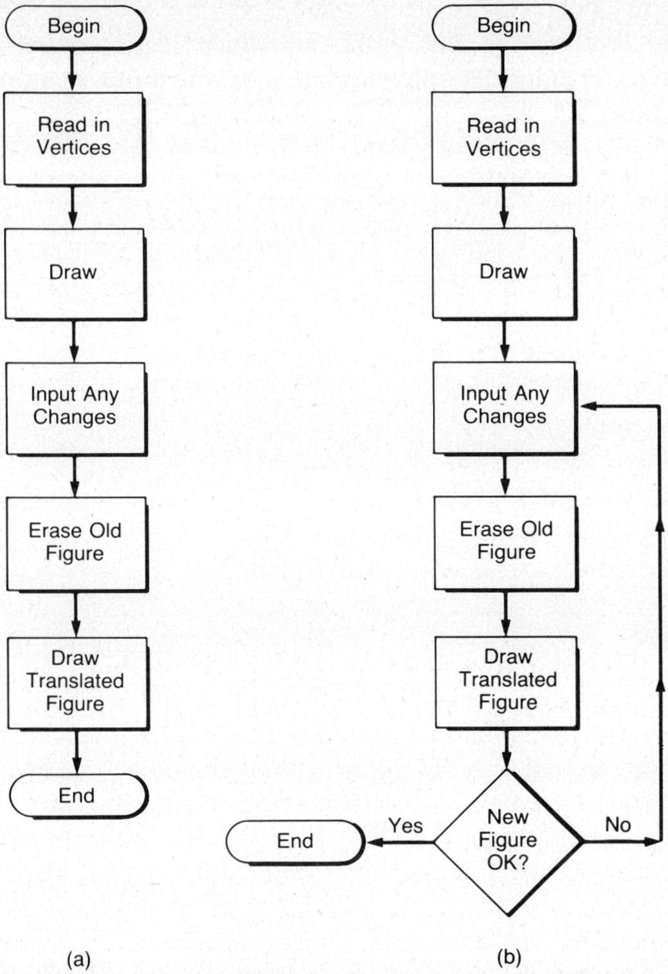

Figure 4.17 Approaches to a simple graphics problem such as translation. (a) Noninteractive approach. (b) Interactive approach.

in this chapter. Video games and computer-produced movies are two important real-world applications of animation. We will give two simple examples showing movement, and we will discuss the question of the speed of image processing.

For the first example, we will need to be able to plot a point on the screen. Although our basic output primitive is the line segment, the IBM system has a procedure called SETPIXEL that lights a given pixel whose coordinates are x and y. Its form is as follows:

```
SETPIXEL (0,x,y,n)
```

When n is 1, the pixel is turned on; when n is 0, the pixel is turned off. (For an explanation of the 0 in the argument, which is not important now, see appendix B.) Consider the following routine, which moves a pixel across the screen:

Program 4.2: A Moving Point

```
PROCEDURE MOVEPOINT;

BEGIN
x := 0;
y := 100;
WHILE x < 640 DO
  BEGIN
    SETPIXEL(0,x,y,1);
    SETPIXEL(0,x,y,0);
    x := x + 1
  END
END;
```

Although this program is quite trivial, you should try running it on your system. You will probably be surprised at how slowly it moves. Can we speed it up? Yes we can, but only by changing the x increment to, say, 10 instead of 1. In other words, if we ask the system to do ten times less work (one-tenth the number of procedure calls to SETPIXEL), it will perform better. This is a good demonstration of how time-consuming graphics tasks are.

The ultimate solution to the speed problem is to abandon the high-level language altogether in favor of **assembly language**. In essence, assembly language is composed of the set of instructions directly executable by the microprocessor. These instructions are elementary by comparison to Pascal; all they can do is move bytes of information and perform a few simple logic and arithmetic operations. Thus, operations that we take for granted, such as READ, WRITE, and MOVETO, must be constructed from scratch in assembly language. However, there is an advantage to this lean design: assembly language is one to two orders of magnitude faster than Pascal. Therefore, when speed is important, assembly language is the only logical choice. It is much easier, however, to convey the *ideas* of computer graphics with a structured, easy-to-read language such as Pascal.

Let us get back to the moving dot and apply it to a demonstration of the optical law of reflection: the angle of incidence equals the angle of reflection. (An object bouncing off a boundary is a fundamental part of computer games.) Figure 4.18 shows the geometry. If we start a dot at P and move it in

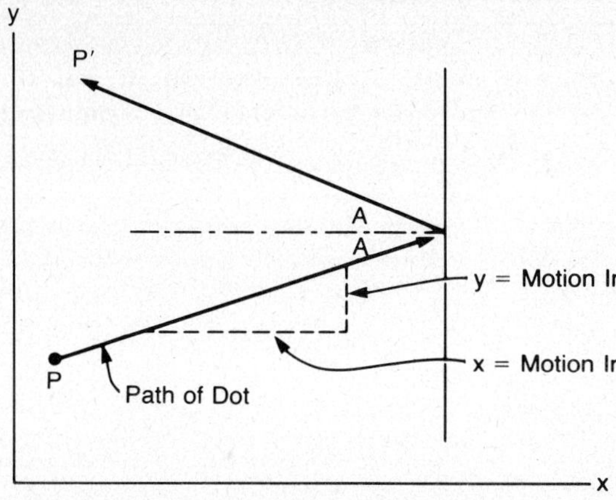

Figure 4.18 Reflection demonstration.

the direction shown, then it should move toward *P'* after it hits the boundary. This is easy to draw, but what are the programming considerations?

1. We must increment both *x* and *y* to move the dot obliquely. That increment requires the use of the *cos* and *sin* functions.
2. We must check the dot's position after each step to make sure it is not past the boundary.
3. We must have a way of reversing the direction of the dot after it hits the boundary.

From the definition of sine and cosine, we can see that the increments are

$$dx = \cos(A)$$

$$dy = \sin(A)$$

The problem with these formulas is that, for most systems, the horizontal and vertical screen resolutions are not equal. Therefore, one pixel in the *y*-direction is equal to *H*/*V* pixels in the *x*-direction. We must keep this in mind when we calculate the increments in terms of pixels.

The check on the dot's position is a matter of an IF–THEN statement. However, checking for equality of the dot's *x*-coordinate and the boundary's *x*-coordinate is dangerous, since they may never be equal. (This is because a boundary *x*-coordinate can fall between dot *x*-coordinate values, which are restricted by the value of the increment.) The safest check is for when the dot is about to exceed the boundary. Then a flag should be set to let the system know that it must reverse the dot's direction. This is easily done by negating the *x* increment.

Program 4.3: Law of Reflection

Assumptions. The dot is at its initial position at left of screen; the reflection angle (ANG) is chosen by the user; the boundary is at $x = L$.

```
PROCEDURE REFLECT;
VAR flag:BOOLEAN;
dx,dy:INTEGER;

BEGIN {1}
  dx := 10*(H/V)*cos(ANG);
  dy := 10*sin(ANG);
  flag := true;
  WHILE x > 0 DO
    BEGIN {2}
     IF (x > L) OR flag      {if dot passes boundary, or flag is set}
     THEN
      BEGIN {3}
       flag := true;      {then set flag, and reverse increment}
       x := x - dx;
       SETPIXEL(0,x,y,1);
      END {3}
    ELSE
      BEGIN {4}
       SETPIXEL(0,x,y,1);      {if not, give positive increment}
       x := x + dx
      END; {4}
  y := y + dy
  END {2}
END; {1}
```

You are urged to do problem 4.8, which suggests a change in the program.

The final program we will offer is one that takes any polygon (drawn with POLY2) and moves it across the screen. Its basic form is extremely simple, but can serve as the model for imparting many types of motion to an object.

Program 4.4: A Moving Box

Assumptions. n vertices entered as $x[0] \ldots x[n-1]$, $y[0] \ldots y[n-1]$; rightmost x coordinate = *max*.

```
PROCEDURE BOX;
```

```
BEGIN
  WHILE max < H DO
    BEGIN
      PENMODE(1);
      PENCOLOR(1);
      POLY2;      {previous boxes not erased}
      TRANSLATE;
      max := max + dx
    END
END;
```

Note that the procedure TRANSLATE could be replaced by a procedure for scaling or one for rotation, and that type of motion would be simulated.

PROBLEMS

4.1. Using the TRANSLATE procedure (program 4.1) as a model, write an analogous procedure for each of the other transformations.

4.2. Write the matrix transformation needed to perform the following operations:

(a) Redraw an image at one-third its size.

(b) Stretch out an object to twice its size in the x-direction, while leaving the size in the y-direction unchanged.

(c) Rotate an object clockwise by a 30-degree angle.

(d) Move an object 10 units to the right, then rotate it 90 degrees counterclockwise.

(e) Rotate an object by 180 degrees about its centroid, then reflect it in a horizontal line passing through the centroid.

4.3. Consider the following diagram (note the symmetry). Write a program to draw it when you are given only the vertices of object A.

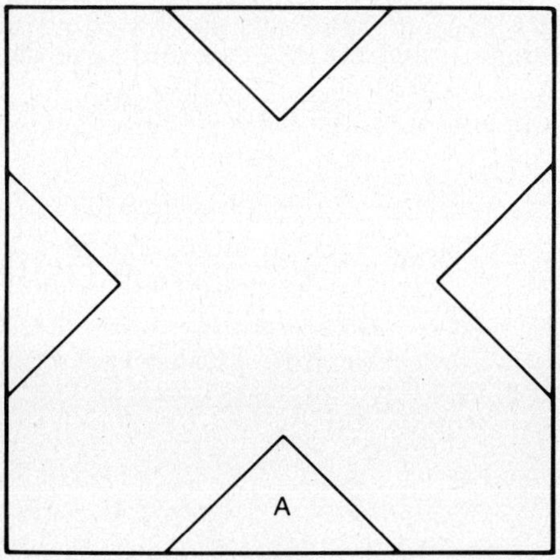

4.4. Write a program that rotates the following triangle about the center of the screen (C).

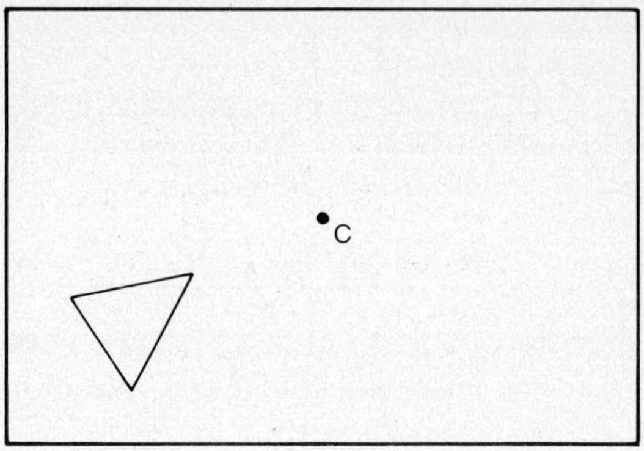

4.5. What is the effect of scaling an object using equal and opposite x and y scaling factors?

4.6. Write a program to create a simple pie chart. Set up a temporary coordinates system that is centered at the center of the screen, and draw a circle centered at the temporary origin. Divide the pie by drawing radii at appropriately chosen locations such that the relative areas of the segments are proportional to the input data. Test your program using the last four months of data from problem 3.3. How would a program for a system that is restricted to the MOVETO command differ from one written for a system that has all four turtle move commands?

4.7. Run the procedure REFLECT with the sin and cos calculations inside the loop instead of outside.

4.8. Write a program that demonstrates the law of refraction (the change in the direction of a light ray when it goes from medium 1 to medium 2):

$$(n_1)\sin(i) = (n_2)\sin(r)$$

where n_1 = index of refraction of medium 1, n_2 = index of refraction of medium 2, and the angles r and i are the ones shown here:

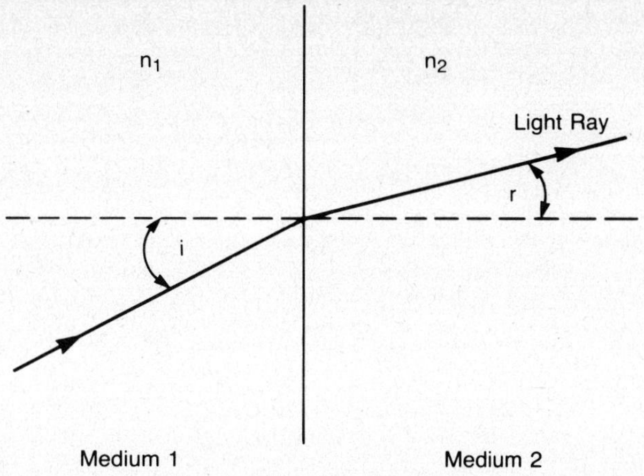

4.9. We have noted that the order of transformations generally cannot be reversed. Can you think of exceptions to this general rule?

4.10. What programming tricks can you use to vary the speed of rotation of an object?

REFERENCES

Foley, J. D., and Van Dam, A. *Fundamentals of Interactive Computer Graphics.* Reading, Mass.: Addison-Wesley, 1982, pp. 245–255.

Harrington, S. *Computer Graphics: A Programming Approach.* New York: McGraw-Hill, 1983, chapter 4.

Kreyszig, E. *Advanced Engineering Mathematics*, 4th ed. New York: Wiley, 1979, pp. 291–301.

Meyers, R. E. *Microcomputer Graphics.* Reading, Mass.: Addison-Wesley, 1982, chapters 4 and 8.

Shoup, R. "Color Table Animation." *Computer Graphics 13*(2), August 1979, 297–317 (SIGGRAPH 79).

Chapter 5

Graphics Data Structures

When you have finished this chapter, you will have important tools for storing and updating graphics information.

Objectives

1. To review the concepts of records and files.
2. To understand the concept of a display file.
3. To develop and work with three types of display files:
   (a) Simple
   (b) Linked list
   (c) Segmented
4. To introduce the concept of a normalized display file.

When we drew a polygon, we set the turtle's pen to draw, then moved the turtle from one point to another until the drawing was completed. At each point in the drawing, we provided the turtle with the coordinates of the next point. The coordinates were stored in an array, then passed to a procedure that executed a MOVETO command. Had we desired to store the resulting picture on a disk, simply writing the array to a disk file would have sufficed. Then, retrieving the picture would have involved reading the coordinates from disk to an array, then passing the coordinates to the drawing routine.

Now, suppose that we have a figure that requires the turtle to plot during some intervals but not during others. In that case, the turtle's pen cannot be set to draw and left that way. The pen status, along with the location of the next point, has to be updated at each point. Clearly, our original drawing routine—as well as the simple storage and retrieval scheme—is no longer viable. In general, if there are *n* quantities that could change at each point in a figure, a drawing routine must allow for updating those *n* quantities at each point. A storage and retrieval scheme must be consistent with that drawing routine.

In this chapter, we will discuss a general method for drawing, storing, and retrieving any picture. We will start with something simple, then get more complex as we approach our goal. Along the way, we will take the opportunity to introduce two major concepts. One is the **display file**—a data structure that contains all the information needed to draw a picture. We will see how a given display file can produce the same figure regardless of a machine's screen resolution. The second concept is **segmentation**, whereby we divide a picture into small modules that can be modified independently of one another. This idea has important real-world applications. For example, an automobile designer can put the major systems (electrical, suspension, fuel, and so on) on separate modules, then concentrate on a particular system as desired. The same principle can be utilized by an architect, with separate modules for the basic systems of a house (electrical, plumbing, frame, and so on.) Whatever the application may be, it requires a familiarity with records and files, so we will review these two data structures.

RECORDS

A **record** is a structured data type with a fixed number of elements. The important characteristics of a record are as follows:

1. The elements do not have to be of the same type.
2. An element is accessed by its name, not by a subscript.

The declaration for a record has the following form:

```
TYPE name = RECORD
            element1:type1;
            element2:type2;
            .
            .
            .
            elementN:typeN
            END;
```

Here, *name* is the name of the data type defined by the record, *element1* is the name of the first element, *type1* is the type of the first element, and so forth. If we declare a variable to be of type *name*

```
VAR z:name;
```

then the elements of *z* are indicated as

```
z.element1
z.element2
```

and so on. The importance of the record type is that we can design it to hold whatever information we please. For example, we can design a record to hold information that the turtle needs at each point:

```
TYPE display = RECORD
               xvalue:REAL;
               yvalue:REAL;
               penstatus:(on,off,erase)
               END;
```

Note that we have defined a field called *penstatus* whose values are easy-to-read English words, rather than numerical codes.

Now we can declare a variable of type *display*:

```
VAR z:display;
```

Here, *z.xvalue* and *z.yvalue* are the coordinates of the next destination of the turtle. The component *z.penstatus* tells the turtle whether or not to plot as it moves.

FILES: GENERAL CONCEPTS

A **file** is nothing more than a named collection of data. We need to know about files of records, so let us discuss how Pascal deals with this concept.

Figure 5.1 illustrates the organization of a file of records. We will assume that this file is named *pic* and that each record has the structure of *display*. Only one record from this file can be accessed at any given time. That record is selected by a hypothetical device called a **window**. In Figure 5.1, for example, the window is over record three. Consequently, the information in record three, *and only record three*, is available to our program. Of course, the position of the window can be changed. Precisely

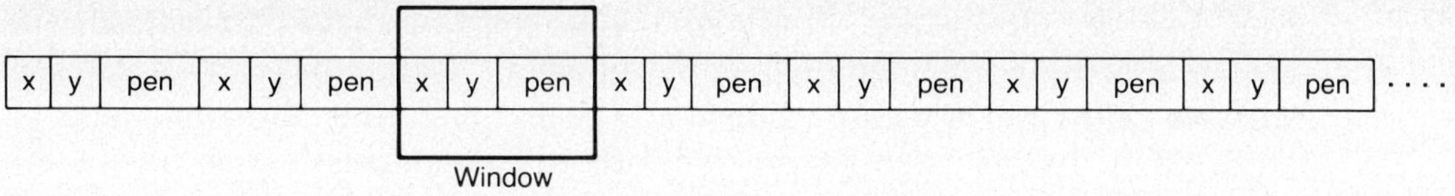

Figure 5.1 A file of records. The window is over record 3.

how depends on whether the file exists or has to be created. For an existing file, we can move the window forward or backward one record at a time. For a new file, records can be created only by moving the window forward.

You should be aware of the two general categories of files (figure 5.2): an **external file** is a file on a disk; an **internal file** is a file in the computer's main memory. Information on a disk is accessed by relatively slow, mechanical means. In contrast, information in main memory is accessed rapidly. Clearly, it makes sense to minimize the number of times we access a disk. A good way to do this, at least for reading from a disk, is to copy from the disk to an internal file. Then all references to the (slow) disk file data can be directed to the (fast) internal file. Similarly, if we wish to write to a disk, we should first write to an internal file, then copy the internal file to the disk when we are finished. For the purposes of the next two sections, we will assume that *pic* is the internal name of our file and that *testdata* is its external name.

Reading from Files

The first step in reading from a file is to declare the internal name in the VAR block:

```
VAR pic:FILE OF display;
```

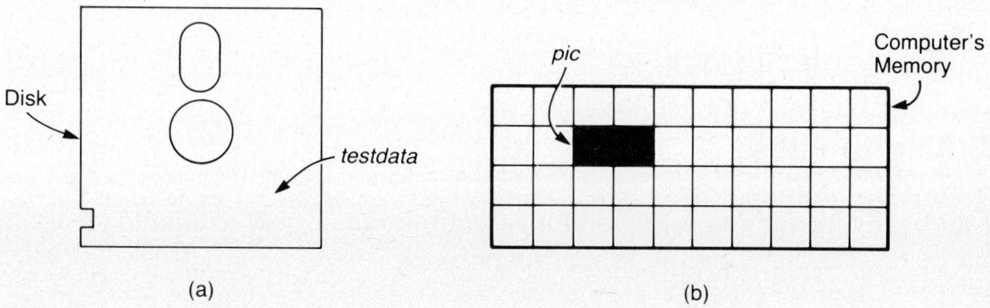

Figure 5.2 Files. (a) An external file is on disk. (b) An internal file is in memory.

This informs the system of the file structure, so that the window will encompass the correct amount of information. It automatically creates a variable called *pic* ^, whose value at any given time is the current contents of the window. In our example, *pic* ^ has three components:

```
pic^.xvalue
pic^.yvalue
pic^.penstatus
```

The second step is to position the window over the first record. In the p-System, this is done with the command

```
RESET(pic, 'testdata');
```

(See appendix C for Turbo Pascal details). RESET also associates the external name with the internal name. In practical terms, this association allows us to proceed as if the disk file *testdata* had been copied into *pic*. Thus, all references to the data in *testdata* are made by specifying the internal name *pic*.

We are now free to use the information in the window as we please. For example, we can assign the values in the window to appropriate variables:

```
var1 := pic^.xvalue;
var2 := pic^.yvalue;
var3 := pic^.penstatus;
```

When we have finished using the values in the current window, we advance the window to the next record with the command

```
GET(pic);
```

This gives us access to the values in the second record. When we have finished using the entire file, or all that we want of it, we let the system know with the command

```
CLOSE(pic);
```

Writing to Files

Writing to a file is almost entirely analogous to reading from one. First, we declare the file in the VAR block:

```
VAR pic:FILE OF display;
```

Then we associate the internal and external files with a statement analogous to RESET:

```
REWRITE(pic, 'testdata');
```

REWRITE sets the window to the beginning of the file. It also associates the internal and external names. In this case, the association lets the system know that information we write to *pic* will eventually be transferred to the disk under the name *testdata*. If *testdata* does not exist, REWRITE creates an empty file on the disk called *testdata*.

At this point, the window is at the beginning of *pic*. We can now assign values to the components of *pic*^:

```
pic^.xvalue := var1;
pic^.yvalue := var2;
pic^.penstatus := var3;
```

Then we send the record to the file with the statement

```
PUT(pic) ;
```

This also advances the window to the next record, enabling us to repeat the procedure and fill the second record. The process of assigning values to *pic*^ and then executing PUT is what creates the file *pic*. However, we have not yet put anything on the disk. That is accomplished by the command

```
CLOSE(pic,LOCK);
```

CLOSE tells the system that we are finished using *pic*; LOCK causes the system to copy *pic* to *testdata*. Figure 5.3 summarizes reading from and writing to a data file.

Operation	Read	Write
Open File	RESET (*int*, '*ext*')	REWRITE (*int*, '*ext*')
Move Window	GET (*int*)	PUT (*int*)
Close File	CLOSE(*int*)	CLOSE (*int*, LOCK)

Figure 5.3 Summary of reading and writing files; *int* = internal file name, *ext* = external file name.

DISPLAY FILES

A **display file** is a file that contains everything needed for drawing an image on the screen. By "everything," we mean not only data, such as coordinates, but also instructions, such as "move," "turn the pen on," "change the color to green," and so forth. This is quite different from our previous arrangement, in which the instructions were in a procedure and the data were brought in from the outside. The display file we shall use is a file of records, with each record containing all the instructions and data needed by the turtle to proceed to the next point. A program called a **display file interpreter** reads each record and directs the turtle accordingly.

A Simple Display File

As a first step, we will construct a display file under the assumption that the turtle is moved only with the MOVETO instruction. This enables us to put the MOVETO command in the display file interpreter, rather than in the display file itself. Of course, this contradicts what was just said about the display file concept, since some information needed for the drawing is not in the display file. However, it is an easy way to illustrate these simple programming concepts:

1. Creating a display file and its interpreter.
2. Effecting modifications of the display file and interpreter.

As we go deeper into the subject, we will develop an increasingly sophisticated display file.

The following program creates a display file according to the aforementioned condition. We have assumed that our drawing has been planned beforehand, so we know exactly what the turtle should do at each point.

Program 5.1: Creating a Simple Display File

Assumptions

```
Display = RECORD
          x:REAL;
          y:REAL;
          penstatus:(on,off,erase)
          END;
```

External file is *testdata*; internal file is *pic*, of type *display*

```
PROCEDURE SIMPLEDISPLAYFILE;
VAR penread: string;

BEGIN
  REWRITE (pic, 'testdata');
  READLN(pic ^ .x,pic ^ .y);
  WHILE pic ^ .x < > 999 DO       {pic ^ .x = 999 is sentinel}
   BEGIN
    READLN(penread);      {penread is input string for penstatus}
    IF penread = 'on'
    THEN pic ^ .penstatus := on
    ELSE IF penread = 'off';
          THEN pic ^ .penstatus := off
          ELSE pic ^ .penstatus := erase;
          PUT(pic);     {advance the window}
          READLN(pic ^ .x,pic ^ .y)
          END,
  CLOSE(pic,LOCK)
END;
```

The next program interprets the display file that was just created.

Program 5.2: A Simple Display File Interpreter

Assumptions. Existence of display file as created in program 5.1; all assumptions of program 5.1.

```
PROCEDURE INTERP1;

BEGIN {1}
  RESET(pic,'testdata');
  PENMODE(0);
   WHILE NOT EOF(pic) DO       {do entire file}
    BEGIN {2}
     MOVETO(pic ^ .x,pic ^ .y);      {go to first vertex with pen off}
     IF pic ^ .penstatus = on
     THEN PENMODE(2)
     ELSE IF pic ^ .penstatus = off
          THEN PENMODE(0)     {sets pen for trip to next vertex}
          ELSE PENMODE(4);
     GET(pic)      {get next record}
    END; {2}
  CLOSE(pic)
END; {1}
```

Note that these routines have no references to the total number of points. The display file interpreter simply executes the instructions in one record after another until the display file runs out of records.

We can test these two routines by considering figure 5.4—an outline of the playing area of a hockey arena. We have designed it so that, given the coordinates of a few points, we can sketch the perimeter and the goals. The arrows indicate the direction of the turtle's motion; the dashed lines indicate that the pen has been turned off. Table 5.1 lists the information for the display file for this drawing. You should verify the accuracy of the information by actually creating the file and running it through the display file interpreter.

Modifying the Display File

It is extremely important that we be able to modify the display file. We will illustrate two simple modifications. First, suppose that some time after creating the hockey arena drawing, we decide to add to the arena by drawing a line at midfield (see figure 5.4). How do we modify the display file so that it produces the updated drawing? It should be evident that only two more moves of the turtle are needed: one to get the turtle to *A*, the other to get it to *B*. Hence, we must add two more records to the end of the original file. This is easily done by the following routine:

Program 5.3: Adding a Record to the End of SIMPLEDISPLAYFILE

Assumptions. Same as program 5.2.

```
PROCEDURE ADDREC;
VAR flag, penread:STRING;
```

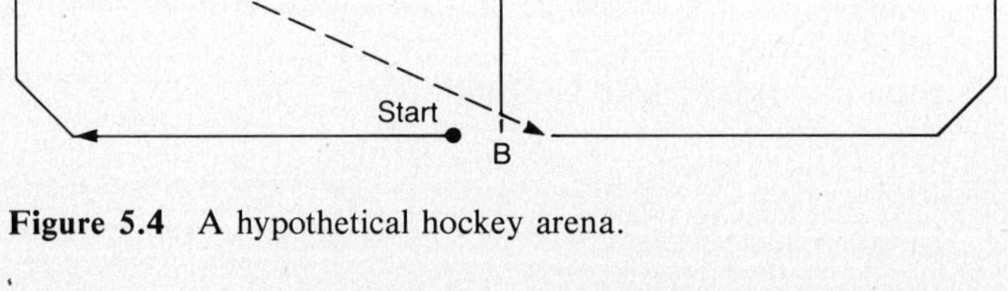

Figure 5.4 A hypothetical hockey arena.

TABLE 5.1 DISPLAY FILE FOR FIGURE 5.4

Point	Coordinates	Pen status
1	180,0	On
2	20, 0	On
3	0, 20	On
4	0, 160	On
5	20, 180	On
6	180, 180	Off
7	50, 100	On
8	40, 100	On
9	40, 80	On
10	50, 80	Off
11	220, 0	On
12	380, 0	On
13	400, 20	On
14	400, 160	On
15	380, 180	On
16	220, 180	Off
17	350, 100	On
18	360, 100	On
19	360, 80	On
20	350, 80	On or off

```
BEGIN
  flag := 'yes'
  RESET(pic,'testdata');
  WHILE NOT EOF(pic) DO
    GET(pic);       {advance window to end of file}
  WHILE flag = 'yes' DO
   BEGIN
    READLN(pic^.x,pic^.y,penread);
    IF penread = 'on'     {evaluate string for penstatus}
    THEN pic^.penstatus := on
    ELSE IF penread = 'off'     {assign penstatus}
          THEN pic^.penstatus := off
          ELSE pic^.penstatus := erase;
    PUT(pic);
    WRITELN('Do you wish to add more data?');
    READLN(flag)
  END;
  CLOSE(pic,LOCK)
END;
```

Finally, what if we discover that there should be another point somewhere in the middle of the drawing? With the present display file structure, there is no way to insert a record for that point without changing all the records that follow (see figure 5.5). If we wish to insert a new record after record two, the new record becomes number three, the old number three becomes the new number four, and so on. We will defer further discussion of insertion and deletion of records until later in this chapter.

A More Versatile Display File

As you know, the p-System has four instructions to move the turtle, not just MOVETO. Suppose that we wish to construct a display file (and interpreter) that can handle all four (or however many your system has). Thanks to the versatility of the record data type, we can do this simply and elegantly. Consider the parameters required by each instruction:

1. MOVETO: two numbers for the coordinates.
2. MOVE: one number for the distance moved.
3. TURNTO: one number for the angular position.
4. TURN: one number for the angular change.

It might appear that we need a fairly large record to accommodate all these possibilities. Actually, we can get away with a record that has only one more field than the record we used before:

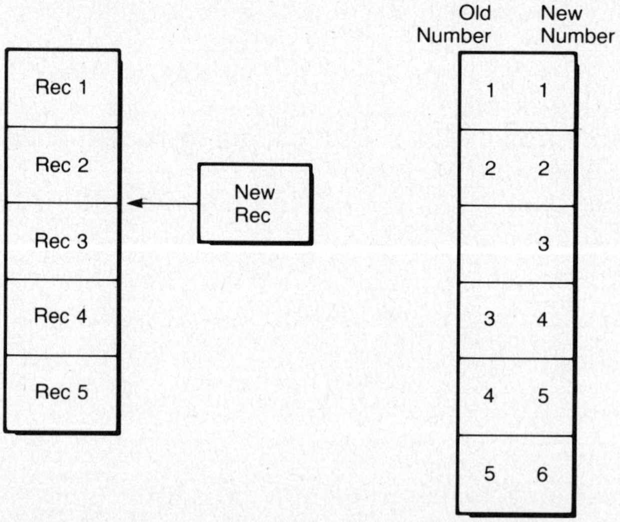

Figure 5.5 When a new record is inserted in the display file, subsequent records must be renumbered.

```
TYPE display = RECORD
               opcode:(movto,mov,turto,tur);
                   {new field—note spelling!}
               penstatus:(on,off,erase);
               v1:REAL;
               v2:REAL
               END;
```

Note that the only item we have added is a component called *opcode*, which contains the move instructions. Also, instead of *xvalue* and *yvalue*, we have *v1* and *v2*. The interpretation of *v1* and *v2* depends on the choice of *opcode*:

opcode	*v1*	*v2*
movto	*x*-coordinate	*y*-coordinate
mov	Distance	Ignored
turto	Angular position	Ignored
tur	Angular change	Ignored

We leave the writing of the programs for this more versatile display file and the corresponding interpreter as an exercise. Both of these programs are similar to the previous versions, but they require an extra IF statement to accommodate the extra information.

LINKED LISTS

Although our existing display file is reasonably sophisticated, it is not convenient for adding or deleting an *arbitrary* record. A display file that allows us to make such additions or deletions is extremely desirable. After a first attempt at a drawing, we often discover details that we missed and wish to include. To obtain such flexibility, we will have to make a significant change in the structure of our display file. A structure called a **linked list** is most appropriate for this task.

Consider the structure illustrated in figure 5.6, which looks almost like the sequence of records shown in figure 5.5. At the left of each record, we have symbolically indicated the address within the memory of the beginning of each record. The only real difference between this structure and that in figure 5.5 is that each record has an extra variable that contains the address of the next record. Any variable that contains an address is called a **pointer**. Hence, we say that each record *points* to the next record. Note that the last record points to an address called *NIL*, which is Pascal's way of indicating that it is, indeed, the last record.

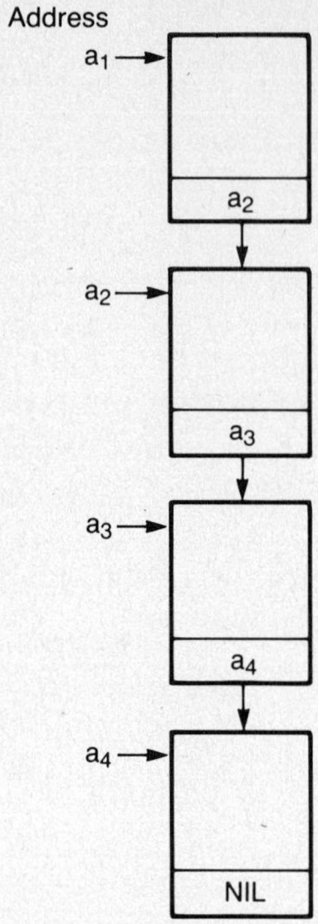

Figure 5.6 A linked list. Each record contains the address of the memory location of the next record.

The pointer is what makes the linked list so desirable. Suppose that we wish to add a record right after the second one, as before. If we assume the location of the new record to be, say, a_9, we can insert it as follows:

1. Change the pointer in record two to a_9.
2. Set the pointer in the new record to a_3.

These steps are illustrated in figure 5.7. Note that the address a_9 can be anywhere in the memory; it need not be contiguous with the original list. It is the pointer that determines the next record, not which record is physically next in line.

Pointers in Pascal

How can we denote the address of a particular variable? Pascal allows us to declare a variable as a pointer type. For example, suppose that we want the variable p to point to a record of type *display*. We simply declare p as follows:

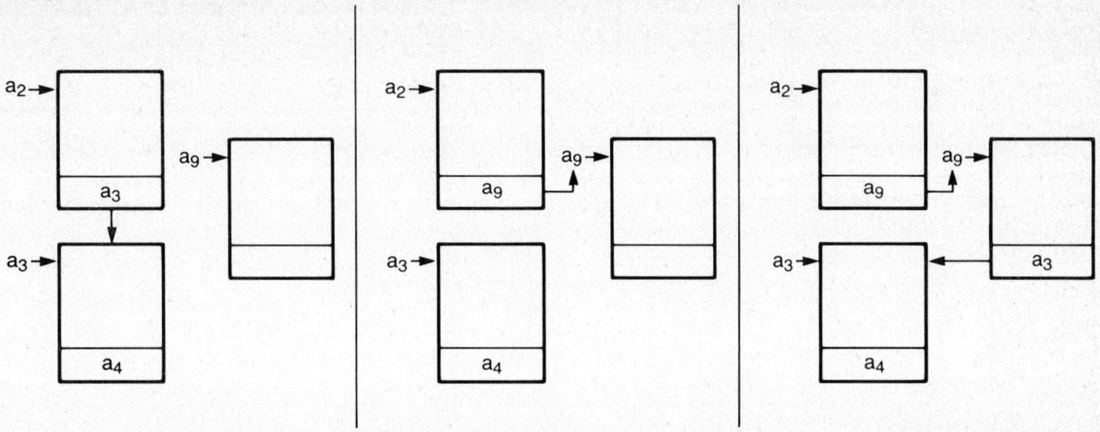

Figure 5.7 Adding a record to a linked list. When a new record is added after a_2, the records from a_3 on are unaffected.

```
p: ^display;
```

This has the following meaning:

1. The address of the variable is *p*.
2. The name of the variable is *p*^.
3. The variable has components *p*^.*opcode*, *p*^.*penstatus*, *p*^.*v1*, and *p*^.*v2*.

How do we actually reserve space in the memory for a record of type *display*? Pascal provides for this with the statement:

```
NEW(p);
```

This sets aside space for a record of type *display* and sets *p* equal to the address of that record. Each time we invoke NEW(p), space for another record is reserved, and *p* takes on a value equal to the address of the new record (figure 5.8). Note that each new record is still referred to as *p*^ and its components as *p*^.*opcode*, and so on. The only way the system knows the difference between this record and any other is by the value of *p*. Just as a file window selects a particular record from a file of records, a pointer selects a particular record from a linked list.

Figure 5.8 Each time NEW(p) is invoked, *p* points to the new record.

Programming a Linked List

We want our linked list to contain the usual turtle information. In addition, each record must have a pointer. Hence we shall define a slightly modified record:

```
TYPE display = RECORD
               opcode:(movto,mov,turto,tur);
               penstatus:(on,off,erase);
               z1:INTEGER;
               z2:INTEGER;
               adr: ^ display
               END;
```

Note that this version of *display* has all the information of the previous *display* plus a new variable, *adr* (address). This is the part of the record that points to the next record.

Now we can make our linked list. Basically, the task consists of the following steps, with steps 2 through 4 repeated:

1. Reserve space in the memory for a record with NEW.
2. Enter the turtle information by assigning values to *p^.opcode, p^.penstatus*, and so forth.
3. Reserve space for another record with NEW.
4. Point the old record to the new one.

Program 5.4 does all this. It is followed here by an analysis of the key steps.

Program 5.4: Creating a Linked List Display File

Assumptions

```
Display = RECORD
          opcode:(mov,movto,tur,turto);
          penstatus:(on,off,erase);
          v1:REAL;
          v2:REAL;
          adr: ^ display
          END;

PROCEDURE LINKLIST;
VAR
  penread,opread,flag:STRING;
  r,p,q,start: ^ display;

BEGIN {1}
  NEW(p);      {create first record}
  start := p;
  WHILE flag = 'yes' DO
  BEGIN {2}
    NEW(q);      {create next record}
    READLN(p ^.v1,p ^.v2,penread);
        {read v1,v2 into first record}
    READLN(opread);
    IF penread = 'on'
    THEN p ^.penstatus; = on       {put pen info into first rec}
    ELSE IF penread = 'off'
         THEN p ^.penstatus; = off
         ELSE p ^.penstatus; = erase;
    IF opread = 'moveto'
    THEN p ^.opcode := movto
    ELSE IF opread = 'move'       {put opcode into first rec}
         THEN p ^.opcode = mov
         ELSE IF opread = 'turn'
                THEN p ^.opcode; = mov
                ELSE IF opread; = 'turn'
    p ^.adr := q;      {point first rec to next}
    r := p;
    p := q;      {advance pointer to next rec}
    WRITELN('More input? Type yes, else no');
    READLN(flag)
  END; {2}
```

```
  p := r;
  p^.adr := NIL      {point last rec to NIL}
END; {1}
```

In this procedure, the statement

```
NEW(p);
```

creates a record pointed to by the variable *p*. Then,

```
start := p;
```

saves this address (we should keep track of where the list starts). The program then enters a loop. The statement

```
NEW(q);
```

creates a second record, this one pointed to by *q*. At this stage, there are two empty records, #1, pointed to by *p*, and #2, pointed to by *q* (see figure 5.9). Now the turtle information is read in and assigned to #1. The last assignment to #1:

```
p^.adr := q;
```

implies that #2 is the next record to be filled. The last line in the loop:

```
p := q;
```

sets the pointer *p* to point to #2. Note that, right now, both *p* and *q* point to the same record. However, when the program enters the loop for the second time, `NEW(q)` creates record #3, so *q* now points to #3. During this execution of the loop, #2 gets filled. After this happens, *p* is changed so that it points to #3. Then a fourth record is created by `NEW(q)`; *q* now points to #4 while #3 gets filled. You should be able to see from the foregoing sequence that record *n* is held in reserve while record $n - 1$ gets filled. The function of *r* is to save the address of the last *filled* record, since the loop always sets the pointer to the unfilled (next) one.

Adding and Deleting Records

Program 5.5 is a procedure to add a record (as demonstrated in figure 5.7).

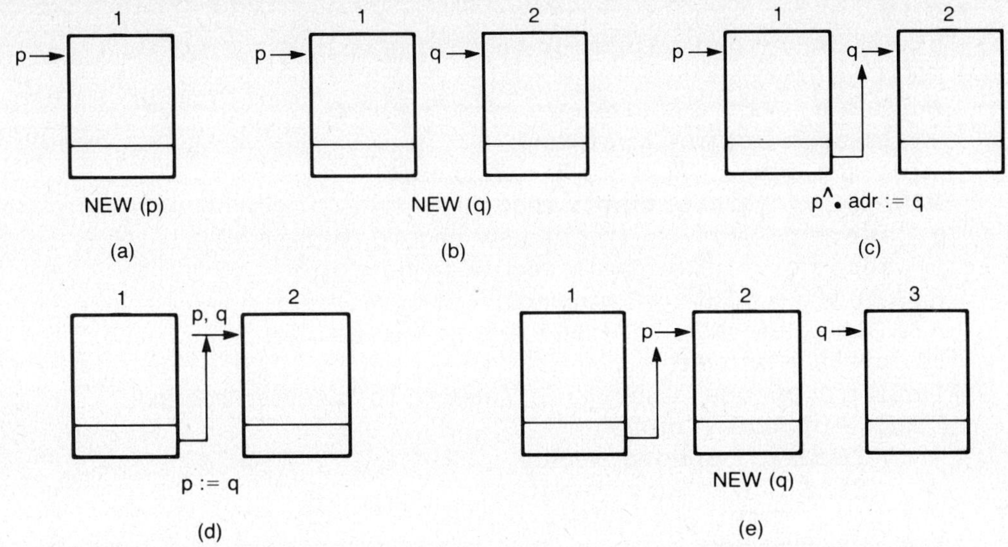

Figure 5.9 Creating a linked list. (a) Record 1 is created. (b) Record 2 is created. (c) Record 1 points to record 2. (d) Both pointers point to record 2. (e) A new record is created, so *q* points to record 3, while *p* still points to record 2. Note that (e) is essentially the same situations as (b).

Program 5.5: Adding a Record to a Linked List Display File

Assumptions

```
Display = RECORD
          opcode:(mov,movto,tur,turto);
          penstatus:(on,off,erase);
          v1:REAL;
          v2:REAL;
          adr: ^ display
          END;
```

Insertion desired after record whose coordinates are *x* and *y* (we call it the *n*th record). Linked list starting at *start*.

```
PROCEDURE ADDTOLIST;
VAR
  p,q,start: ^ display;
  x,y: real;
```

```
BEGIN
  p := start;       {set pointer to beginning of list}
  READLN(x,y);
  WHILE(p^.v1 <> x) OR (p^.v2 <> y) DO
      {search list until pointer}
    p := p^.adr;      {points to nth record}
  NEW(q);       {create empty record}
  q^.adr := p^.adr;       {point new record to old n+1}
  p^.adr := q;       {point nth record to new one}
  READLN(q^.v1,q^.v2,opread);
  READLN(penread);       {read record values and}
  IF opread = 'moveto'
  THEN q^.opcode := movto       {assign to inserted record}
  ELSE IF opread = 'move'
        THEN q^.opcode := mov
        ELSE IF opread = 'turnto;
              THEN q^.opcode := turto
              ELSE q^.opcode := tur;
  IF penread = 'on'
  THEN q^.penstatus := on
  ELSE IF penread = 'off'
        THEN q^.penstatus := off
        ELSE q^.penstatus := erase
END;
```

To delete the record after the *n*th record, we reset its pointer so that it points to *n*+2, not to *n*+1 (figure 5.10).

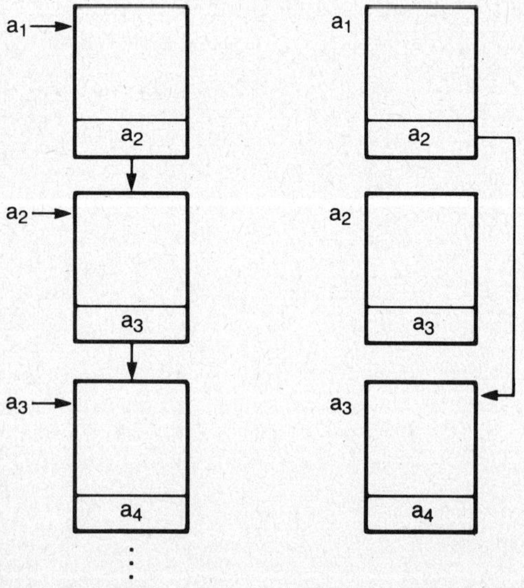

Figure 5.10 Deleting a record from a linked list. To delete the second record, set the first record to point to the third record.

Program 5.6: Deleting a Record from a Linked List Display File

Assumptions. Same as for program 5.5.

```
PROCEDURE DELETEFROMLIST;
VAR
  p,q start: ^display;
  x,y:real;

BEGIN
  p := start;
  READLN(x,y);      {read coordinates of nth record}
  WHILE (p^.v1 <> x) OR (p^.v2 <> y) DO
    p := p^.adr;      {stop when p points to nth record}
  q := p^.adr;      {set q to point to n+1 record}
  p^.adr := q^.adr      {since q^.adr points to n+2, this}
END;    {causes nth record to point to n+2}
```

Disk Files and Linked Lists

Suppose that we stored the foregoing linked list on a disk and then read it into an internal file similar to *pic*. We would not be able to use it as a linked list! The reason for this is quite simple. Each record has a component that is the address of the following record—the address it had when it was created. When an operating system loads a disk file into the computer, that file starts at an address of the system's choosing. Unless a freak accident occurs, the file will not be loaded into the same area of memory where it was originally created. Hence, each record will be in a location different from that promised by the previous record's pointer.

This does not mean that we cannot make use of data files to create a linked list. We can always obtain *opcode, penstatus, v1*, and *v2* from a disk file instead of from the keyboard. However, the program itself must assign the pointer. With a slight modification (see problem 5.4), the program LINKLIST can create a linked list from a disk file. As demonstrated by the following routine, we can store a linked list on disk by storing all of the record's components except the pointer.

Program 5.7: Storing Information from a Linked List on a Disk

Assumptions. Linked list as created by program 5.4.

```
Display2 = RECORD
            opcode:(mov,movto,tur,turto);
            penstatus:(on,off,erase);
            v1:REAL;
```

```
          v2:REAL
          END;

Display = RECORD
          z:display2;
          adr: ^.display
          END;
```

Internal file *pic*; external file *testdata*.

```
PROCEDURE STORLIST;
VAR
  p,q,start: ^display;      {display is linked list structure}
  pic:FILE OF display2;      {display2 is disk file structure}

BEGIN
  p := start;
  REWRITE(pic,'testdata');      {open pic for writing}
  WHILE p < > NIL DO      {for every record in list}
   BEGIN
    pic^.v1 := p^.z.v1;      {assign those values to pic}
    pic^.v2 := p^.z.v2;
    pic^.penstatus := p^.z.penstatus;
    pic^.opcode := p^.z.opcode;
    PUT(pic);      {write values to pic}
    p := p^.adr      {advance pointer}
   END;
  CLOSE(pic,LOCK)
END;
```

Using a Linked List as a Display File

We have one more programming task before we summarize the use of the linked list as a display file: we must write a display file interpreter for it.

Program 5.8: Display File Interpreter for Linked List Display File

Assumptions. Linked list created as in program 5.4.

```
PROCEDURE INTERP3;
VAR p,start: ^display;

BEGIN
  p := start;
  PENMODE(0);
```

```
  MOVETO(p^.v1,p^.v2);
  WHILE p <> NIL DO
   BEGIN
    IF p^.penstatus = on
    THEN PENMODE(2)
    ELSE IF p^.penstatus = off
          THEN PENMODE(0)
          ELSE PENMODE(4);
    p := p^.adr;
    IF p^.opcode = movto
    THEN MOVETO(p^.v1,p^.v2)
    ELSE IF p^.opcode = mov
          THEN MOVE(p^.v1)
          ELSE IF p^.opcode = tur
                THEN TURN (p^.v1)
                ELSE TURNTO(p^.v1)
   END
END;
```

This program is very similar to program 5.2, except that records are accessed by moving a pointer instead of a window.

Now consider figure 5.11—a flowchart that outlines a sequence of steps for the creation, modification, and storage of an image using a linked list. Naturally, the first step is to create the linked list. This is the display file. Input is from the keyboard if the drawing is just being created, or from a disk file if the drawing already exists. The linked list is then fed to the display file interpreter, which produces the drawing. At this point, the user has the option of adding to, deleting from, or storing the list. If the user chooses one of the modifications, he or she can either send the modified display file back to the interpreter so that the new drawing can be displayed or store it directly on disk.

SEGMENTATION

Perhaps you noticed a flaw in our system for handling a linked list display file. When we try to modify the display file and then elect to see the updated drawing, we must redisplay the entire file, even though only a small piece of it may have been changed. Also, suppose that we have a cutaway drawing of an automobile showing the major systems: electrical, fuel, exhaust, suspension, and so on. What if we wish to view only the suspension system or only the fuel or electrical systems? That would be extremely inconvenient with the system we have already discussed. The reason for each of these difficulties is the

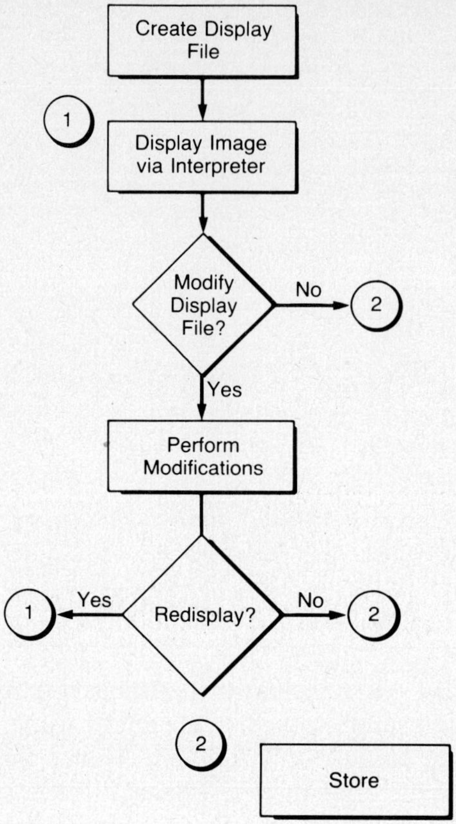

Figure 5.11 Flowchart for use of linked list display file.

same: we have not yet developed a way of dealing exclusively with a given portion of the display file. As we shall see, it is very easy to divide our display file into individually manageable units called **segments** (figure 5.12). We can then think of the display file as being composed of a relatively small number of segments, rather than a large number of records. In this section, we will develop routines that enable us to use a segmented display file. In particular, we want to be able to perform the following functions:

1. Draw an arbitrary segment.
2. Remove an arbitrary segment from the screen.
3. Remove an arbitrary segment from the display file.
4. Add a segment to the display file.

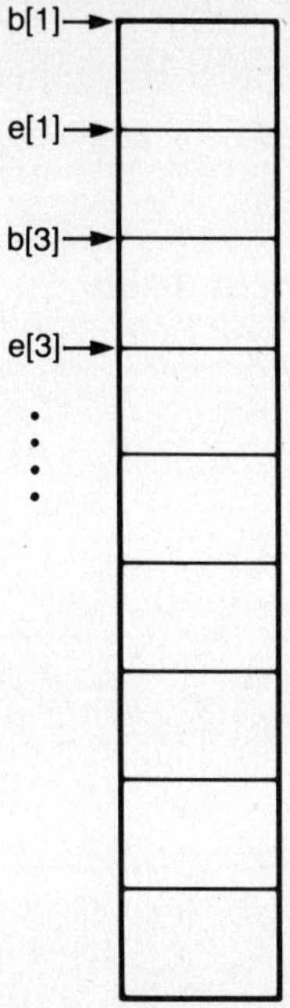

Figure 5.12 Segmented display file. Each box represents a segment of the list; $b =$ address of first record in the segment, $e =$ address of last record in the segment.

Creating a Segmented Display File

The first step in segmenting the display file is to modify our old friend *display* so that a record can be identified as belonging to a particular segment. This is done with an additional field, which we have called *segnum*:

```
TYPE display = RECORD
               segnum:INTEGER;     {segment number goes here}
               opcode:(movto,mov,turto,tur);
               penstatus:(on,off,erase);
               v1:REAL;
               v2:REAL;
               adr: ^ display
               END;
```

Clearly, as we create the segmented list, we must read the segment number for each record into *segnum*. However, there is an additional consideration. After we create the list, we must have a means of selecting a particular segment for the desired processing. This is best done using an arrangement called a **segment table**. A segment table contains the location in memory of the beginning and end of each segment. How do we get these locations? As we create the display file, we keep track of the pointer's value. When it points to a first or a last record of a segment, we record that value. If we then store those values in an array, we can access a segment simply by specifying an index. Program 5.9 creates the display file and segment table.

Program 5.9: Creating a Segmented Linked List with Segment Table

Assumptions

```
Display = RECORD
          segnum:INTEGER;
          opcode:(mov,movto,tur,turto);
          penstatus:(on,off,erase);
          v1:REAL;
          v2:REAL;
          adr: ^ display
          END;

PROCEDURE SEGLIST;
VAR
  start,p,q: ^ display;
  penread,opread:string;
  b,e:array [1..20] of ^ display;      {e[n] points to the end of the}
  flag:char;                           {nth segment}
  n:integer;      {b[n] points to the beginning of
                   the nth segment}

BEGIN
  NEW(p);
  start := p;
  b[1] := start;      {initialize counters, pointers}
  flag := 'c';
  n := 1;
  WHILE flag < > 'e' DO      {makes linked list}
   BEGIN {while}
    NEW(q);
    READLN(p ^ .v1,p ^ .v2,opread);
    READLN(penread);
    IF penread = 'on'
    THEN p ^ .penstatus := on
    ELSE IF penread = 'off'
          THEN p  ^ .penstatus := off
          ELSE p  ^ .penstatus := erase;
    IF opread = 'moveto'
    THEN p ^ .opcode := movto
    ELSE IF opread = 'move'
```

```
            THEN p^.opcode := mov
            ELSE IF opread = 'turnto'
                 THEN p ^.opcode := turto
                 ELSE p^.opcode := tur;
     p^.segnum := n;
     WRITELN('Type c = continue, s = end of segment, e = end of
         input');
     READLN(flag);
     IF flag = 's'    {end of segment?}
     THEN
      BEGIN     {then put pointer to its}
       e[n] := p;     {beginning and end in table}
       n := n + 1;
       b[n] := q
      END
     ELSE IF flag = 'e'     {end of input?}
          THEN e[n] := p;     {then assign last e[n]}
     p^.adr := q;
     p := q
   END; {while}
p := e[n];     {set pointer to last record}
p^.adr := NIL     {set last record to point to NIL}
END;
```

When the user indicates the end of the nth segment, several things happen:

1. The current value of p is saved as $e[n]$.
2. n is incremented to $n + 1$.
3. The current value of q, which points to the next record, is saved as $b[n + 1]$, the beginning of the next record.

Note that $b[1]$, the beginning of the first segment, is equal to *start.*

Deleting a Segment from the Display File

To learn how to delete a segment from the foregoing display file, we will suppose that we wish to delete the fourth segment. We set a pointer p to $e[3]$, the end of the previous segment (figure 5.13a). Note that this record points to the beginning of the fourth segment. We must change it so that it points to $b[5]$, the beginning of the fifth segment (figure 5.13b). The programming is very similar to that for deleting a record from a linked list (program 5.6).

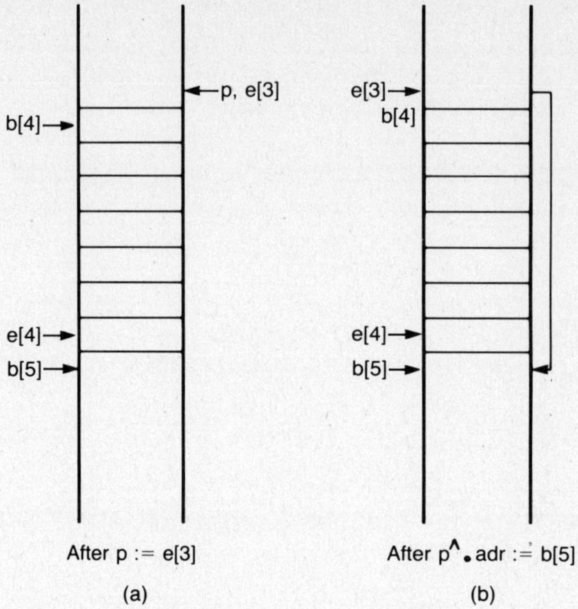

Figure 5.13 Deletion of the fourth segment. The end of segment 3 is changed to point to the beginning of segment 5.

Adding a Segment to the Display File

A segment is most easily added to the end of the file. Suppose that the last record in the original file is *L*. Since we know its address from the segment table, we set a pointer *p* to point to it (figure 5.14a). Note that *e*[*L*] points to *NIL*, as expected. We then use `NEW(q)` to create a new record, *R*, and change *L* so that it points to *R* (figure 5.14b). Finally, we change *p* so that it points to *R*, then invoke `NEW(q)` (Figure 5.14c). We now have two empty records—one pointed to by *p*, the other by *q*. Therefore, we can use the same programming scheme to create this segment that we used to create the original display file.

Displaying a Segment on the Screen

To display a segment on the screen, we use the display file interpreter for a linked list. However, instead of starting from *start* and ending at *NIL*, we start at *b*[*n*] and end at *e*[*n*], where *n* is the segment number (see problem 5.7).

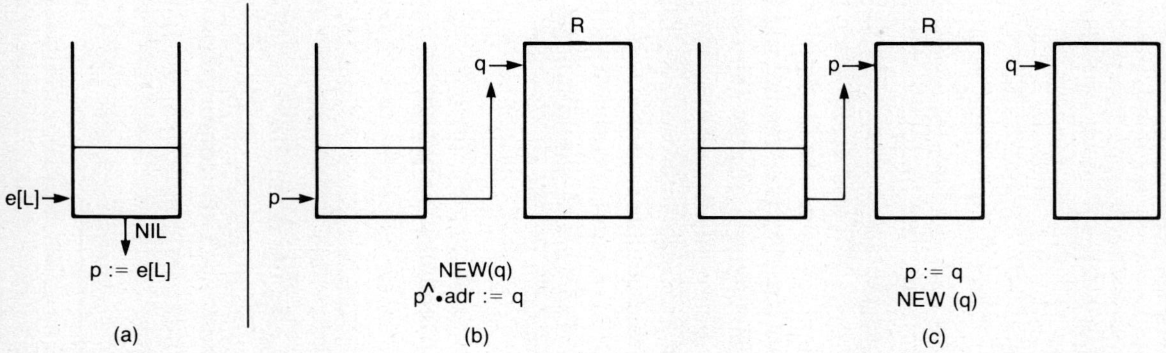

Figure 5.14 Adding a segment. (a) Set a pointer, p, to the end of the list. (b) Create a new record, R; point the end of the list to it; then point p to it. (c) Create another record and use the linked list creation method from this point on.

Erasing a Segment from the Screen

The process for erasing a segment from the screen is virtually identical to that for displaying a segment. The only (and crucial!) difference is that the display file interpreter always sets *penstatus* to the erase mode (see problem 5.7).

A NORMALIZED DISPLAY FILE

Now that we know how to create a fairly sophisticated display file, let us put some icing on the cake. Suppose that we are asked to run our display file on an unknown machine (but one that has an identical display file interpreter). Since the data in each record are in device coordinates, we can only hope that the new machine has the same screen resolution as ours. If not, the resultant drawing will be on a different scale, since the meaning of a coordinate value varies from system to system. In fact, part of the drawing might even be off the screen. Thus, we say that our display file is not portable.

How can we create a display file that *is* portable? Recall that we must plan our drawing carefully before entering coordinates in the display file. This means mapping it out on some sort of grid that is a duplicate of the screen. Suppose, now, that computer graphics people agree to draw all their pictures on a grid whose maximum coordinate is 1 and whose minimum is 0 (figure 5.15). Then all display files would appear to have been created on the same machine. Coordinates in this system are called **normalized coordinates.** If the display file interpreter converts them to the host machine's device coordinates, the same display file can be used on all machines with the same results. The conversion is very simple:

$$x_d = H \cdot x_n$$

$$y_d = V \cdot y_n$$

where x_n and y_n are the normalized *x*- and *y*-coordinates, respectively. Note that the display file interpreter is tailored to a given machine by the particular values of H and V. This combination of a customized interpreter and normalized coordinates enables us to make a portable display file.

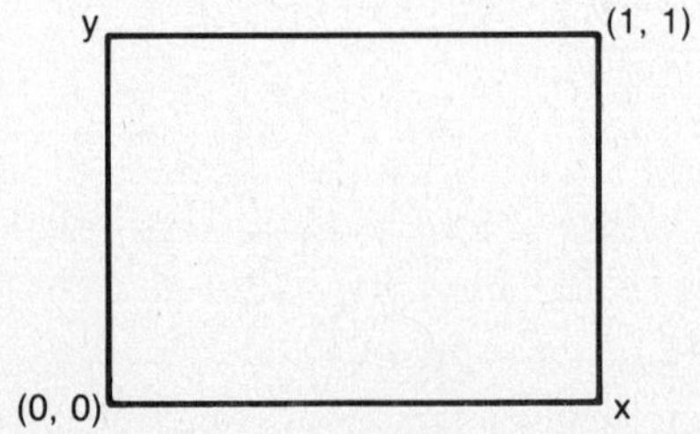

Figure 5.15 A normalized coordinate system.

PROBLEMS

5.1. What is the advantage of this declaration:

```
opcode:(mov,movto,tur,turto);
penstatus:(on,off,erase);
```

as opposed to this one:

```
opcode:INTEGER;
penstatus:INTEGER;
```

What is the disadvantage of the first declaration? Why does it use different spellings for MOVE, TURN, and so forth?

5.2. Explain clearly the advantages of a linked list display file instead of one using an array. Comment on any inconveniences inherent in this choice.

5.3. **(a)** Write a program to create a linked list for the hockey arena in figure 5.4.
(b) After the arena is projected, add the line across the middle of the arena.
(c) Modify the program so that the goals can be moved, say, 10 units toward the center of the arena.

5.4. Write a program that creates a linked list for information stored in a disk file. Assume that the disk file consists of records with the following structure:

```
Display = RECORD
          opcode:(mov,movto,tur,turto);
          penstatus:(on,off,erase);
          x:REAL;
          y:REAL
          END;
```

5.5. Write a program that plots the tide data in chapter 3 (problem 3.1), but only for the odd-numbered hours. Use a linked list and design the program so that data points can be added to it. Test the program by using points from the even-numbered hours as additions.

5.6. Write a program that plots the layout of a bedroom. Use a segmented linked list with five segments: wall outline, bed, bookcase, dresser, and television console. Make sure that the user can move the furniture around the room at will (assume that "move" means rotate and/or translate).

5.7. Write procedures for the following tasks:
(a) Create a display file and interpreter for a linked list that can accommodate the TURN, TURNTO, and MOVE commands.
(b) Create a display file that accepts input from a disk file.
(c) Delete a segment from a linked list.
(d) Display a segment on the screen.
(e) Erase a segment from the screen.

REFERENCES

Hume, J. N. P., and Holt, R. C. *UCSD Pascal: A Beginner's Guide to Programming Microcomputers.* Reston, Va.: Reston, 1982, chapter 17.

IBM Pascal Reference Manual, p-System. Boca Raton, Fla.: IBM Corporation, 1982, part 2, chapter 3.

Tenenbaum, A., and Augenstein, M. *Data Structures Using Pascal.* Englewood Cliffs, N.J.; Prentice-Hall, 1981, chapter 4.

Chapter 6

Windows and Viewports

When you have finished this chapter, you will be able to select an arbitrary portion of a drawing and display it on any desired part (or all) of the screen.

Objectives

1. To understand the concepts of window and viewport and the difference between them.
2. To be able to map a window to a viewport.
3. To understand and implement clipping.
4. To introduce the concepts of zooming and panning.

Imagine that you are an engineer using a computer graphics system to modify the design of a circuit board. This circuit performs four functions, and the components for each function are neatly separated into four distinct areas of the board. When you create the display file or the circuit board, you naturally put each of these areas into a separate segment. When all four segments of the file are displayed, an image of the board fills the entire screen (see figure 6.1).

Suppose that you normally study only one area at a time, hoping to get a better view of the many details that characterize these circuits. Using the system developed in the preceding chapter, you could select the desired segment for display and ignore the others. Unfortunately, very little is gained

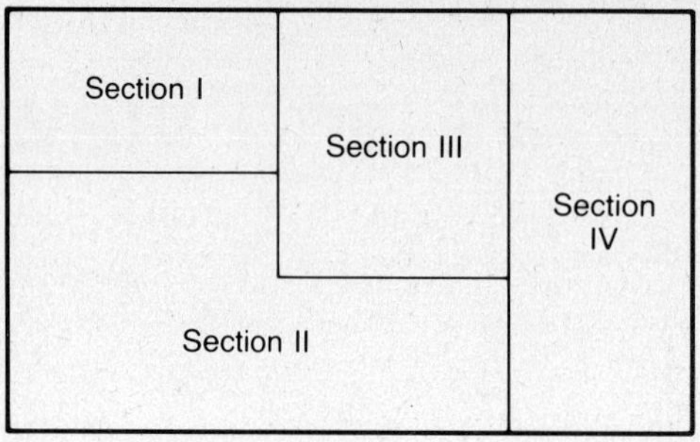

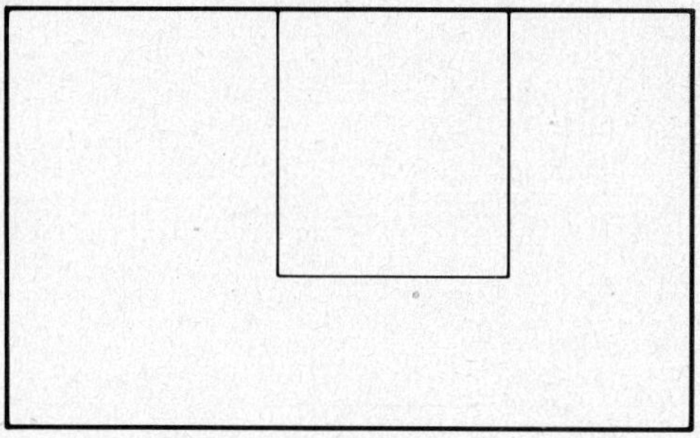

Figure 6.1 A hypothetical circuit board. (a) The four sections take up the entire screen. (b) If only one section is displayed, it is restricted to the same area it occupied in (a).

by doing this. The desired area is, indeed, singled out for attention, but it is displayed in the same rather small area of the screen that it would occupy if all segments were displayed at once. We need a system that not only singles out a given area for display, but can fill the entire screen with the contents of that area.

In this chapter, we will develop methods that give our system this capabililty. Before doing so, however, we must introduce some additional terminology. The circuit board in the foregoing example is called the **object**. The object exists in a real coordinate system called **object space**, where distances are measured in physical units, such as centimeters. As you might guess, the drawing displayed on the screen is called the **image**; the extent of the screen is called **image space**. Note that there is theoretically no limit on the extent of object space, whereas image space extends no farther than the limits of the screen.

WINDOWS

A **window** is an area of object space that is selected for display on the screen. For convenience, we use windows with two horizontal and two vertical sides.

Since object space is theoretically infinite in extent, choosing a window is an essential first step in making a drawing. We have been doing this unwittingly all along. For example, in making a graph of real-world data, we selected values of *xmin, xmax, ymin,* and *ymax.* These quantities determine how much of the data gets plotted. Figure 6.2 shows that they also fix the lower left and upper right corners of a window; everything in the window is displayed on the screen. The polygons and other shapes we drew were assumed to exist in a space defined by, for example, a drawing board or a digitizer. The boundaries of such a board form the window.

In the example of the circuit board, it is the window that enables the engineer to zero in on part of the board. Note that the window can be anywhere on the board and that it can be of any size; it has nothing to do with segments in the display file. Figure 6.3 shows a window that includes parts of all four segments of the circuit board.

Program 6.1: Setting the Window

Assumptions. Lower left coordinates of window are *xmin, ymin*; upper right coordinates are *xmax, ymax.*

```
PROCEDURE WINDOW;

BEGIN
  READLN(xmin,xmax,ymin,ymax)
END;
```

VIEWPORTS

A **viewport** is an area of the screen in which the contents of the window are displayed. Viewports and windows should not be confused; the window

Figure 6.2 A window in object space bounded by *xmin*, *xmax*, *ymin*, *ymax*.

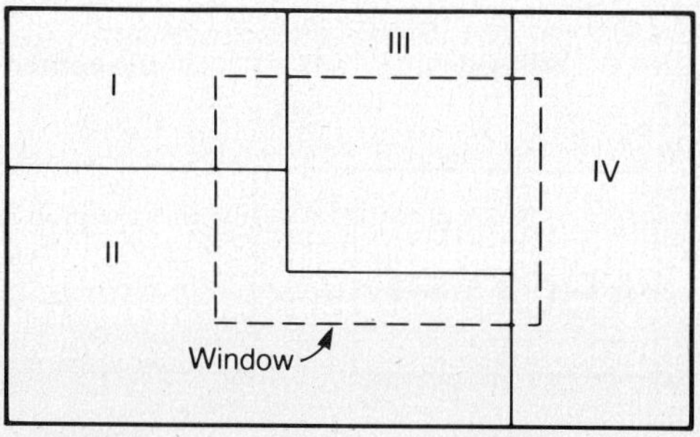

Figure 6.3 A window can be anywhere in object space.

determines *how much* information is displayed, while the viewport determines *where* the information is displayed. Thus, the area of a viewport may change, but the information contained therein stays the same. Figure 6.4 shows two window/viewport combinations. Figure 6.5 shows a window/viewport combination that does not fit our definition of a viewport. It is *not* the function of a viewport to take a screenful of information and eliminate from view everything outside the selected area.

For either a window or a viewport, the ratio of the width to the height is called the **aspect ratio**. An image will have the same proportions as its corresponding object only if the window has the same aspect ratio as the viewport. (This is the case illustrated in figure 6.4b.) If the aspect ratios differ, the image is compressed or expanded along one of the axes.

Program 6.2: Setting the Viewport Parameters

Assumptions. Screen is H pixels wide, V pixels high. Lower left coordinates of viewpoint are x_l, y_b; upper right coordinates of viewport are x_r, y_t.

```
PROCEDURE VIEWPORT;

BEGIN
  READLN(xl,xr,yb,yt);
  IF (xl < 0) OR (xr > H) OR (yb < 0) OR (yt > V)
  THEN
```

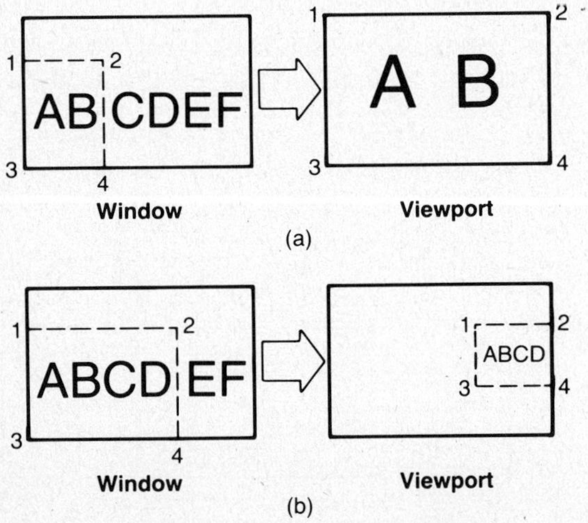

Figure 6.4 Two window/viewport combinations.

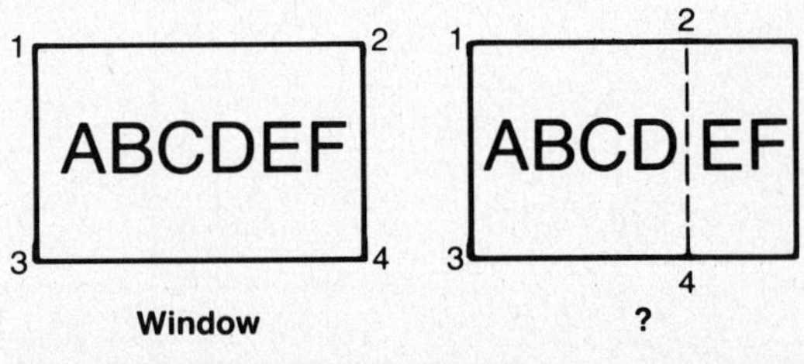

Figure 6.5 The dashed line cannot be the right boundary of the viewport, because it cuts off part of the window.

```
      BEGIN
        WRITELN('VIEWPORT OFF THE SCREEN. TRY AGAIN');
        VIEWPORT
      END
    END;
```

WINDOW-TO-VIEWPORT MAPPING

The process of displaying the window contents in the viewport is called **window-to-viewport mapping**. What, exactly, does this entail? Consider figure 6.6, which shows an arbitrary window in object space and an arbitrary viewport in image space. The mapping of window to viewport is such that a point A appears on the screen at A', B appears at B', and so on. All other points are mapped according to their relative positions between these boundaries. This problem is very similar to that for conversion from the world system to the device system. In fact, we can solve it the same way. We calculate the ratio M_1/M_2 for the window and the ratio M_1'/M_2' for the viewport and set them equal. The expressions for these are as follows (see figure 6.6 for labeling):

$$M_1 = x - xmin, \qquad M_1' = x' - x_l$$

$$M_2 = xmax - xmin, \qquad M_2' = x_r - x_l$$

Setting the two ratios equal gives:

$$(x - xmin)/(xmax - xmin) = (x' - x_l)/(x_r - x_l)$$

Solving for x' in terms of x yields:

$$x' = x_l + (x - xmin)(x_r - x_l)/(xmax - xmin)$$

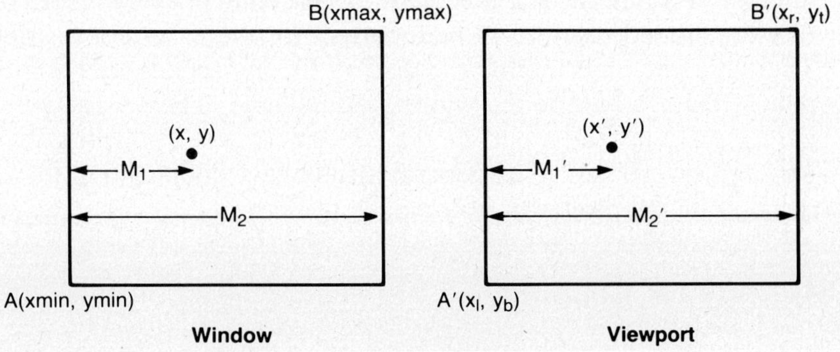

Figure 6.6 Geometry for window-to-viewport mapping derivation.

For the y-coordinates, we have an analogous procedure, with y's replacing x's in the equations. The result is

$$y' = y_b + (y - ymin)(y_t - y_b)/(ymax - ymin)$$

Program 6.3: Window-to-Viewport Conversion

Assumptions. Same as for programs 6.1 plus 6.2. *xw, yw* = coordinates in object space; *xv, yv* = coordinates in image space.

```
PROCEDURE MAP;

BEGIN
  xv := xl + (xr - xl)*(xw - xmin)/(xmax - xmin);
  yv := yb + (yt - yb)*(yw - ymin)/(ymax - ymin)
END;
```

Note that MAP converts only one pair of coordinates in object space to one pair of coordinates in image space. To map an entire window, we would have to call this procedure for each record of a linked list.

CLIPPING

Thus far, we have been making two assumptions about the drawing process:

1. The window is large enough to contain all points on an object.
2. The viewport is the entire screen.

In practice, these assumptions may not be true, and if they are not, the display file contains points that are not in the window. Since the display file interpreter is designed to execute the instruction in every record of the display file, the plotted results will be incorrect for the case of a restricted window. Therefore, we must modify the display file interpreter so that it does not plot points that are outside the window boundaries. The process of eliminating a part of a figure that is outside the window is called **clipping**. In this section, we shall investigate some general ideas about clipping and then write a new display file interpreter to accomplish the task.

General Strategy for Clipping

A computer drawing is basically a collection of line segments. Four such segments, with endpoints A and B, are shown in figure 6.7. Segment (a) is entirely outside the window; it is ignored. Segment (b) is entirely inside the

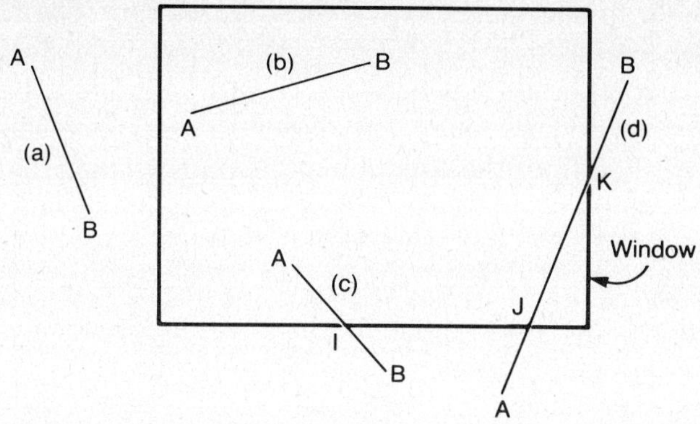

Figure 6.7 Line segments in the vicinity of a window. (a) Not plotted. (b) Completely plotted. (c) Plotted from A to I. (d) Plotted from J to K.

window; it is plotted from A to B. Segment (c) lies partially inside the window; the computer must calculate the intersection point I and plot only from A to I. Segment (d) is also partially inside, but there are two intersection points for the computer to calculate; it must plot only from J to K.

It should be evident from this brief discussion that the key property of a line segment is the number of times the segment intersects a window boundary. This is strongly, but not completely, related to the location of the endpoints. If both endpoints are inside, there can be no intersection with a boundary. If only one of the endpoints is inside, there must be one intersection. However, if both endpoints are outside, there could be either two intersections or none. With these basic ideas in mind, we can give a broad outline of how a clipping routine proceeds. First, it checks whether both endpoints of a segment are inside the window. If they are, the turtle plots directly from one endpoint to the other (assume `PENMODE(2)` for this example). If they are not, then the segment is checked for an intersection against each boundary. The number of intersections is counted and interpreted as follows:

1. If there are none, ignore the segment.
2. If there is one, record the intersection point and plot from the interior endpoint to the intersection.
3. If there are two, record both intersections and plot from one to the other.

Pascal Clipping Procedure and Related Procedures

Before we look at the programming aspects of clipping, let us briefly consider how we can determine the intersection of two line segments. In figure 6.8, we see a line segment in the vicinity of a vertical window boundary. The x-coordinate of the intersection is x_l. The y-coordinate, whatever it is, meets two simultaneous conditions: it is between y_1 and y_2 and also between y_b and y_t. The computer can do a two-step calculation to determine whether there is an intersection. First, it finds the equation of the line of which the line segment is a part:

$$y - y_1 = (x - x_1)(y_2 - y_1)/(x_2 - x_1)$$

Then it substitutes x_l, the x-coordinate of the intersection, for x and solves for y_i, the corresponding y-coordinate:

$$y_i = y_1 + (x_l - x_1)(y_2 - y_1)/(x_2 - x_1)$$

Then y_1 is checked to see if it meets the aforementioned conditions.

For the intersection of a line segment and a horizontal boundary (figure 6.9), the treatment is virtually identical. The intersection has a y-coordinate of y_t and an x-coordinate that is between x_l and x_r and between x_1 and x_2. (We leave the derivation of the conditions that correspond to the horizontal boundary case as an exercise.)

For the program itself, we assume that a linked list display file already exists and that a pointer to its beginning is stored in the variable *start*. In addition, we restrict ourselves to the MOVETO instruction. This simplifies the programming and allows us to concentrate on the clipping logic. The main routine is listed in program 6.4. It consists of repeated calls to a few other procedures, which are described after the main program.

Program 6.4: Main Clipping Routine

Assumptions (for this and following routines). Linked list display file. (x_1, y_1) and (x_2, y_2) are coordinates of endpoint of segment to be clipped. 'E' means point is outside the window; 'I' means point is inside the window.

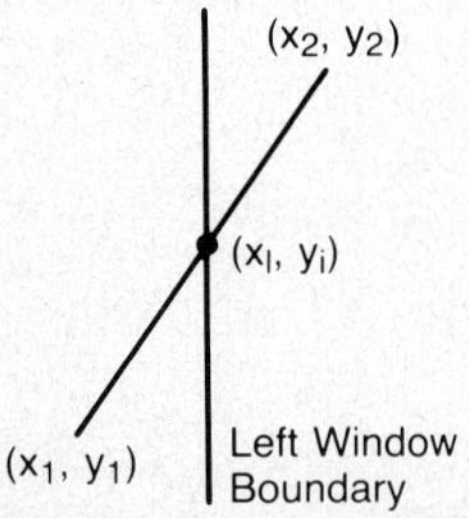

Figure 6.8 A line segment intersecting the left window boundary.

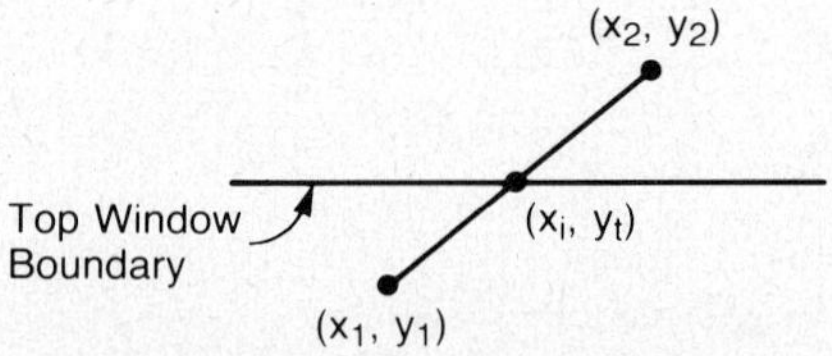

Figure 6.9 A line segment intersecting the top window boundary.

```
PROCEDURE CLIP;
VAR n:integer;       {counts intersections}

BEGIN
  p := start;
  q := p^.adr;
  x1 := p^.v1;       {x-coordinate of first endpoint}
  x2 := p^.v2;       {y-coordinate of first endpoint}
  y1 := q^.v1;       {x-coordinate of second endpoint}
  y2 := q^.v2;       {y-coordinate of second endpoint}
  WHILE q <> NIL DO
    BEGIN
      n := 0;
      LOCTEST;       {check location of endpoints}
      IF (loc1 = 'I') AND (loc2 = 'I')      {both inside?}
      THEN NEXTPOINT        {then plot and get next point}
      ELSE BOUNDTEST        {otherwise analyze possible}
    END                     {intersections}
END;
```

This routine is very simple in outline. It first calls the procedure LOCTEST:

```
PROCEDURE LOCTEST;

BEGIN
  IF (x1 < xmin) OR (x1 > xmax) OR (y1 < ymin) OR (y1 > ymax)
  THEN loc1 := 'E'     {any coordinate outside the window? if yes}
  ELSE loc1 := 'I';    {loc1 is 'E', if not loc1 = 'I'}
  IF (x2 < xmin) OR (x2 > xmax) OR (y2 < ymin) OR (y2 > ymax)
  THEN loc2 := 'E'     {same idea for loc2 as for loc1}
  ELSE loc2 := 'I'
END;
```

The procedure LOCTEST checks for any one of the following conditions:

$x < x_l, \qquad x > x_r, \qquad y < y_b, \qquad y > y_t$

If none of these conditions holds, then both points are inside and no checking for intersections is necessary. The procedure NEXTPOINT (described later) does the appropriate plotting and gets the next point from the display file. If any one of the foregoing conditions is true, then at least one of the points is outside the window. The procedure BOUNDTEST is then called to analyze the possible intersections:

```
PROCEDURE BOUNDTEST;

BEGIN      {xi, yi are coordinates of intersection points}
xi := xmin;
VERT;      {this checks for intersection with left boundary}
yi := ymin;
HORIZ;      {this checks for intersection with bottom boundary}
IF n < > 2      {if fewer than two intersections, keep checking}
THEN
  BEGIN
  xi := xmax;
  VERT      {this checks for intersection with right boundary}
  END;
IF n < > 2      {still fewer than two intersections? check top}
THEN
  BEGIN
  yi := ymax;
  VERT
  END;
IF n < > 2
THEN NEXTPOINT      {must have been only one intersection}
END;
```

BOUNDTEST uses HORIZ or VERT to check a line segment for an intersection with the left, bottom, right, and top boundary (it does the checking in that order). It keeps track of the number of intersections with the variable *n*. When HORIZ or VERT finds the first intersection, it calls SETINT to record the coordinates as (*ax, ay*). When it finds the second, it calls SETINT again, but this time to record the coordinates as (*bx, by*). At this point, the program exits BOUNDTEST via NEXTPOINT. If there are fewer than two intersections after all four boundaries have been checked, the program simply calls NEXTPOINT.

The procedure SETINT assigns the intersection coordinates to (*ax, ay*) or (*bx, by*) according to the value of *n*.

```
PROCEDURE SETINT;

BEGIN
  IF n = 2      {first intersection called (ax,ay)}
  THEN
    BEGIN      {second intersection called (bx, by)}
      bx := xi;
      by := yi;
```

```
        NEXTPOINT
      END;
    IF n = 1
    THEN
      BEGIN
        ax := xi;
        ay := yi
      END
END;
```

The procedure NEXTPOINT also uses the value of *n* in determining the correct plot commands. Then it calls the next point by advancing the pointer to the next record in the display file.

```
PROCEDURE NEXTPOINT;

BEGIN
  CASE n OF      {depending on number of intersects}
  0: PLOT (x1,y1,x2,y2);      {0: plot between endpoints}
  1: IF locl = 'I'      {1: plot from inside endpoint}
     THEN PLOT (x1,y1,ax,ay)      {to intersection point}
     ELSE PLOT (x2,y2,ax,ay);
  2: PLOT(ax,ay,bx,by)      {2: plot between intersection points}
  END;
  q := q^.adr;
  x1 := x2;
  y1 := y2;
  x2 := q^.v1;      {advance pointer; get new endpoint}
  y2 := q^.v2
END;
```

The procedures to check for intersections (HORIZ and VERT) and the PLOT routine are as follows:

```
PROCEDURE HORIZ;

BEGIN
  xi := x1 + (yi - y1)*(x2 - x1)/(y2 - y1);
  IF x1 < x2
  THEN IF (xi >= x1) AND (xi <= x2)
         THEN BEGIN
                n := n + 1;
                SETINT
                END;
  IF x1 >x2
```

```
  THEN IF (xi >= x2) AND (xi <= x1)
         THEN BEGIN
                n := n + 1;
                SETINT
                END
END;


PROCEDURE VERT;

BEGIN
  yi := y1 + (y2 - y1)*(xi - x1)/(x2 - x1);
  IF y1 < y2
  THEN IF (yi >= y1) AND (yi <= y2)
         THEN BEGIN
                n := n + 1;
                SETINT
                END;
  IF y1 > y2
  THEN IF (yi >= y2) AND (yi <= y1)
    THEN BEGIN
           n := n + 1;
           SETINT
           END
END;


PROCEDURE PLOT (z1,z2,z3,z4:real);

BEGIN
  PENMODE(0);
  MOVETO(z1,z2);
  PENMODE(2);
  MOVETO(z3,z4)
END;
```

ZOOMING AND PANNING

When a window is mapped to a viewport, a figure that occupies a certain fraction of the window occupies the same fraction of the viewport. If the window surrounding this figure is made larger, the figure will appear smaller in the new viewport. Similarly, if the window is made smaller, the figure will appear larger. We can take advantage of this simple idea to simulate the cinematic effect of **zooming**. In zooming, a given figure can be made to appear progressively larger by making the window progressively smaller. This is called zooming in. Similarly, we can make the window progressively larger, thereby zooming out. In both cases, we keep the center of the window fixed. Theoretically, we can zoom in or out until the figure becomes unrecognizable.

We can accomplish zooming with a simple modification to the window-to-viewport mapping process. Assume that a particular window is in effect. Suppose that we increase the height of the window by D. Then we should increase its width by $R \cdot D$ to keep the window's proportions constant (where R is the aspect ratio, width/height). To keep the center of the window fixed, we make the change to the height and width in the following way:

$$xmax \rightarrow xmax + R \cdot D/2$$

$$xmin \rightarrow xmin - R \cdot D/2$$

$$ymax \rightarrow ymax + D/2$$

$$ymin \rightarrow ymin - D/2$$

If we pass these new window dimensions to the mapping routine, our hypothetical figure in the window will appear to be reduced in size. The zooming effect results when the foregoing procedure is repeated, as illustrated in figure 6.10.

The other cinematic effect, **panning**, is accomplished by keeping the size of the window fixed but moving it through object space. For example, if the window in figure 6.11a starts at position A, the viewport would look like figure 6.11b. If we execute the following changes to the window dimensions:

$$xmin \rightarrow xmin + D$$

$$xmax \rightarrow xmax + D$$

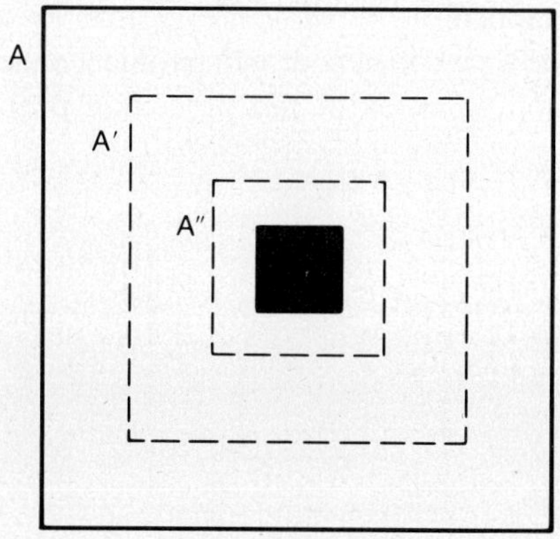

Figure 6.10 Zooming in on an object. As window A is reduced in size, the dark square in the center appears larger on the screen. It takes up about 3 percent of window A but about 25 percent of window A''.

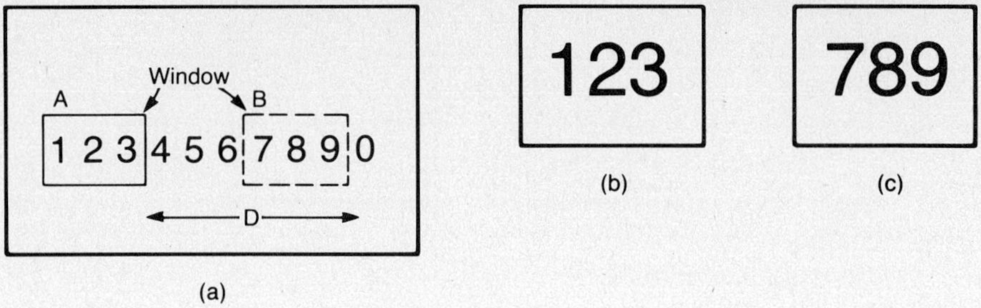

Figure 6.11 Planning. As the window in (a) is moved from *A* to *B*, the screen changes from (b) to (c).

and then map the new window to the viewport, we get the image shown in figure 6.11c. Panning is accomplished by repeating this process.

Figure 6.12 is a flowchart of the zooming or panning process. We leave the programming details, which consist of procedures already defined, as an exercise.

PROBLEMS

6.1. Given a window with the following boundaries:

$x_l = 20, \quad y_b = 0, \quad x_r = 130, \quad y_t = 80$

For each of the following line segments, state exactly which part gets plotted:

A: (0,60) → (40,100) *B:* (10,30) → (60,40)
C: (90,10) → (110,40) *D:* (140,30) → (110,90)

6.2. Write a program that allows the user to map one or two different windows to one or two different viewports. The image in the first viewport should not disappear when the second viewport is mapped.

6.3. The figure on the left below shows two objects drawn in object space. Using one of the window-to-viewport mapping cases of the preceding problem, write a

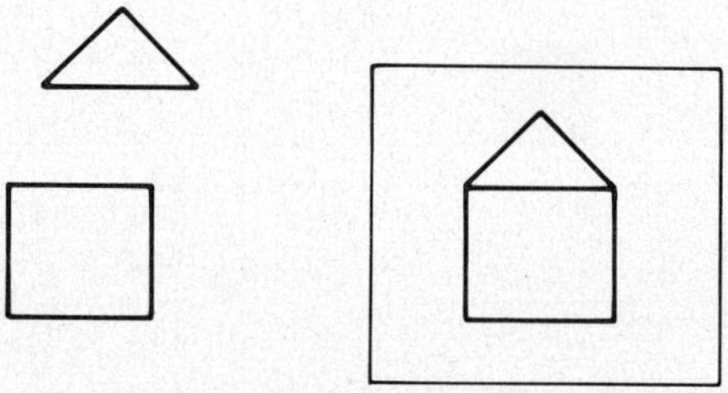

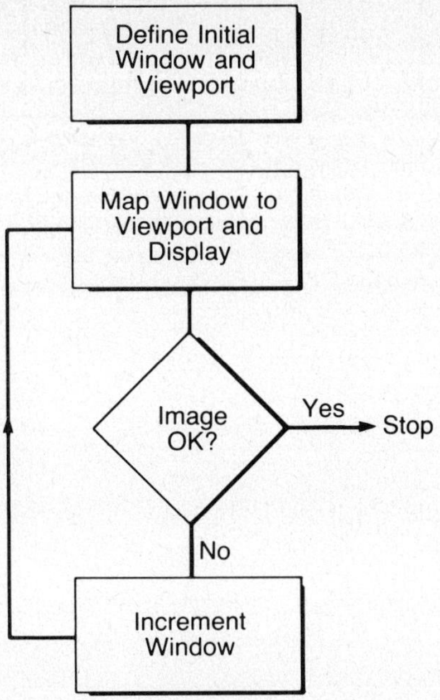

Figure 6.12 Flowchart for implementing zooming or panning.

program that draws the figure on the right (the image is centered at the center of the screen).

6.4. In each of the following cases, write the explicit mapping equation that accomplishes the indicated transformation:

	Window	*Viewport*
A:	$xmin = 10,\ xmax = 80$	$x_l = 0,\ y_b = 0$
	$ymin = 0,\ ymax = 50$	$x_r = 640,\ y_b = 200$
B:	$xmin = -30,\ xmax = 100$	$x_l = 40,\ y_b = 20$
	$ymin = 10,\ ymax = 60$	$x_r = 100,\ y_t = 100$

6.5. Derive the equation for clipping against a vertical boundary.

6.6. Implement a procedure that performs the user's choice of zooming or panning.

6.7. **(a)** Write a program that erases everything in a viewport.
(b) Write a program that erases everything outside a viewport.

REFERENCES

Harrington, S. *Computer Graphics: A Programming Approach.* New York: McGraw-Hill, 1983, chapter 6.

Hearn, D., and Baker, M. P. *Microcomputer Graphics.* Englewood Cliffs, N.J.: Prentice-Hall, 1983, chapter 8.

Pavlidis, T. *Algorithms for Graphics and Image Processing.* Potomac, Md.: Computer Science Press, 1982, chapter 15.

Chapter 7

Three-Dimensional Graphics: Part One

When you have finished this chapter, you will be able to draw (with some limitations) a realistic image of a three-dimensional object on the two-dimensional screen.

Objectives

1. To develop elementary analytic geometry concepts, such as coordinate systems, lines, planes, and vectors in three dimensions.
2. To understand the difference between parallel and perspective projections.
3. To develop formulas for simple cases of parallel and perspective projections.

Many useful graphics applications require no more than the two-dimensional techniques we have studied. A bar chart, used often in business, is a good example. Suppose, however, that we are designing a critical part for a jet engine. This part must mesh smoothly with many others. To judge the fit of the part, we need views of it from different angles. As another example, if we wanted to train pilots using flight simulators, we would certainly need a good deal of three-dimensional realism in our graphics. These and other problems force us to consider the complex and interesting problem of three-dimensional graphics. Some of the two-dimensional concepts have relatively straightforward analogs in three dimensions, but there are problems that are unique to three-dimensional graphics. First, every three-dimensional object must be represented on a two-dimensional screen. This entails a transformation from three to two dimensions. Second, we cannot see all sides of a three-dimensional object at one time. Finally, it is possible for one object to block the view of another. In this and the remaining two chapters, we shall extend the two-dimensional concepts already presented and address the issues mentioned here.

THREE-DIMENSIONAL COORDINATE SYSTEMS

Representing a point in three dimensions requires a three-dimensional coordinate system. We can establish such a system with a set of three perpendicular axes—two in the plane of the paper, one perpendicular to it. There are two possible choices for the latter axis, as indicated in figure 7.1, which lead to two distinct types of coordinate systems. Figure 7.1a shows a **left-handed coordinate system**; if you curl the fingers of your left hand in the direction of the arrow, the thumb will point in the positive *z*-direction. The same principle applies to figure 7.1b, but for the right hand; thus, it is a **right-handed coordinate system.**

When three-dimensional objects are represented on a CRT screen, the third dimension appears to be inside the tube. Therefore, it is reasonable to imagine a third axis extending into the tube. Since we are so used to seeing a

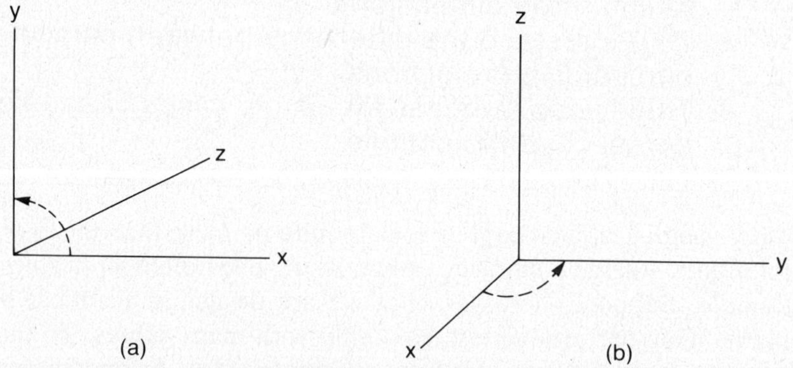

Figure 7.1 Three-dimensional coordinate systems. (a) Left-handed coordinate system; if the fingers of the left hand are curled along the arrow, the thumb points in the *z*-direction (into the paper). (b) Right-handed coordinate system; if the fingers of the right hand are curled along the arrow, the thumb points in the *z*-direction (upward).

two-dimensional system labeled x–y, as in figure 7.1a, many computer graphics systems use the left-handed coordinate system. In mathematics, we often use a right-handed system. In this text, we will use the right-handed system, letting the y-axis extend into the screen while the screen itself is the x–z plane.

VECTORS IN THREE DIMENSIONS

Having chosen our coordinate system, we can define three unit vectors that point along the coordinate axes (figure 7.2a). The vectors **i** and **j** have the same meaning as before; the additional vector, **k**, points in the positive z-direction.

Any vector in three dimensions can be represented in the form shown in figure 7.2b:

$$\mathbf{V} = a\mathbf{i} + b\mathbf{j} + c\mathbf{k}$$

Two vectors

$$\mathbf{V}_1 = a_1\mathbf{i} + b_1\mathbf{j} + c_1\mathbf{k}$$
$$\mathbf{V}_2 = a_2\mathbf{i} + b_2\mathbf{j} + c_2\mathbf{k}$$

have a sum, difference, and dot product entirely analogous to their respective two-dimensional cases:

$$\mathbf{V}_1 + \mathbf{V}_2 = (a_1 + a_2)\mathbf{i} + (b_1 + b_2)\mathbf{j} + (c_1 + c_2)\mathbf{k}$$
$$\mathbf{V}_1 - \mathbf{V}_2 = (a_1 - a_2)\mathbf{i} + (b_1 - b_2)\mathbf{j} + (c_1 - c_2)\mathbf{k}$$
$$\mathbf{V}_1 \cdot \mathbf{V}_2 = a_1a_2 + b_1b_2 + c_1c_2$$

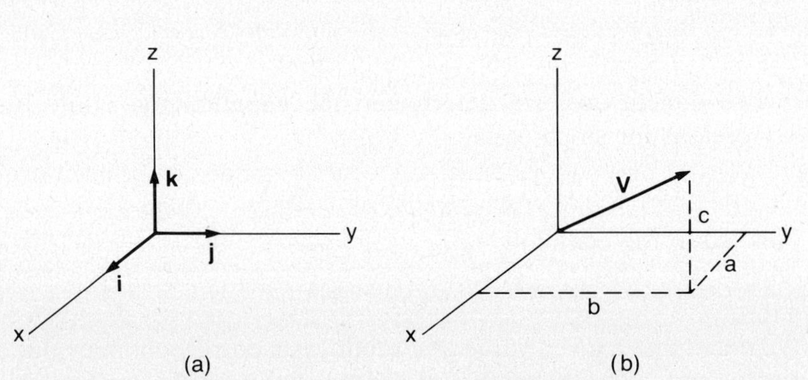

Figure 7.2 Vectors in three dimensions. (a) Unit vectors. (b) Vector **V** has components a, b, and c in the x-, y-, and z-directions.

The cross product

$$\mathbf{V}_1 \times \mathbf{V}_2 = (a_1\mathbf{i} + b_1\mathbf{j} + c_1\mathbf{k}) \times (a_2\mathbf{i} + b_2\mathbf{j} + c_2\mathbf{k})$$

is perpendicular to both $\mathbf{V}_1$ and $\mathbf{V}_2$ and is the sum of nine separate cross products of the form:

$$\begin{array}{lll} \mathbf{i}\times\mathbf{i} & \mathbf{i}\times\mathbf{j} & \mathbf{i}\times\mathbf{k} \\ \mathbf{j}\times\mathbf{i} & \mathbf{j}\times\mathbf{j} & \mathbf{j}\times\mathbf{k} \\ \mathbf{k}\times\mathbf{i} & \mathbf{k}\times\mathbf{j} & \mathbf{k}\times\mathbf{k} \end{array}$$

The angles between these products are either 0 degrees ($\mathbf{i}\times\mathbf{i}$, $\mathbf{j}\times\mathbf{j}$, and $\mathbf{k}\times\mathbf{k}$) or 90 degrees (all the others). Hence, the three cross products with 0-degree angles are zero, while the remaining ones have magnitudes of one and directions determined by a right-hand rule (see figure A.16):

$$\begin{array}{lll} \mathbf{i}\times\mathbf{j} = \mathbf{k} & \mathbf{j}\times\mathbf{k} = \mathbf{i} & \mathbf{k}\times\mathbf{i} = \mathbf{j} \\ \mathbf{j}\times\mathbf{i} = -\mathbf{k} & \mathbf{k}\times\mathbf{j} = -\mathbf{i} & \mathbf{i}\times\mathbf{k} = -\mathbf{j} \end{array}$$

With the correct coefficients plugged in, the cross product is

$$\mathbf{V}_1 \times \mathbf{V}_2 = (b_1c_2 - b_2c_1)\mathbf{i} + (a_2c_1 - a_1c_2)\mathbf{j} + (a_1b_2 - a_2b_1)\mathbf{k}$$

We leave it to you to show that this is the result obtained when the following determinant:

$$\begin{vmatrix} \mathbf{i} & \mathbf{j} & \mathbf{k} \\ a_1 & b_1 & c_1 \\ a_2 & b_2 & c_2 \end{vmatrix}$$

is evaluated according to the rules of determinants (see appendix A).

LINES

In two dimensions, we determined the equation for a line by setting two expressions for slope equal:

$$(y - y_1)/(x - x_1) = (y_2 - y_1)/(x_2 - x_1) \qquad (7.1)$$

This led to the equation

$$y - y_1 = (y_2 - y_1)(x - x_1)/(x_2 - x_1)$$

We noted that a given value of x produces a corresponding value of y. In three dimensions, z is also related to x according to a similar equation:

$$(z - z_1)/(x - x_1) = (z_2 - z_1)/(x_2 - x_1) \qquad (7.2)$$

or

$$z - z_1 = (z_2 - z_1)(x - x_1)/(x_2 - x_1)$$

Therefore, in three dimensions, a given value of x produces corresponding values of both y and z. We can rewrite equations (7.1) and (7.2) slightly:

$$(y - y_1)/(y_2 - y_1) = (x - x_1)/(x_2 - x_1)$$
$$(z - z_1)/(z_2 - z_1) = (x - x_1)/(x_2 - x_1)$$

If we let

$$\alpha = (x - x_1)/(x_2 - x_1)$$

then we can write a set of **parametric** equations for the line:

$$x = \alpha(x_2 - x_1) + x_1$$
$$y = \alpha(y_2 - y_1) + y_1$$
$$z = \alpha(z_2 - z_1) + z_1$$

This is another, and sometimes more convenient, way to express a line in three dimensions. At every point on the line, α has a certain value. Once we determine that value, plugging it into the foregoing equations determines x, y, and z for that point.

Let us pursue the parametric formulation a bit further. Suppose that we draw vectors from the origin to points (x_1, y_1, z_1) and (x_2, y_2, z_2). If we call these, respectively, $\mathbf{V}_1$ and $\mathbf{V}_2$, then

$$\mathbf{V}_1 = x_1\mathbf{i} + y_1\mathbf{j} + z_1\mathbf{k}$$
$$\mathbf{V}_2 = x_2\mathbf{i} + y_2\mathbf{j} + z_2\mathbf{k}$$

If we perform the subtraction

$$\mathbf{V}_2 - \mathbf{V}_1 = (x_2 - x_1)\mathbf{i} + (y_2 - y_1)\mathbf{j} + (z_2 - z_1)\mathbf{k}$$

then $\mathbf{V}_2 - \mathbf{V}_1$ points in the direction of the line (figure 7.3). However, the components of $\mathbf{V}_2 - \mathbf{V}_1$ are clearly the same as the coefficients of α in the parametric equations. Therefore, if we have a vector

$$\mathbf{V} = xd\mathbf{i} + yd\mathbf{j} + zd\mathbf{k}$$

which points in the direction of the line, then the parametric equations look like this:

$$x = \alpha \cdot xd + x_1$$
$$y = \alpha \cdot yd + y_1$$
$$z = \alpha \cdot zd + z_1$$

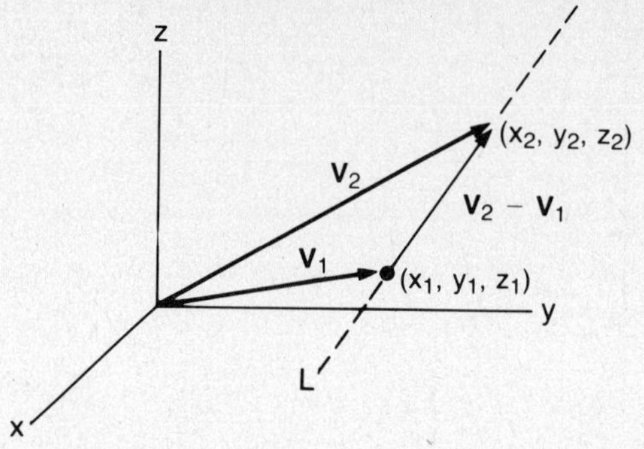

Figure 7.3 $\mathbf{V}_2 - \mathbf{V}_1$ points along line L.

Hence, we can write equations for a line if we know a vector in its direction and the coordinates of *one* point.

PLANES

Just as it takes two points to determine a unique line, it takes three points to determine a unique plane. For our purposes, however, it is less important to determine the plane itself than to determine its orientation. We can do this easily using vectors.

Consider a line that is perpendicular to the plane. Along this line, we can draw two vectors pointing outward from the plane (figure 7.4). These vectors, called **normal vectors** (or **normals**), change direction as the orientation of the plane changes. Hence, either of them could be used to specify the plane's orientation. The question is, which one? When we look at a particular face (plane) of an object, we can see one side but not the other. We shall use the normal to the side we can see to indicate the orientation of the plane. Note that we have labeled the vertices of the face in counterclockwise order. If we form vectors between successive vertices (figure 7.5), the cross product of any vector with the one following it will be in the direction of the desired normal;

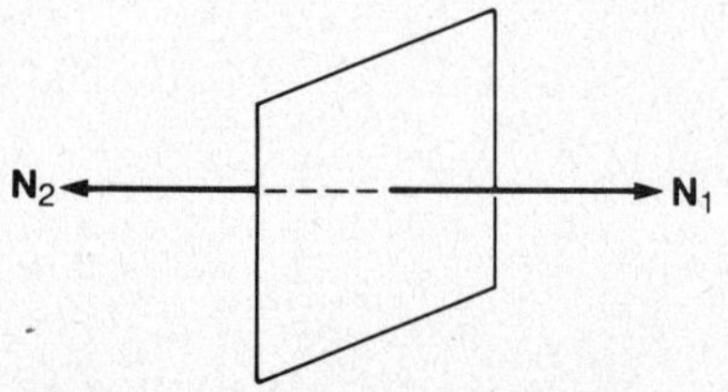

Figure 7.4 Every plane has two normal directions.

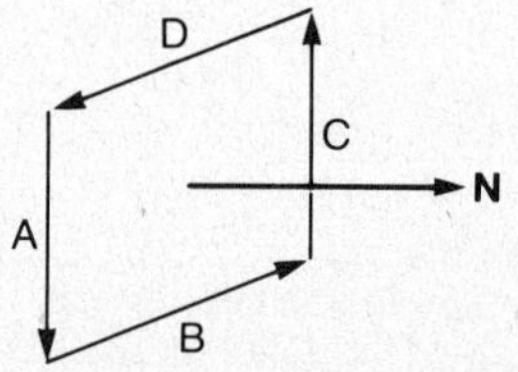

Figure 7.5 Establishing a convention for choosing a normal.

that is, $\mathbf{A} \times \mathbf{B}$, $\mathbf{B} \times \mathbf{C}$, $\mathbf{C} \times \mathbf{D}$, and $\mathbf{D} \times \mathbf{A}$ are all suitable for defining the orientation of the plane.

PROJECTIONS

The problem of representing a point from a three-dimensional object on a two-dimensional plane is solved by a mathematical technique called **projection**. Figure 7.6 shows examples of two projections, each illustrating the projection of two points onto a plane. In both cases, we move along lines, called **projectors**, to get from A to A' and from B to B'. In figure 7.6a, the lines converge to a point called the **center of projection**; this is a **perspective projection**. In figure 7.6b, the lines are parallel (the center of projection is at infinity); this is a **parallel projection**. In this chapter, we shall study a special case of each type—that in which the plane of projection is parallel to the screen.

Parallel Projections

When we are dealing with parallel projections, we must have a way of specifying the direction of the projectors. Let us consider a unit vector, PP', in the direction of an arbitrary projector (figure 7.7). Note that PP' is not parallel to any of the axes. It makes angle B with the x–z plane, while its projection onto the x–z plane makes an angle A with the horizontal. Both of these angles are specified for a given projection. We will derive formulas for the lengths RQ, QP, and $P'R$, since these are the magnitudes of the xd, yd, and zd components, respectively, of the projector's direction. From the diagram, we have:

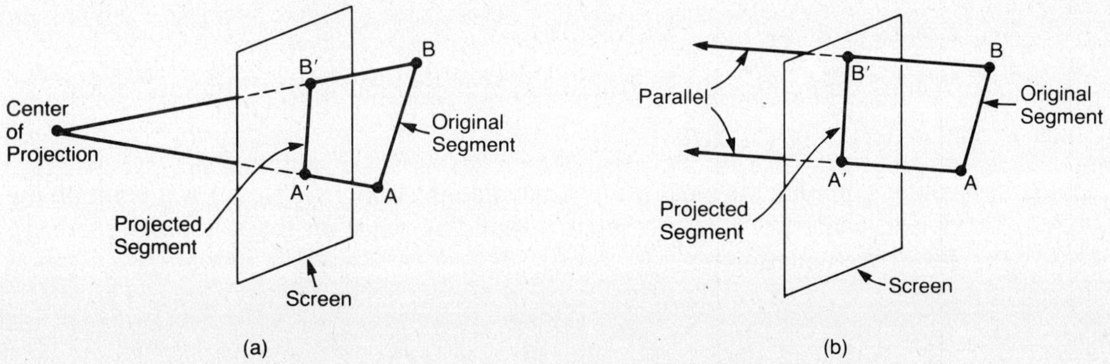

Figure 7.6 (a) Perspective projection: projectors converge at center of projection. (b) Parallel projection: projectors do not converge, but are parallel.

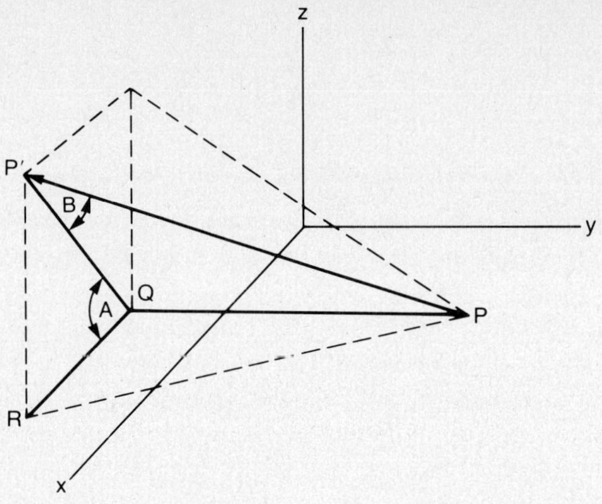

Figure 7.7 Geometry for parallel projection derivation. *PP′* is the projector, and can be considered a unit vector.

$$yd = QP = -\sin B$$
$$P'Q = \cos B$$
$$xd = RQ = P'Q \cdot \cos A = \cos B \cdot \cos A$$
$$zd = P'R = P'Q \cdot \sin A = \cos B \cdot \sin A$$

Having taken care of the direction, we can turn our attention to the general formula for a parallel projection. We start with the parametric equations for a line:

$$x = xd \cdot \alpha + x_1$$
$$y = yd \cdot \alpha + y_1 \quad (\text{with } y = 0)$$
$$z = zd \cdot \alpha + z_1$$

We are assuming that the direction of projection is given by the vector

$$\mathbf{V} = xd\mathbf{i} + yd\mathbf{j} + zd\mathbf{k}$$

whose components we have just calculated. Also, (x_1, y_1, z_1) is a point on the object, while $(x, y, 0)$ is the corresponding point on the x–y plane (screen). From the equation

$$0 = yd \cdot \alpha + y_1$$

we can solve for the parameter α:

$$\alpha = -y_1/y_2$$

Then:

$$x = -y_1 \cdot xd/yd + x_1$$
$$z = -y_1 \cdot zd/yd + z_1$$

In other words, given the components of the projector's direction and the coordinates of a point, we can find the corresponding point on the screen, provided that the projection is made onto the x–z plane.

Now we are ready to look at some special cases of parallel projection. For this purpose, we will use the cube whose coordinates are indicated in figure 7.8. First, a word is necessary about the orientation of the cube. Imagine a coordinate system in the cube such that two of the axes lie in a face and the third extends inside. These are called **principal axes**. Our cube is oriented so that the principal axes are in the same directions as our coordinate axes. In the examples that follow, we have chosen various combinations of A and B, and we show what a user sees on the screen. In addition, we use the foregoing formulas to calculate the screen coordinates of certain points.

Case 1: $A = B = 90°$, **Orthographic Projection.** In an orthographic projection, the projector is normal to the projection plane. Also, the projector is along one of the principal axes. Figure 7.9 shows top and side views of this projection. From the direction formulas, it should be clear that

$$xd = zd = 0$$
$$yd = -1$$

The projection formulas are then

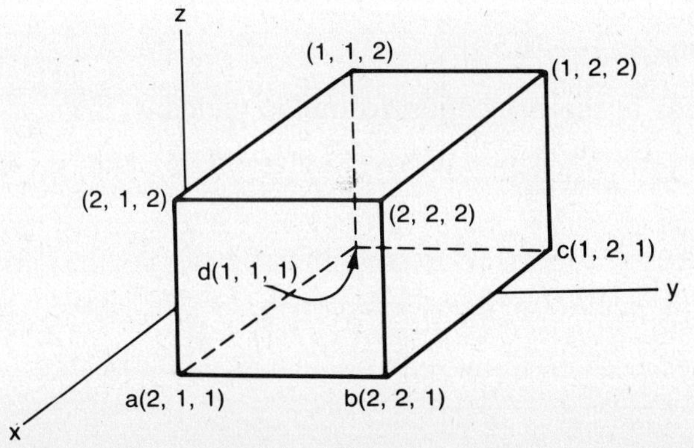

Figure 7.8 Cube for projection examples. Here, *ab* is a line segment perpendicular to the screen; *ad* is a line segment parallel to the screen.

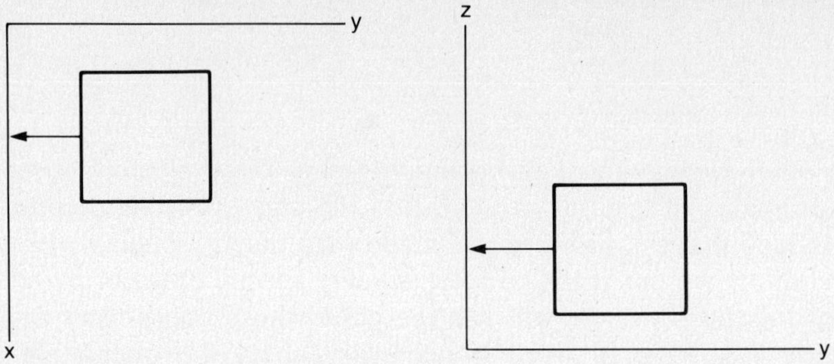

Figure 7.9 Two views of an orthographic projection.

$$x = x_1$$
$$z = z_1$$

The x- and z-coordinates on the screen are therefore identical to those of the point in space, and we see an exact duplicate of the front of the cube (figure 7.10).

Case 2: $B = 45°$, Oblique Projection (Cavalier). In an oblique projection, the projector is not normal to the projection plane, nor is it parallel to any of the principal axes (figure 7.11). The cavalier projection has interesting properties, as we shall see. Let us calculate the direction for an angle $A = 45°$:

$$xd = \cos(45) \cdot \cos(45) = 0.5$$
$$yd = -\sin(45) = -0.707$$
$$zd = \cos(45) \cdot \sin(45) = 0.5$$

Using these values in the projection formulas yields:

$$x = (0.707)y_1 + x_1$$
$$z = (0.707)y_1 + z_1$$

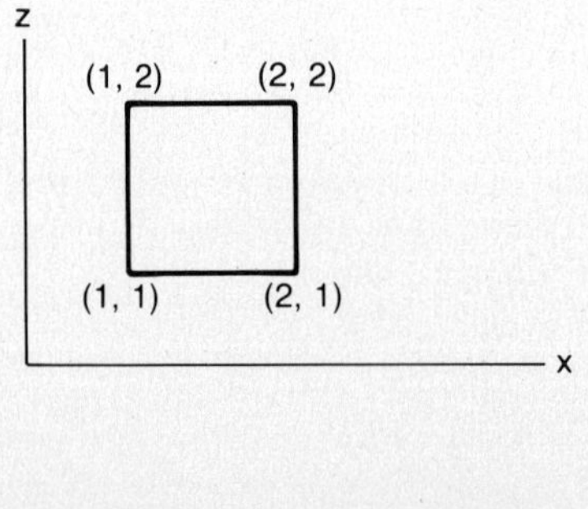

Figure 7.10 Screen view of the orthographic projection in case 1.

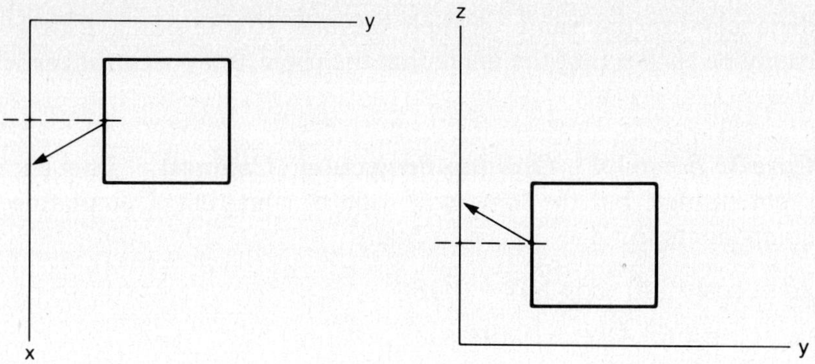

Figure 7.11 Two views of an oblique projection.

It is very instructive to calculate the coordinates of the projections of points *a*, *b*, and *d*:

$$a: \quad x = 0.707 + 2 = 2.707$$
$$z = 0.707 + 1 = 1.707$$
$$b: \quad x = 2(0.707) + 2 = 3.414$$
$$z = 2(0.707) + 1 = 2.414$$
$$d: \quad x = 0.707 + 1 = 1.707$$
$$z = 0.707 + 1 = 1.707$$

Figure 7.12 shows the projected view of the cube for this case. If you calculate the distance between the projected points *a* and *d*, it is the same—1—as that for the original cube. This may not surprise you, since the segment *ad* was originally parallel to the projection plane. Now calculate it for the projected segment *ab*; it is also 1, even though this segment was originally perpendicular to the projection plane. In the cavalier projection, all projected

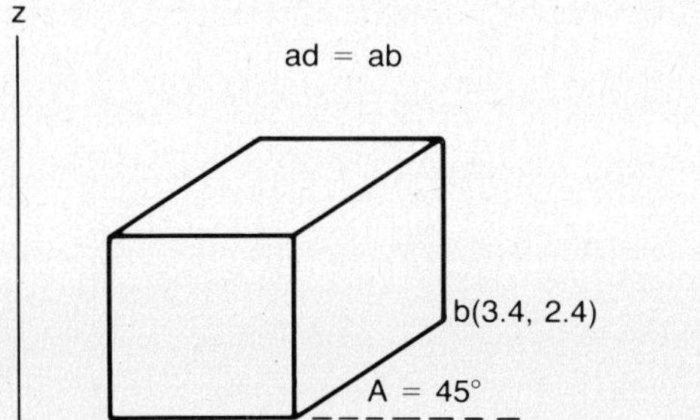

Figure 7.12 Screen view of the oblique projection in case 2 (cavalier).

distances are the same as their original counterparts. Furthermore, it can easily be shown that the angle that the projected y-axis makes with the x-axis is A.

Case 3: $B = 63.4°$, **Oblique Projection (Cabinet).** This choice of B may seem strange, but the logic will soon be apparent. Calculating the direction components for $A = 30°$, we obtain:

$$xd = \cos(63.4) \cdot \cos(30) = 0.388$$
$$yd = -\sin(63.4) = -0.894$$
$$zd = \cos(63.4) \cdot \sin(30) = 0.224$$

Plugging these values into the projection formulas gives:

$$x = (0.388/0.894)y_1 + x_1$$
$$= 0.434y_1 + x_1$$
$$z = (0.224/0.894)y_1 + z_1$$
$$= 0.251y_1 + z_1$$

Let us calculate the projected coordinates for the points a and b:

$$a: \quad x = 0.434 \cdot 1 + 2 = 2.434$$
$$z = 0.251 \cdot 1 + 1 = 1.251$$
$$b: \quad x = 0.434 \cdot 2 + 2 = 2.868$$
$$z = 0.251 \cdot 2 + 1 = 1.502$$

From these values, you can determine that the distance between the projected points a and b is 0.5. This projection is shown in figure 7.13. In the cabinet projection, the projected distances of segments that are perpendicular to the projection plane are one-half those of the original figure. As in the cavalier

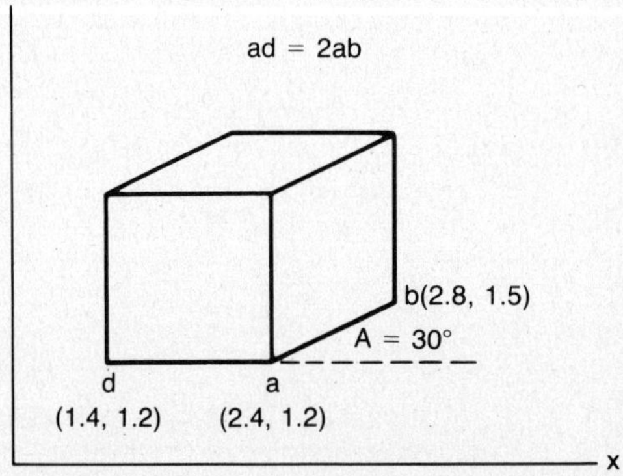

Figure 7.13 Screen view of the oblique projection in case 3 (cabinet).

projection, segments that are originally parallel to the projection plane project to the same length as the originals. Note that segments perpendicular to the plane of projection make an angle of 30 degrees with the *x*-axis.

Programming Considerations for Parallel Projections

Now that we have discussed the basics of projecting three-dimensional objects, we can attend to the matter of developing the necessary programming. As you might guess, the first order of business is creating a display file. What should the display file structure look like? We certainly want fields for the three coordinates of a vertex and the pen mode. For simplicity, we will use only the MOVETO instruction, so we can leave out the *opcode* field. We will often deal with more than one object, so we should put each object in a separate segment. Hence, we shall need a field for segment number.

So far, this looks like a repeat of a two-dimensional display file. However, a three-dimensional object is assumed to be composed of planar faces (polygons), rather than line segments. Therefore, our display file should somehow be organized into faces. We can do this by first entering the vertices for one side into the display file, then doing the same for the second side, and so on. Note that with this system, a given vertex will be entered more than once, since a vertex belongs to more than one side. Therefore, we shall include one more field for side number in the display file. A reasonable structure for the display file is as follows:

```
TYPE Display = RECORD
               x:REAL;
               y:REAL;
               z:REAL;
               penstatus:(on,off,erase);
               segnum:INTEGER;
               side:INTEGER
               END;
```

The meaning of the first four variables should be obvious. We also use *segnum* to number the objects and *side* to number the sides.

Now that we have set the structure of the display file, we can outline a simple procedure to project three-dimensional objects according to the methods we have discussed:

1. Create the display file.
2. For each record in a side, transform the three vertex coordinates to

two projection coordinates, then plot that side on the screen.

3. Perform the preceding step for each side in the display file.

The procedure to project an object is simple in outline; it calculates the necessary parameters, then calls two other procedures. We will give all three procedures here.

Program 7.1: Parallel Projection of a Three-Dimensional Object onto the Screen

Assumptions

```
Display = RECORD
          x:REAL;
          y:REAL;
          x:REAL;
          penstatus:(on,off,erase);
          segnum:INTEGER;
          side:INTEGER
          END;
```

Segmented linked list with structure as given here. *xd, yd, zd*: direction of projection. *A* and *B* angles as in figure 7.7.

```
PROCEDURE PARALLELPROJECTION;

BEGIN
  READLN(A,B);
  xd :=cos(B)*cos(A);        {calculates}
  yd:= -sin(B);              {projection}
  zd:= cos(B)*sin(A);        {direction}
  TRANSFORM;       {calculates projected coordinates}
  DRAWIT     {draws projected figure}
END;
```

The procedure TRANSFORM goes through the display file and calculates the two screen coordinates for each vertex of the object. It uses the *x* and *z* fields of the original display file to store the results.

```
PROCEDURE TRANSFORM;         {general parallel projection}

BEGIN
  p:= start;       {set pointer to first record}
  WHILE p < > NIL DO
    BEGIN
```

```
      p^.x:= -(p^.y)*xd/yd + p^.x;      {calculate projected x}
      p^.z:= -(p^.y)*zd/yd + p^.z;      {calculate projected z}
      p:= p^.adr     {advance pointer}
    END
END;
```

The procedure DRAWIT goes through the newly transformed display file and draws the projected figure.

```
PROCEDURE DRAWIT;

BEGIN
  PENMODE(0);
  p:= start;
  WHILE p <> NIL DO
    BEGIN
      MOVETO(p^.x,p^.y);       {go to first point without plotting}
      IF p^.penstatus = on     {but go to all others according to
                                           PENMODE}
      THEN PENMODE(2)
      ELSE PENMODE(0);
      p:= p^.adr
    END
END;
```

Perspective Projections

Although parallel projections convincingly suggest a three-dimensional quality, they lack the realism of the perspective projection. In a perspective projection, objects in the foreground are drawn larger than those in the distance. This mirrors the situation in the real world, where an object close to an observer appears larger than the same object located far away. In addition, certain lines that are parallel in the real world converge in a perspective drawing. Figure 7.14 shows a perspective representation of a cube. Lines that are normally parallel to the x-axis (AE, CG, BF) converge in the drawing at Q. Similarly, lines that are normally parallel to the y-axis (AB, DC, FE) converge at Q'. The points Q and Q' are called **vanishing points**; the line connecting them is called the **horizon**.

How can we make a perspective drawing? Imagine standing in one spot, closing one eye, and viewing an object through a picture window (Figure 7.15). The window is the projection plane, and the eye is the center of projection. A projector connects a point Q on the object with the eye; the projector that is perpendicular to the projection plane is called the **line of sight**. Using the window as a sketchpad, we can trace the outline of the object

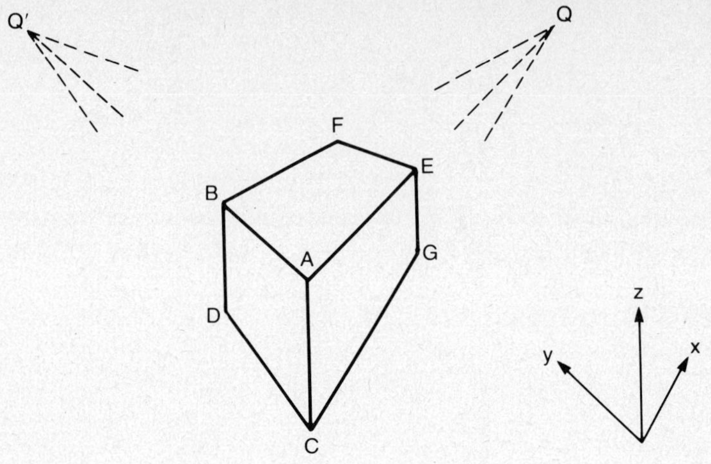

Figure 7.14 Perspective drawing of a cube.

with a marking pen. What results is a perspective drawing of that object. Before jumping into the mathematics of perspective, we must first understand the factors that influence the final perspective drawing of an object. For example, suppose that an observer looks at the object while standing on his head. Obviously, his perspective drawing will be inverted. Similarly, if the observer moves to a window in a different room, he will draw a different view of the object. Finally, suppose that the window is moved farther from the observer's eye (figure 7.16). Then the object takes up a greater fraction of the

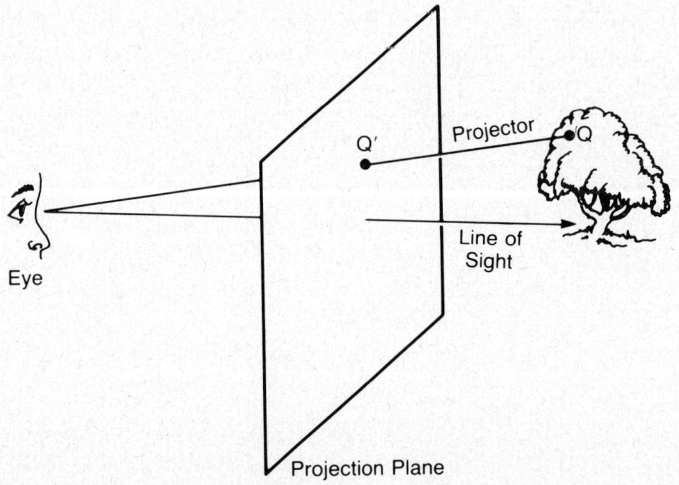

Figure 7.15 Relationship of observer, projection plane, and object.

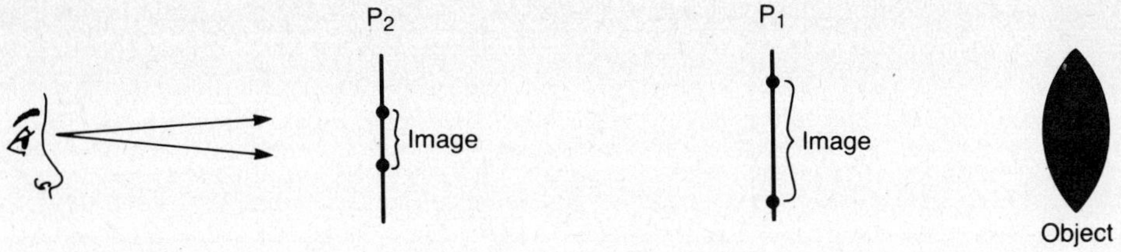

Figure 7.16 Projection of an object onto two different planes. Projection onto P_1 takes up a greater fraction of the plane than projection onto P_2.

viewing area; the observer draws it larger. These examples illustrate, respectively, the three factors that determine the final perspective drawing:

1. The angular orientation of the eye.
2. The position of the eye relative to the object.
3. The distance of the eye from the projection plane.

The last two items on this list are easy to understand, but what do we mean by "angular orientation of the eye"? Assume that the observer is a bird with two perpendicular unit vectors sticking out of it (figure 7.17). Vector **b** points in the direction the bird faces. Vector **n** points straight up through the top of its head. We have drawn the bird so that **b** points in the positive *y*-direction and **n** points in the positive *z*-direction. Note that this forces the wings to be parallel to the *x*-axis.

The angular orientation of the bird is determined by the amount of its rotation about the *x*-, *y*-, and *z*-axes. A rotation about the *z*-axis (figure 7.18a) is called its **heading**, *H*. A rotation about the *x*-axis (figure 7.18b) is called its **pitch**, *P*. A rotation about the *y*-axis (figure 7.18c) is called its **bank**, *B*. An angle is positive (or negative) if the bird is turned counterclockwise (or clockwise) in the plane of rotation. The plane must be viewed by sighting

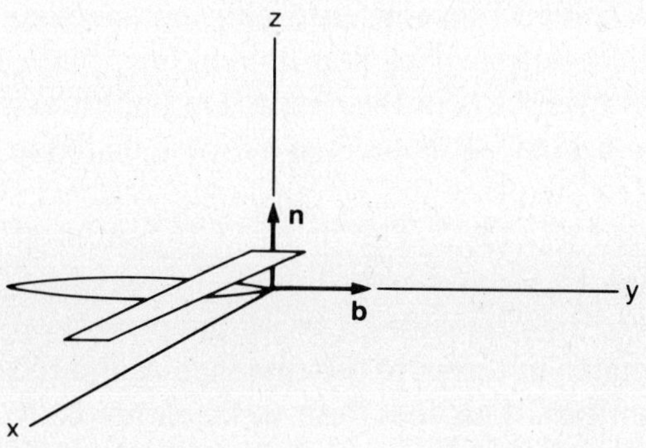

Figure 7.17 Imaginary "bird" for defining the orientation of an observer.

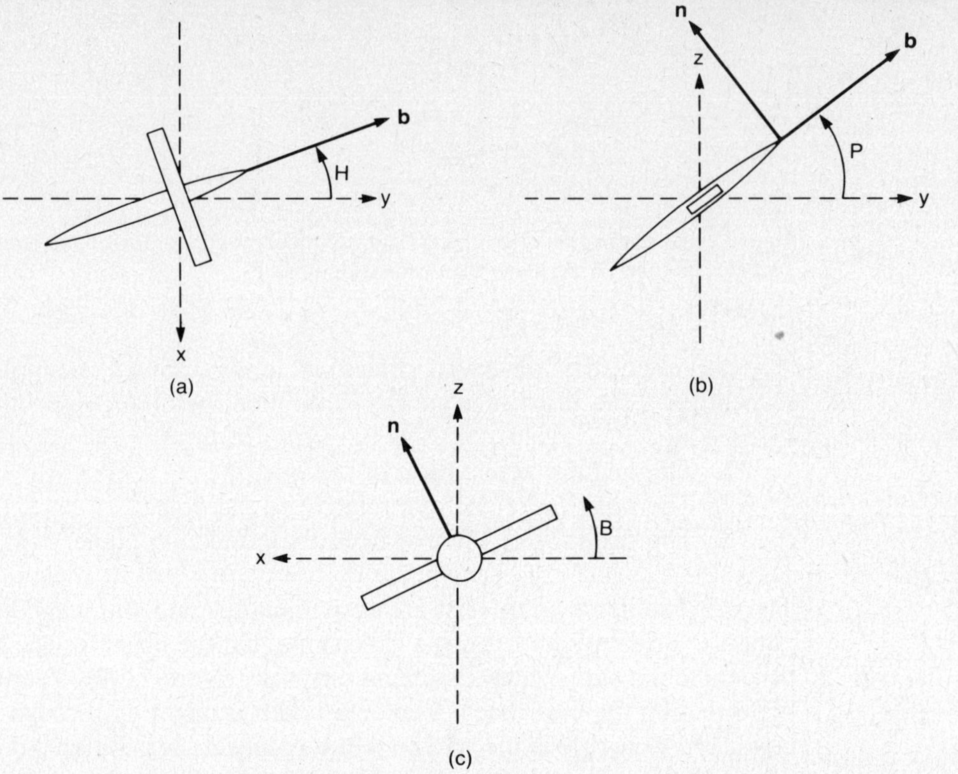

Figure 7.18 Angular orientation. (a) Heading: the z-axis is out of the paper. (b) Pitch: the x-axis is out of the paper. (c) Bank: the y-axis is out of the paper.

along the axis of rotation from positive to negative values. In figure 7.18, the angles are all positive. In figure 7.17, all the angles are zero.

Perspective Projection Formulas

We now have enough information to solve a special case of a perspective drawing. In figure 7.19, the observer is positioned so that its heading, pitch, and bank are all zero. Furthermore, its eye, E, is at the origin. By definition, the projection plane is parallel to the x–z plane. It is located at some distance S from the observer. Note that the projection plane has a coordinate system of its own, with perpendicular axes labeled x' and z'. The origin is the point of intersection with the y-axis. The point Q', whose coordinates in the x', z' system are (x'_p, z'_p), is the intersection of the projector EQ with the projection plane. Our goal is to find these coordinates in terms of the distance S and the coordinates x_o, y_o, z_o—all known quantities. This turns out to be rather easy

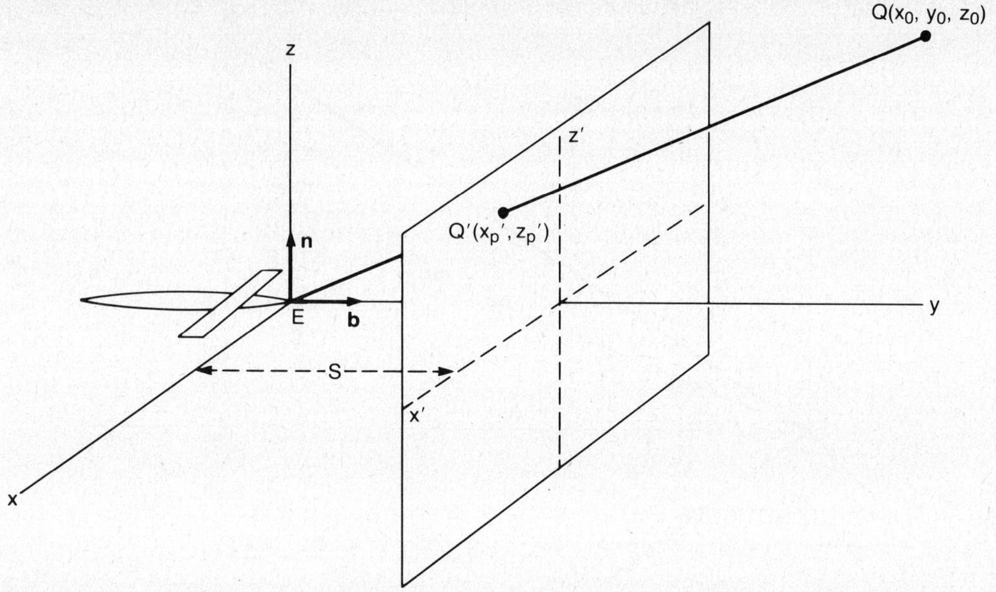

Figure 7.19 Projection of a point Q onto the projection plane. The observer is at the origin, with $H = P = B = 0°$.

because of all the conditions we have imposed. In figure 7.20, we have projected EQ onto the y–z and x–z planes, respectively, to obtain the right triangles EYA and EYB. Looking carefully at EYA, we can use similar triangles to write

$$\frac{z'_p}{S} = \frac{z_o}{y_o}$$

Solving for z'_p we get:

$$z'_p = \frac{S \cdot z_o}{y_o} \tag{7.3}$$

For triangle EYB, we can do the same:

$$\frac{x'_p}{S} = \frac{x_o}{y_o}$$

Solving for x'_p we get:

$$x'_p = \frac{S \cdot x_o}{y_o} \tag{7.4}$$

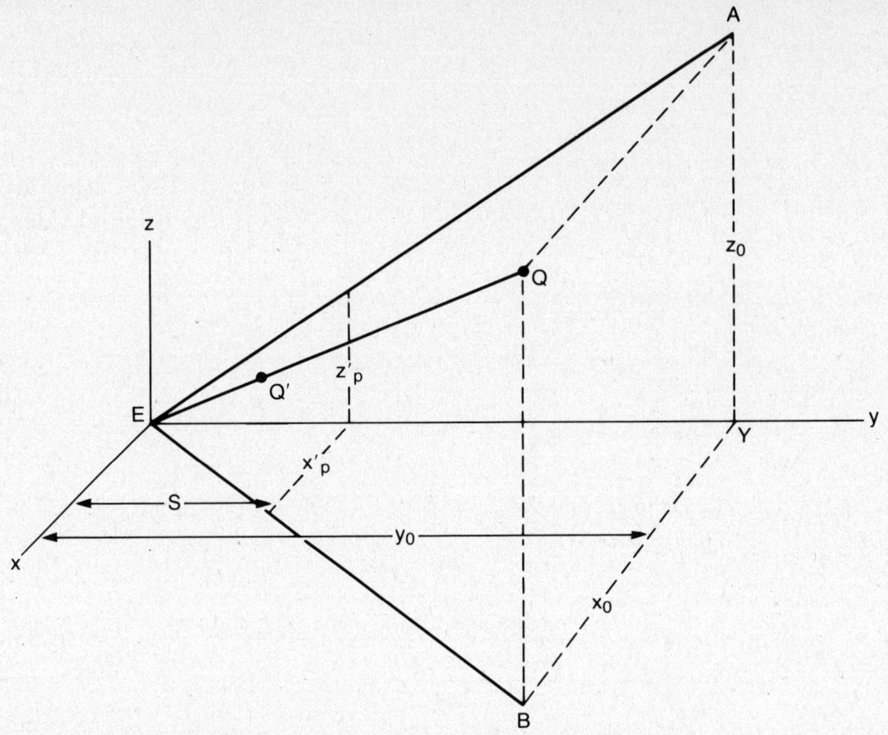

Figure 7.20 Construction used to derive formulas (7.3) and (7.4).

We have therefore accomplished what we set out to do: get the coordinates of Q in the projection plane's system. Keep in mind, however, that we can use these equations only if the observer is at the origin, with heading, pitch, and bank equal to zero.

Example. Consider the cube in figure 7.8. We wish to project the bottom face onto the projection plane. The xyz-coordinates of each point are indicated in the figure. We assume that the observer is at the origin, with $H = P = B = 0°$, and that the projection plane is 4 units from the observer. The x- and z-coordinates of each point are as follows:

a: $x = 4 \cdot 2/1 = 8$

$z = 4 \cdot 1/1 = 4$

b: $x = 4 \cdot 2/2 = 4$

$z = 4 \cdot 1/2 = 2$

c: $x = 4 \cdot 1/2 = 2$

$$z = 4 \cdot 1/2 = 2$$

$$d{:}\quad x = 4 \cdot 1/1 = 4$$

$$z = 4 \cdot 1/1 = 4$$

The plot of these four points in the x'–z' plane is shown in figure 7.21. The two characteristics of perspective drawings discussed earlier are evident here. Side $a'd'$ is larger than side $b'c'$, even though the original sides ab and cd are equal. Since ad is closer than bc, it appears longer and is drawn that way. Furthermore, we can easily see that the parallel lines ab and cd converge when they are drawn as $a'b'$ and $c'd'$. Finally, if S were increased to 6 units, each coordinate would be increased in magnitude by 50 percent. This demonstrates that as the projection plane is moved farther from the observer, the image that is drawn gets larger.

Programming Considerations for Perspective Projections

Although the ideas behind perspective projections are significantly different from those of parallel projections, the programming strategies are quite similar, at least for now. As in the parallel projection procedure, we assume that we have a linked list display file. However, the procedure TRANSFORM must be rewritten.

Program 7.2: Perspective Transformation

Assumptions. Same as program 7.1.

```
PROCEDURE TRANSFORM2;

BEGIN
```

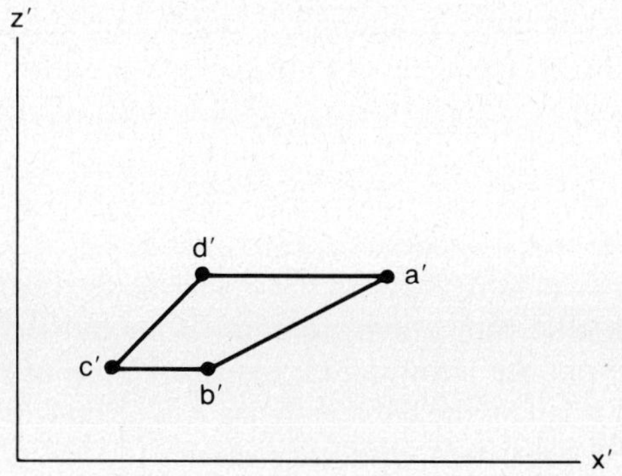

Figure 7.21 Perspective projection of bottom face of the cube in figure 7.8. The observer is at the origin, with $H = P = B = 0°$.

```
  p := start;
  WHILE p <> NIL DO
    BEGIN
      p^.x := S*p^.x/p^.y;
      p ^.z := S*p ^.z/p ^.y;
      p := p^.adr
    END
END;
```

Also, the distance from the viewing plane, S, must be input. Otherwise, the program follows the same path as the parallel projection routine.

PROBLEMS

7.1. Verify that the formula for the cross product can be represented by the determinant indicated in the text.

7.2. Consider the triangular surface defined by the following three points:

p_1: (10, 20, 5) p_2: (5, 10, 20) p_3: (20, 40, 20)

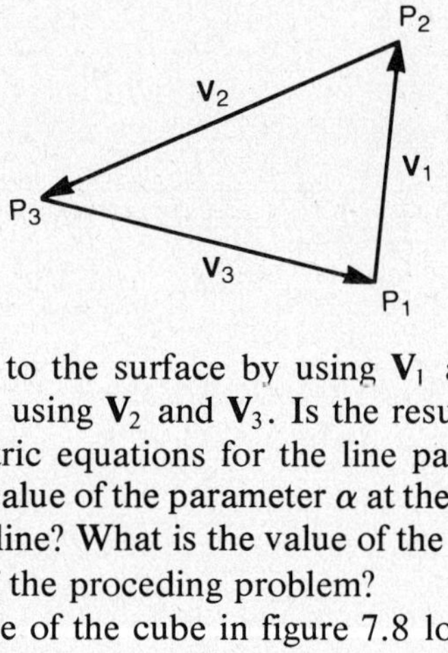

Find a vector normal to the surface by using $\mathbf{V}_1$ and $\mathbf{V}_2$ in your calculation. Repeat the calculation using $\mathbf{V}_2$ and $\mathbf{V}_3$. Is the result the same? Explain.

7.3. What are the parametric equations for the line passing through (1, 2, 6) and (4, 1, 0)? What is the value of the parameter α at the point where $y = 1.5$? What is the direction of this line? What is the value of the scalar product between this line and the normal of the proceding problem?

7.4. What does the top face of the cube in figure 7.8 look like when it is projected under the following conditions? (You should not have to program to answer.)

(a) $A = B = 90°$
(b) $A = B = 45°$
(c) $A = 0°$, $B = 45°$
(d) $A = 30°$, $B = 63.4°$

7.5. Implement a complete parallel projection program. It should first construct a linked list with all the appropriate information, then make use of the projection procedure in the text. Test it out on the cube in figure 7.8. (You will have to scale the given coordinates to be consistent with your screen.)

7.6. For perspective projection, derive equations that convert from the temporary system (x'–z') to the screen system (x–z).

7.7. Rewrite the procedure TRANSFORM so that the transformed coordinates are saved in a new list, rather than in the original one. This allows us to keep a list of the original coordinates.

7.8. Implement a complete perspective projection program for the case where $H = P = B = 0°$. It should be very similar to the program in problem 7.5, but with a different procedure for the transformation. Design the program so that you can investigate the effect of moving the projection plane with respect to the observer. In other words, when the program finishes, it should allow the same coordinate data to be repeated, but with a different value of S.

7.9. On a sheet of paper, sketch a simple house (a box with a pitched roof, a few windows, and a door). Save the coordinates of all vertices in a disk file for future reference. Then use those coordinates to project the house on the screen using a parallel projection.

REFERENCES

Foley, J. D., and Van Dam, A. *Fundamentals of Interactive Computer Graphics.* Reading, Mass.: Addison-Wesley, 1982, pp. 267–279.

French, T., and Vierck, C. *Engineering Drawing and Graphics Technology*, 12th ed. New York: McGraw-Hill, 1978, pp. 265–323.

Greco, S. *The Art of Perspective Drawing.* New York: Grumbacher, 1975.

Meyers, R. *Microcomputer Graphics.* Reading, Mass.: Addison-Wesley, 1982, chapter 6.

Chapter 8

Three-Dimensional Graphics: Part Two

When you have finished this chapter, you will be able to select the angle from which an object is viewed and then project the image, using the formulas of the preceding chapter.

Objectives

1. To determine the viewing angles: heading, pitch, and bank.
2. To learn how to translate and rotate an object in three dimensions so that the projection formulas of the preceding chapter can be used.

In this chapter, we will continue our discussion of perspective projection, lifting the restriction that the projection plane be the x–z plane. This restriction, imposed so that the projection formulas come out simple, essentially constrains us to one view of an object. Clearly, we would benefit from being able to represent an object from any view. To do so, we must first be able to calculate the viewing parameters H, P, and B for an arbitrary viewpoint.

DETERMINATION OF HEADING, PITCH, AND BANK

When the "bird" is not oriented as it was in figure 7.17, determination of the heading, pitch, and bank can be tricky, and intuition is often unreliable in these matters. Fortunately, there is a simple way of determining these angles. Assuming the bird to be at the origin of an xyz-coordinate system:

1. Rotate the bird about the z-axis until **b** is in the y–z plane. The negative of the rotation angle is the heading.
2. Then rotate the bird about the x-axis until **b** is in the positive y-direction. The negative of the rotation angle is the pitch.
3. Finally, rotate the bird about the y-axis until **n** points in the positive z-direction. The negative of the rotation angle is the bank.

Example 1. The bird in figure 8.1a is facing in the negative z-direction. Vector **n** is in the positive y-direction. Since **b** is already in the y–z plane, no rotation about z is needed. Therefore, the heading is zero. To face the bird in the positive y-direction, it must be rotated by 90 degrees about the x-axis. Hence, its pitch is −90 degrees. After this rotation (figure 8.1b), **n** points in the positive z-direction, so no rotation about y is necessary. The bank is therefore zero. To summarize: $H = 0°$, $P = -90°$, $B = 0°$.

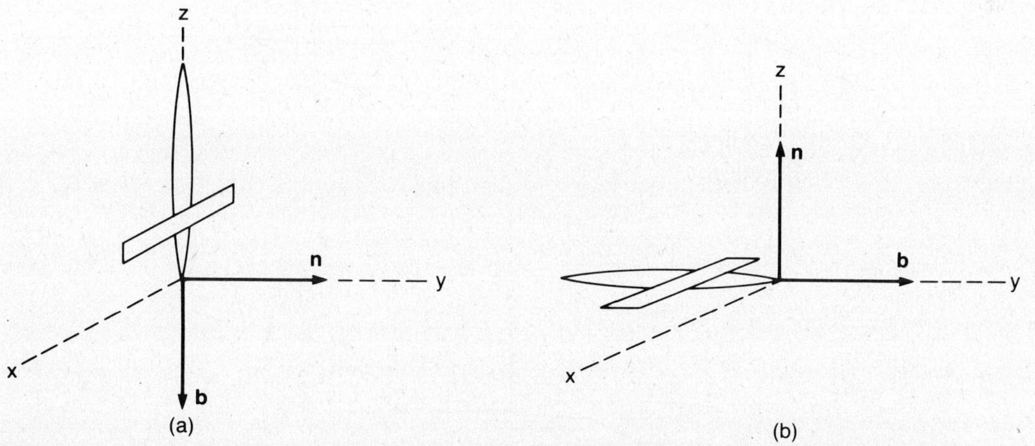

Figure 8.1 Example 1. (a) Initial orientation of bird. (b) Orientation after 90-degree rotation about x.

Example 2. The bird in figure 8.2a is oriented so that it faces in the negative z-direction. Vector **n** points in the positive x-direction. Since vector **b** lies in the y–z plane, the heading is zero. A rotation of 90 degrees about the x-axis is needed to face the bird in the positive y-direction (figure 8.2b). Hence, the pitch is −90 degrees. After a rotation of −90 degrees about the y-axis (figure 8.2c), vector **n** points in the positive z-direction. Hence, the bank is 90 degrees. To summarize: $H = 0°$, $P = -90°$, $B = 90°$.

Example 3. In figure 8.3a, the bird is oriented so that both vectors lie in the x–y plane and point as shown. A rotation of 45 degrees about the z-axis brings **b** into the y–z plane. Hence, the heading is −45 degrees. At this point, the bird is facing in the positive y-direction (figure 8.3b). Hence, its pitch is zero. Finally, a rotation of −90 degrees about the y-axis brings **n** to the positive z-direction (figure 8.3c). Hence, the bank is 90 degrees. To summarize: $H = -45°$, $P = 0°$, $B = 90°$.

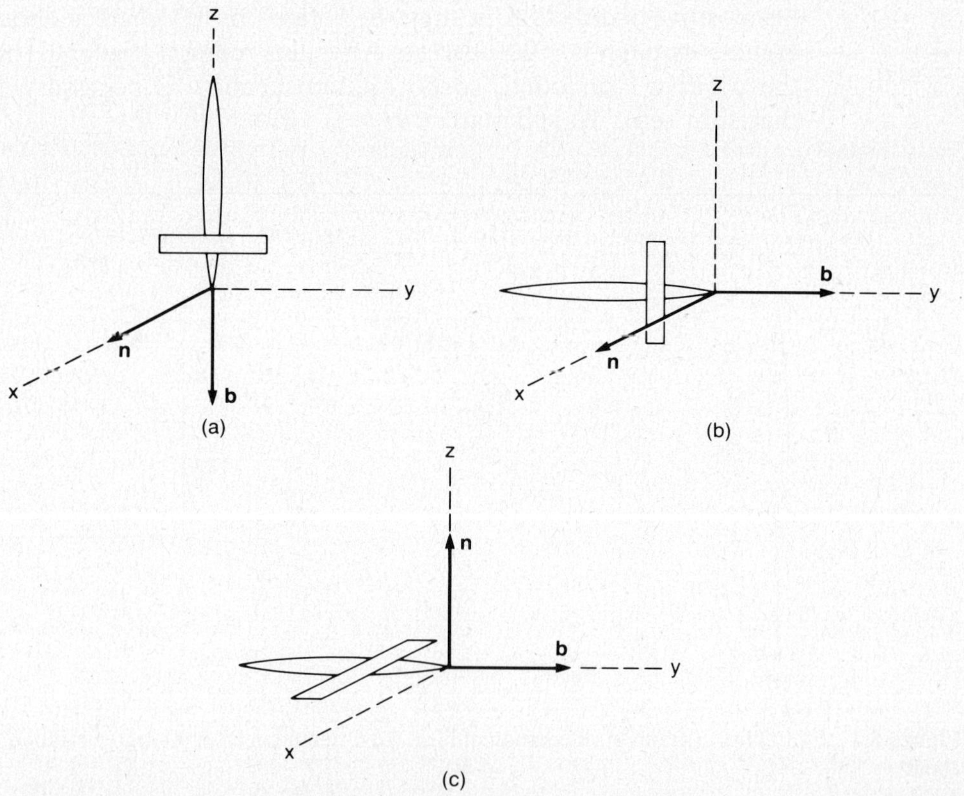

Figure 8.2 Example 2. (a) Initial orientation of bird. (b) Orientation after 90-degree rotation about x. (c) Orientation after 90-degree rotation about y.

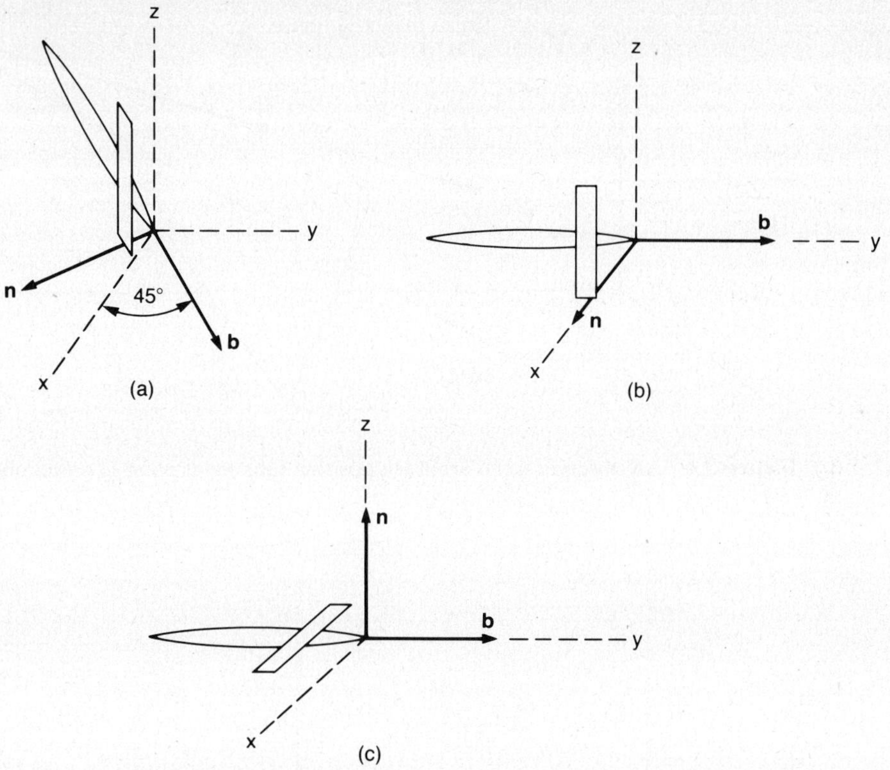

Figure 8.3 Example 3. (a) Initial orientation of bird. (b) Orientation after 45-degree rotation about z. (c) Orientation after -90-degree rotation about y.

A General Viewing Case

The general case of an observer viewing an object is illustrated in figure 8.4. The differences between this and the restricted case are immediately apparent. The eye is located at some point (x_e, y_e, z_e), not at $(0, 0, 0)$, and it has nonzero values of heading, pitch, and bank. Also, the projection plane is not parallel to any of the coordinate planes. Although it is possible to calculate the coordinates of a projected point under these circumstances, it is not worth the effort. Instead, we will transform the problem so that it looks like the x–z plane projection we have already solved.

Consider an observer looking at an object, as shown in figure 8.5a. For simplicity, we assume that the line of sight is in the negative z-direction and that the heading and bank (but not pitch) are zero. Suppose that the observer is translated to the origin without changing his line of sight (figure 8.5b); obviously, he no longer sees the object. If the object is translated by the same amount as the observer (figure 8.5c), the observer sees the object exactly as

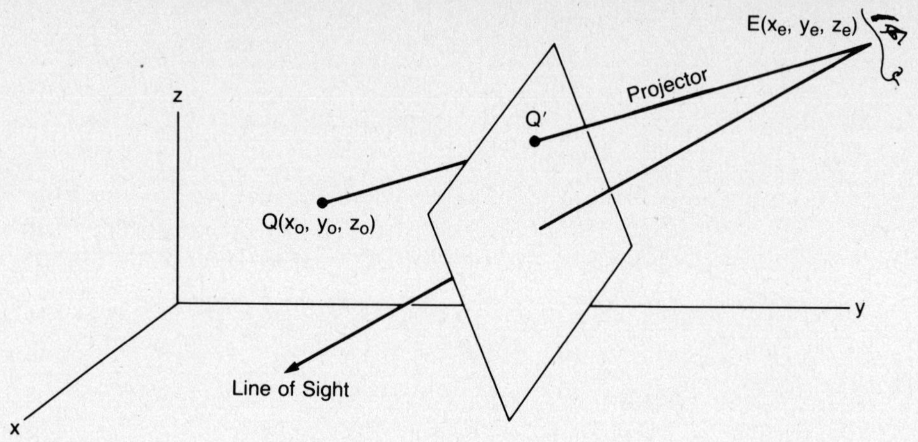

Figure 8.4 An observer in an arbitrary position looking at point Q on an object.

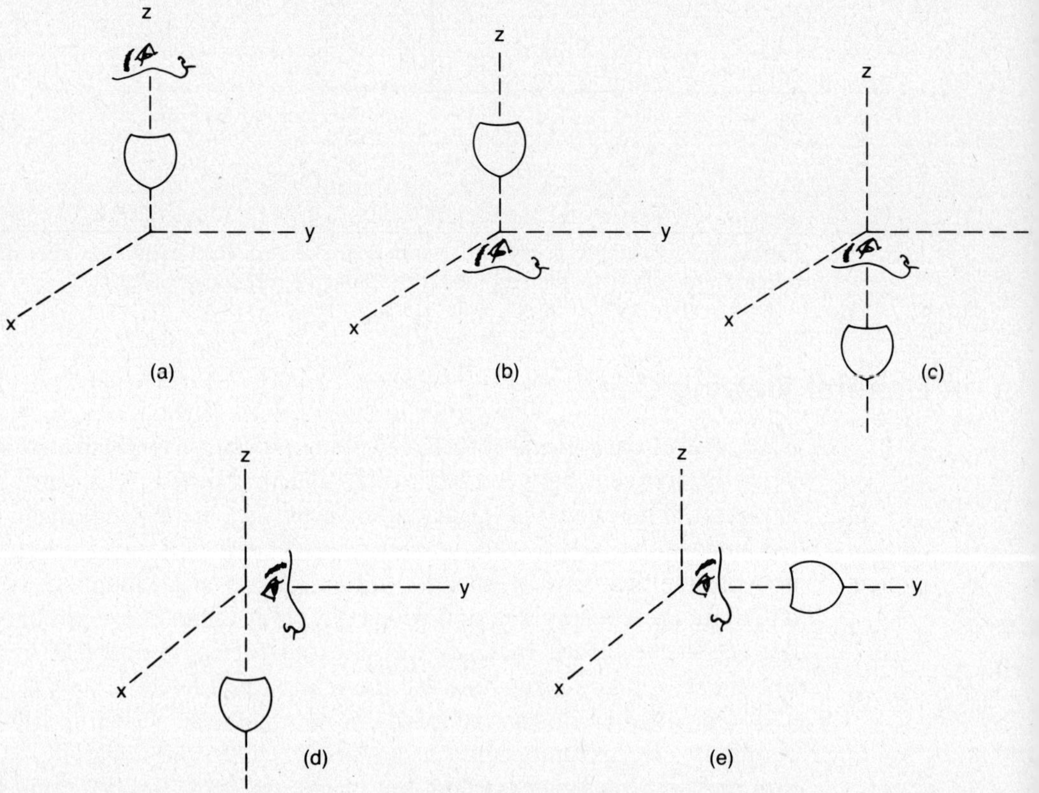

Figure 8.5 (a) Initial position of observer and object. (b) Observer translated by $-z$ to origin. (c) Object translated by $-z$. (d) Observer rotated 90 degrees about x. (e) Object rotated 90 degrees about x.

before. Suppose that the observer is now rotated so that his line of sight is in the positive y-direction (figure 8.5d); once again, the object is out of view. However, the observer's pitch, heading, and bank are now all zero. Finally, if the object is rotated by the same amount (figure 8.5e), the observer's view is again back to normal.

It might appear that we have gained absolutely nothing by these motions, but quite the contrary is true. By moving the observer to the origin, with heading, pitch, and bank equal to zero, we have fulfilled the conditions necessary to use formulas (7.3) and (7.4). This is what we mean by transforming the problem so that it looks like the special case we already solved. Of course, simply moving the observer changes his view of the object. Moving the object by the same amount ensures that the observer's view of it remains the same. For our example, we chose a simple case in which only a translation and a rotation were required. In general, a translation and three rotations are required. If an observer is at (x_e, y_e, z_e), then every point (x, y, z) on the object must undergo the following transformations (in order):

1. A translation to the point $(x-x_e, y-y_e, z-z_e)$.
2. A rotation about the z-axis by an amount $-H$.
3. A rotation about the x-axis by an amount $-P$.
4. A rotation about the y-axis by an amount $-B$.

After these steps, formulas (7.3) and (7.4) can be used to get the coordinates in the projection plane.

THREE-DIMENSIONAL TRANSFORMATIONS

How do we carry out the foregoing transformations in three dimensions? We simply extend the two-dimensional techniques already developed. Recall that in chapter 4, we used homogeneous coordinates, so that both rotation and translation could be represented by matrices. Since a 3 by 3 matrix was needed for the two-dimensional case, it should come as no surprise that a 4 by 4 matrix is needed for three dimensions. The extra row and column are for z-coordinate information.

A two-dimensional translation of t_x in the x-direction and t_y in the y-direction was represented by the set of equations

$$X_T = x + t_x$$
$$Y_T = y + t_y$$

where T is the transformed coordinate, and by the matrix formulation

$$\begin{pmatrix} X_T \\ Y_T \\ 1 \end{pmatrix} = \begin{pmatrix} 1 & 0 & t_x \\ 0 & 1 & t_y \\ 0 & 0 & 1 \end{pmatrix} \begin{pmatrix} x \\ y \\ 1 \end{pmatrix}$$

For the three-dimensional case, there is an additional translation of t_z in the z-direction, so:

$$Z_T = z + t_z$$

Therefore, an arbitrary translation in three dimensions can be represented by the matrix equation

$$\begin{pmatrix} X_T \\ Y_T \\ Z_T \\ 1 \end{pmatrix} = \underbrace{\begin{pmatrix} 1 & 0 & 0 & t_x \\ 0 & 1 & 0 & t_y \\ 0 & 0 & 1 & t_z \\ 0 & 0 & 0 & 1 \end{pmatrix}}_{\tilde{T}} \begin{pmatrix} x \\ y \\ z \\ 1 \end{pmatrix}$$

where $\tilde{T}$ is the translation operator.

The three-dimensional rotation matrices are also similar to the two-dimensional case already discussed. This is because a rotation about one of the coordinate axes is the same as a rotation about the origin in a plane perpendicular to the axis. Recall that a rotation of a point (x, y) about the origin in the x–y plane (figure 8.6) was given by the equations

$$X_T = x \cos(\theta) - y \sin(\theta) \tag{8.1}$$

$$Y_T = x \sin(\theta) + y \cos(\theta) \tag{8.2}$$

and in matrix form, by

$$\begin{pmatrix} X_T \\ Y_T \\ 1 \end{pmatrix} = \begin{pmatrix} \cos(\theta) & -\sin(\theta) & 0 \\ \sin(\theta) & \cos(\theta) & 0 \\ 0 & 0 & 0 \end{pmatrix} \begin{pmatrix} x \\ y \\ 1 \end{pmatrix}$$

A rotation of a point Q about the z-axis takes place in a plane parallel to the x–y plane. The z-coordinate stays constant, while the x- and y-coordinates

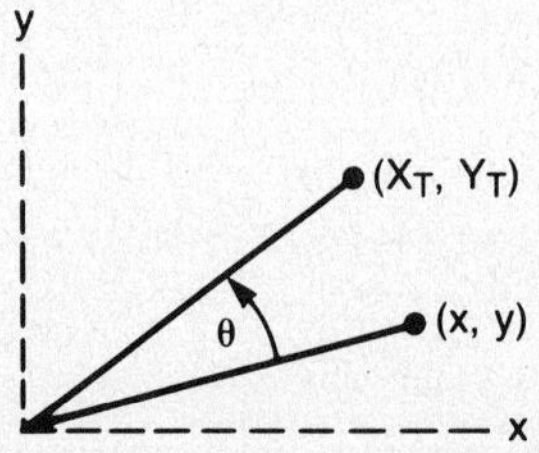

Figure 8.6 Rotation of a point about the origin in the x–y plane

change as if the point were in the x–y plane rotating about the origin. Hence, equations (8.1) and (8.2) describe the x and y changes of the three-dimensional rotation about z. The three transformation equations are as follows:

$$X_T = x\cos(\theta) - y\sin(\theta)$$
$$Y_T = x\sin(\theta) + y\cos(\theta)$$
$$Z_T = z$$

The matrix formulation is

$$\begin{pmatrix} X_T \\ Y_T \\ Z_T \\ 1 \end{pmatrix} = \underbrace{\begin{pmatrix} \cos(\theta) & -\sin(\theta) & 0 & 0 \\ \sin(\theta) & \cos(\theta) & 0 & 0 \\ 0 & 0 & 1 & 0 \\ 0 & 0 & 0 & 1 \end{pmatrix}}_{R_z} \begin{pmatrix} x \\ y \\ z \\ 1 \end{pmatrix}$$

where R_z is the z-axis rotation operator.

We now turn our attention to a rotation about the x-axis. This takes place in a plane parallel to the y–z plane. Hence, the x-coordinate remains fixed, while the y- and z-coordinates change as if the point were in the y–z plane rotating about the origin (figure 8.7). We need not derive equations for this new situation. It is just like figure 8.6 except that the vertical axis is labeled z and the horizontal axis is labeled y. We can use equations (8.1) and (8.2) to describe the y and z changes, provided that $x \rightarrow y$ and $y \rightarrow z$. Therefore:

$$Y_T = y\cos(\theta) - z\sin(\theta)$$
$$Z_T = y\sin(\theta) + z\cos(\theta)$$
$$X_T = x$$

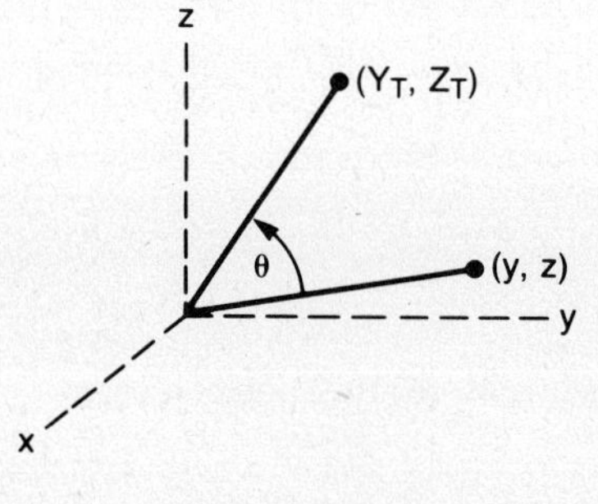

Figure 8.7 Rotation of a point about the x-axis.

It is easily verified that the matrix form of these equations is

$$\begin{pmatrix} X_T \\ Y_T \\ Z_T \\ 1 \end{pmatrix} = \underbrace{\begin{pmatrix} 1 & 0 & 0 & 0 \\ 0 & \cos(\theta) & -\sin(\theta) & 0 \\ 0 & \sin(\theta) & \cos(\theta) & 0 \\ 0 & 0 & 0 & 1 \end{pmatrix}}_{R_x} \begin{pmatrix} x \\ y \\ z \\ 1 \end{pmatrix}$$

where R_x is the x-axis rotation operator.

The final step is a rotation about the y-axis (figure 8.8a). Following the logic of the previous discussions, we consider a rotation in the x–z plane (figure 8.8b), since the y-coordinate remains constant. Using the same reasoning as before, $x \to z$ and $y \to x$ in equations (8.1) and (8.2). Therefore:

$$X_T = x\cos(\theta) + z\sin(\theta)$$
$$Z_T = -x\sin(\theta) + z\cos(\theta)$$
$$Y_T = y$$

The matrix equations are

$$\begin{pmatrix} X_T \\ Y_T \\ Z_T \\ 1 \end{pmatrix} = \underbrace{\begin{pmatrix} \cos(\theta) & 0 & \sin(\theta) & 0 \\ 0 & 1 & 0 & 0 \\ -\sin(\theta) & 0 & \cos(\theta) & 0 \\ 0 & 0 & 0 & 1 \end{pmatrix}}_{R_y} \begin{pmatrix} x \\ y \\ z \\ 1 \end{pmatrix}$$

where R_y is the y-axis rotation operator.

To get combinations of translation and rotations, we do exactly what we did in the two-dimensional case: we multiply the matrices together. For the following values:

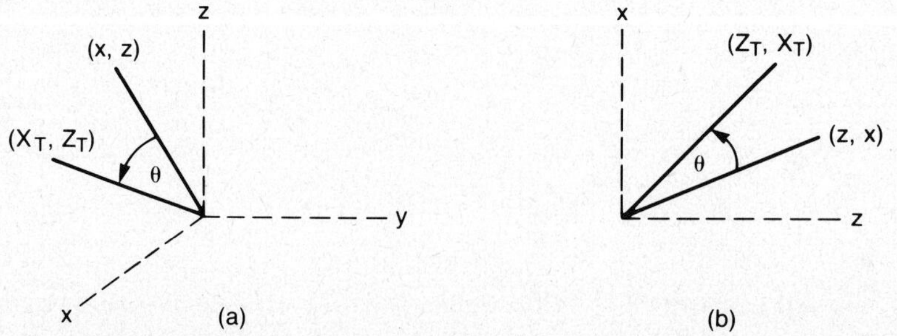

Figure 8.8 (a) Rotation of a point about the y-axis. (b) Rotation of a point in the x–z plane.

$t_x = -x_e, \quad t_y = -y_e, \quad t_z = -z_e \quad \text{in } \tilde{T}$

$\theta = -H \quad \text{in} \quad R_z$

$\theta = -P \quad \text{in} \quad R_x$

$\theta = -B \quad \text{in} \quad R_y$

we get the matrix equation for the most general transformation of a point (x, y, z):

$$\underset{\text{New}}{\begin{pmatrix} X_T \\ Y_T \\ Z_T \\ 1 \end{pmatrix}} = \underset{R_y}{\begin{pmatrix} \cos(B) & 0 & -\sin(B) & 0 \\ 0 & 1 & 0 & 0 \\ \sin(B) & 0 & \cos(B) & 0 \\ 0 & 0 & 0 & 0 \end{pmatrix}} \underset{R_x}{\begin{pmatrix} 1 & 0 & 0 & 0 \\ 0 & \cos(P) & \sin(P) & 0 \\ 0 & -\sin(P) & \cos(P) & 0 \\ 0 & 0 & 0 & 1 \end{pmatrix}} \underset{R_z}{\begin{pmatrix} \cos(H) & \sin(H) & 0 & 0 \\ -\sin(H) & \cos(H) & 0 & 0 \\ 0 & 0 & 1 & 0 \\ 0 & 0 & 0 & 1 \end{pmatrix}} \underset{\tilde{T}}{\begin{pmatrix} 1 & 0 & 0 & -x_e \\ 0 & 1 & 0 & -y_e \\ 0 & 0 & 1 & -z_e \\ 0 & 0 & 0 & 1 \end{pmatrix}} \underset{\text{Old}}{\begin{pmatrix} x \\ y \\ z \\ 1 \end{pmatrix}}$$

Example 4. An observer, E, is located 5 units above the origin on the z-axis (figure 8.9), with $H = 0°$, $P = -90°$, $B = 0°$. A point Q_0 on an object has coordinates $(1, 0, 0)$. The observer is translated to the origin and rotated until $H = P = B = 0°$. What will be the coordinates of Q_0 after the equivalent transformations?

From the given information, we can see that $x_e = 0$, $y_e = 0$, and $z_e = 5$. Furthermore $x = 1$, $y = 0$, and $z = 0$. Plugging in these values and those of the angles, we can write the matrix formulation of the transformation:

$$\begin{pmatrix} X_T \\ Y_T \\ Z_T \\ 1 \end{pmatrix} = \underset{R_y}{\begin{pmatrix} 1 & 0 & 0 & 0 \\ 0 & 1 & 0 & 0 \\ 0 & 0 & 1 & 0 \\ 0 & 0 & 0 & 1 \end{pmatrix}} \underset{R_x}{\begin{pmatrix} 1 & 0 & 0 & 0 \\ 0 & 0 & -1 & 0 \\ 0 & 1 & 0 & 0 \\ 0 & 0 & 0 & 1 \end{pmatrix}} \underset{R_z}{\begin{pmatrix} 1 & 0 & 0 & 0 \\ 0 & 1 & 0 & 0 \\ 0 & 0 & 1 & 0 \\ 0 & 0 & 0 & 1 \end{pmatrix}} \underset{\tilde{T}}{\begin{pmatrix} 1 & 0 & 0 & 0 \\ 0 & 1 & 0 & 0 \\ 0 & 0 & 1 & -5 \\ 0 & 0 & 0 & 1 \end{pmatrix}} \begin{pmatrix} 1 \\ 0 \\ 0 \\ 1 \end{pmatrix}$$

The operation with $\tilde{T}$ gives:

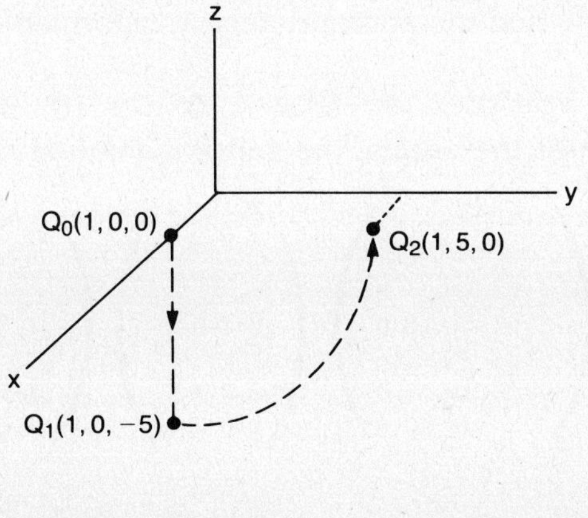

Figure 8.9 Transformations for example 4. Q_0 is translated -5 units in the z-direction to Q_1. Q_1 is rotated 90 degrees about the x-axis to Q_2.

$$\begin{pmatrix} 1 & 0 & 0 & 0 \\ 0 & 1 & 0 & 0 \\ 0 & 0 & 1 & -5 \\ 0 & 0 & 0 & 1 \end{pmatrix} \begin{pmatrix} 1 \\ 0 \\ 0 \\ 1 \end{pmatrix} = \begin{pmatrix} 1 \\ 0 \\ -5 \\ 1 \end{pmatrix}$$

Operating on the new coordinates with R_z gives:

$$\begin{pmatrix} 1 & 0 & 0 & 0 \\ 0 & 1 & 0 & 0 \\ 0 & 0 & 1 & 0 \\ 0 & 0 & 1 & 1 \end{pmatrix} \begin{pmatrix} 1 \\ 0 \\ -5 \\ 1 \end{pmatrix} = \begin{pmatrix} 1 \\ 0 \\ -5 \\ 1 \end{pmatrix}$$

This result should not be surprising. R_z is a unit matrix, so multiplying by it leaves the coordinates unchanged. Continuing with the next matrix, we get:

$$\begin{pmatrix} 1 & 0 & 0 & 0 \\ 0 & 0 & -1 & 0 \\ 0 & 1 & 0 & 0 \\ 0 & 0 & 0 & 1 \end{pmatrix} \begin{pmatrix} 1 \\ 0 \\ -5 \\ 1 \end{pmatrix} = \begin{pmatrix} 1 \\ 5 \\ 0 \\ 1 \end{pmatrix}$$

Since R_y is a unit matrix, operating with it will leave this result unchanged. Therefore, the coordinates of Q_0 after all the transformations are $x = 1$, $y = 5$, and $z = 0$. We can see from figure 8.9 that this is the correct result. To bring the observer to the origin with $H = P = B = 0°$, we had to translate it by -5 units along the z-axis and rotate it 90 degrees about the x-axis. Translating Q_0 by the same amount brings it to Q_1. A subsequent rotation about the x-axis brings it to Q_2, whose coordinates are (1, 5, 0). This point appears to the observer at the origin exactly the same as the original point appears to the original observer.

Example 5. An observer located 5 units below the origin on the z-axis has a heading of -45 degrees, a pitch of 0 degrees, and a bank of 90 degrees. A point Q_0 on an object is located at (10, 10, 0). If the observer is moved to the origin, with $H = P = B = 0°$, find the appropriately transformed coordinates of Q_0.

In this example, $x_e = y_e = 0$, $z_e = -5$, $x = 10$, $y = 10$, $z = 0$. With these values, and the values of the angles, the matrix equation is

$$\begin{pmatrix} X_T \\ Y_T \\ Z_T \\ 1 \end{pmatrix} = \begin{pmatrix} 0 & 0 & -1 & 0 \\ 0 & 1 & 0 & 0 \\ 1 & 0 & 0 & 0 \\ 0 & 0 & 0 & 1 \end{pmatrix} \begin{pmatrix} \frac{\sqrt{2}}{2} & \frac{-\sqrt{2}}{2} & 0 & 0 \\ \frac{\sqrt{2}}{2} & \frac{\sqrt{2}}{2} & 0 & 0 \\ 0 & 0 & 1 & 0 \\ 0 & 0 & 0 & 1 \end{pmatrix} \begin{pmatrix} 1 & 0 & 0 & 0 \\ 0 & 1 & 0 & 0 \\ 0 & 0 & 1 & 5 \\ 0 & 0 & 0 & 1 \end{pmatrix} \begin{pmatrix} 10 \\ 10 \\ 0 \\ 1 \end{pmatrix}$$

Notice that we have left out the R_x matrix, since it is a unit matrix. Performing the translation, we get

$$\begin{pmatrix} 1 & 0 & 0 & 0 \\ 0 & 1 & 0 & 0 \\ 0 & 0 & 1 & 5 \\ 0 & 0 & 0 & 1 \end{pmatrix} \begin{pmatrix} 10 \\ 10 \\ 0 \\ 1 \end{pmatrix} = \begin{pmatrix} 10 \\ 10 \\ 5 \\ 1 \end{pmatrix}$$

The rotation R_z gives:

$$\begin{pmatrix} \frac{\sqrt{2}}{2} & \frac{-\sqrt{2}}{2} & 0 & 0 \\ \frac{\sqrt{2}}{2} & \frac{\sqrt{2}}{2} & 0 & 0 \\ 0 & 0 & 1 & 0 \\ 0 & 0 & 0 & 1 \end{pmatrix} \begin{pmatrix} 10 \\ 10 \\ 5 \\ 1 \end{pmatrix} = \begin{pmatrix} 0 \\ 10\sqrt{2} \\ 5 \\ 1 \end{pmatrix}$$

The rotation R_y gives:

$$\begin{pmatrix} 0 & 0 & -1 & 0 \\ 0 & 1 & 0 & 0 \\ 1 & 0 & 0 & 0 \\ 0 & 0 & 0 & 1 \end{pmatrix} \begin{pmatrix} 0 \\ 10\sqrt{2} \\ 5 \\ 1 \end{pmatrix} = \begin{pmatrix} -5 \\ 10\sqrt{2} \\ 0 \\ 1 \end{pmatrix}$$

The result of each transformation is indicated in figure 8.10. The final coordinates are $(-5, 10\sqrt{2}, 0)$. The transformed observer sees this point the same way the original observer sees the original point.

PROGRAMMING CONSIDERATIONS

Having gone through all this mathematics, it might seem that we have an enormous programming task ahead of us. Actually, however, we already have almost all the necessary techniques at hand. If we assume a segmented linked list, then the steps we must take for the general perspective transformation are as follows:

1. Read in the viewing parameters: t_x, t_y, t_z, H, P, B, and S.
2. Translate by t_x, t_y, t_z.
3. Rotate around z by the amount $-H$.
4. Rotate around x by the amount $-P$.
5. Rotate around y by the amount $-B$.

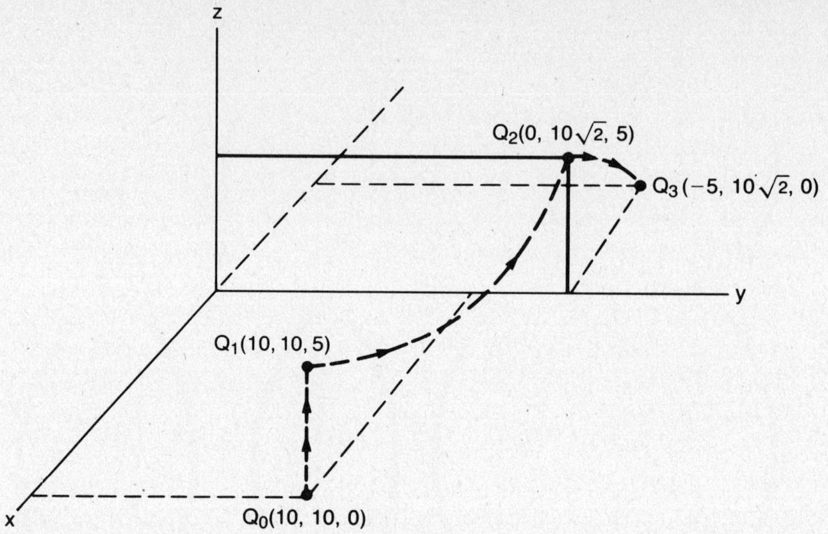

Figure 8.10 Transformations for example 6. Q_0 is translated 10 units in the z-direction to Q_1. Q_1 is rotated 45 degrees to Q_2. Q_2 is rotated -90 degrees to Q_3.

6. Project using TRANSFORM2.
7. Draw.

Since the coding for these steps is quite straightforward, we will introduce a small twist to make things more interesting. When we programmed the parallel projection case, we placed the transformed x- and z-coordinates into the x and z fields of the original linked list. Suppose we had wanted to execute a different projection of the original coordinates? They would be gone! In the present treatment, we will create a separate list when we do the first transformation, then use that list to store the transformed variables. The original list will remain intact. Since the first transformation is translation, we will create the new list in that procedure.

Program 8.1: Translation with a New List

Assumptions. Segmented linked list.

```
Display = RECORD
          x:REAL;
          y:REAL;
          z:REAL;
          penstatus:(on,off,erase);
```

```
          segnum:INTEGER;
          side:INTEGER
          END;
```

Viewing parameters established. *r, s, t, start2* point to new list.

```
PROCEDURE TRANSLATE 2;

BEGIN
  NEW(s);
  p := start;                {s and t used here as p and q were}
  WHILE p < > NIL DO         {used in program 5.4}
   BEGIN
    NEW(t);
    s ^.x := p ^.x - tx;     {put transformed coordinates in the}
    s ^.y := p ^.y - ty;     {coordinate fields of s}
    s ^.z := p ^.z - tz;
    s ^.penstatus := p ^.penstatus;    {copy untransformed fields
                                       ffrom p directly into s}
    s ^.side := p ^.side;
    s ^.segnum := p ^.segnum;
    p := p ^.adr;        {advance p}
    s ^.adr := t;        {point this record to next one}
    r := s;      {r saves last value of s}
    s := t        {point s to next empty record}
  END;
s := r;
s ^.adr := NIL      {last s points to NIL}
END;
```

Having established a new list, *s*, we can transform it any way we please and not worry about losing the original coordinates. The rotations come next. Program 8.2 is for a rotation about the *z*-axis.

Program 8.2: Rotation

Assumptions. New linked list as program 8.1, and assumptions stated in program 8.1.

```
PROCEDURE ROTz;
VAR ch,sh:real;

BEGIN
  ch := cos(-H);      {calculate sin and cos outside loop!}
```

```
  sh:= sin(-H);
  s:= start2;
  WHILE s <> NIL DO
   BEGIN
    s^.x:= s^.x*ch + s^.y*sh;     {only x and y fields change}
    s^.y:= -s^.x*sh + s^.y*ch;     {due to this rotation}
    s:= s^.adr
   END
END;
```

We leave the writing of the procedures for the other two rotations, ROTy and ROTx, as an exercise. The main routine for the transformation would look like this:

Program 8.3: Main Perspective Transformation Routine

Assumptions. As in programs 8.1 and 8.2

```
PROCEDURE PERSPEC;

BEGIN
  READLN(tx,ty,tz,H,P,B,S);
  TRANSLATE2;
  ROTz;
  ROTx;
  ROTy;
  TRANSFORM2;
  DRAWIT
END;
```

MISCELLANEOUS PROJECTIONS

Before leaving the topic of projection, let us apply the ideas just presented to parallel projections. There is an important class of parallel projections called **axonometric projections**, in which the projector is perpendicular to the screen, but not in the same direction as any of the principal axes. If the projector makes equal angles with each of the principal axes, the projection of the cube looks like that in figure 8.11. This is called an **isometric projection**. (If we project onto the x–z plane as usual, then the cube is oriented so that none of its faces is parallel to a coordinate plane. Figure 8.12 shows this orientation.) All projected edges of the cube are shortened as compared to their original lengths, and the shortening is the same for all edges. If the normal makes equal angles with only two of the axes, edges parallel to these axes are shortened the same amount (figure 8.13). This is called a **dimetric**

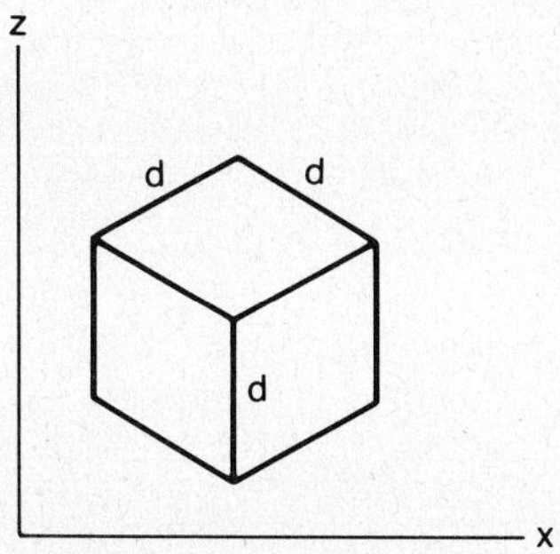

Figure 8.11 Isometric projection of a cube.

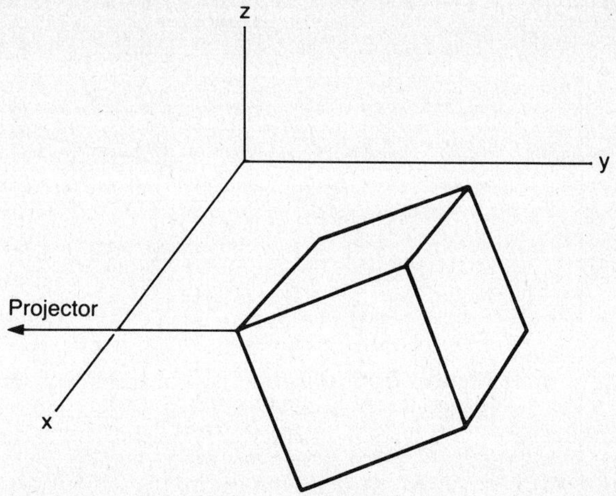

Figure 8.12 Orientation of the cube to produce the projection in figure 8.11.

projection. Finally, if the normal makes three different angles with the axes, edges parallel to these axes are shortened by different amounts (figure 8.14). This is called a **trimetric projection**.

If the projection plane is initially something other than the *x–z* plane, we can always rotate it so that it ends up parallel to the *x–z* plane. Of course, we have to rotate the object by the same amounts. Once we do this, we can then use the parallel projection formulas previously developed. How much should those rotations be? Figure 8.15 shows a normal to an arbitrary projection plane. We want the normal **N** to end up in the positive *y*-direction. Figure

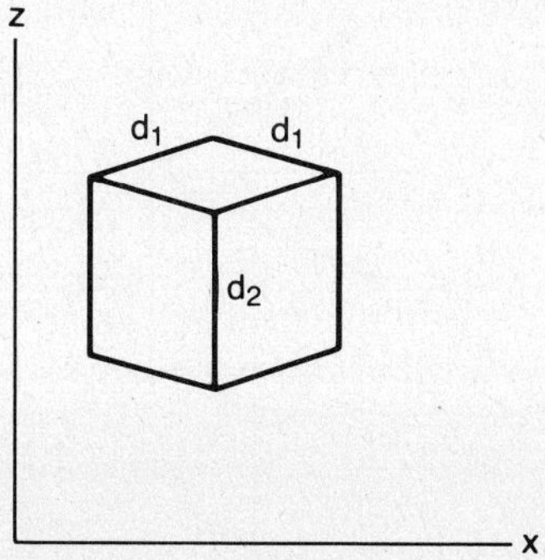

Figure 8.13 Dimetric projection of a cube.

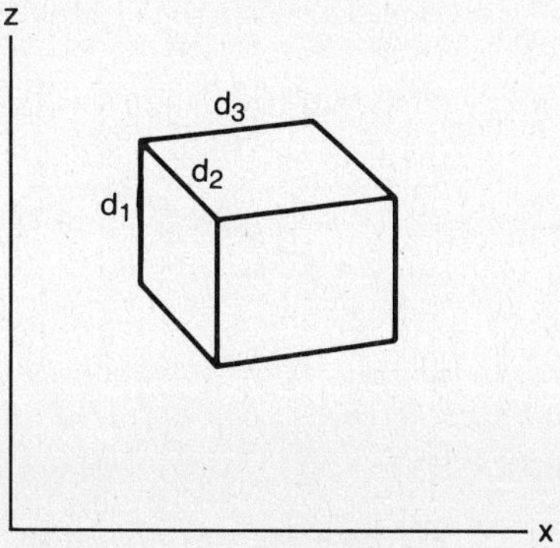

Figure 8.14 Trimetric projection of a cube.

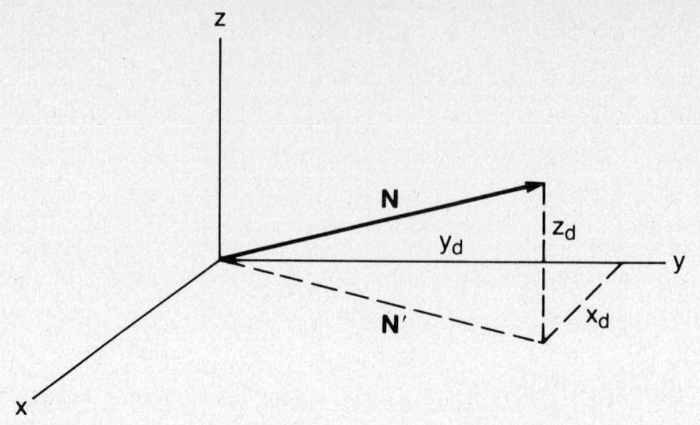

Figure 8.15 Normal to an arbitrary projection plane.

8.16a shows four possible starting positions of the line *N′* from figure 8.15. In any of these cases, a rotation of the normal about the *z*-axis by $-A$:

$A = \arctan(x_n/y_n)$

will bring the normal into the *y–z* plane. There are four possible orientations for *N′* in the *y–z* plane (figure 8.16b). For the two cases where *N′* has a positive *y* component, a rotation by $-B$:

$B = \arctan(zd/yd)$

brings it into the positive *y*-direction. For the two cases where *N′* has a negative *y* component, a rotation by $B - \pi$ will do the trick.

To summarize, we can make an axonometric projection onto an arbitrary plane in the following way:

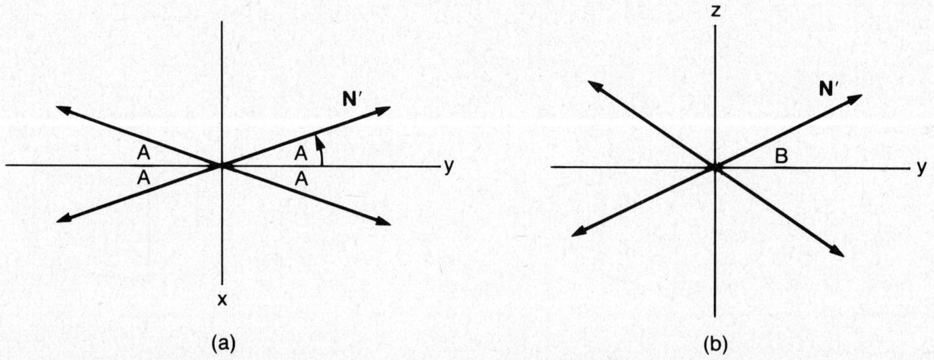

Figure 8.16 (a) For an angle *A*, there are four possible orientations of **N′** from figure 8.15. A rotation of $-A$ always brings **N′** into the *y–z* plane. (b) Once **N′** is in the *y–z* plane, a rotation of either $-B$ or $B - \pi$ brings it to the positive *y*-direction.

1. Determine the angles A and B.
2. Rotate the object by these amounts.
3. Apply the parallel projection formulas to the rotated object.

PROBLEMS

8.1. Write procedures ROTx and ROTy for rotations about the x-axis and the y-axis.

8.2. Write rotation procedures to transform an arbitrary axonometric projection problem into one where the projection plane is the x–z plane.

8.3. If a cube has a side of length S, what length will each side project to for the isometric case?

8.4. For each of the following situations, determine the orientation of the bird:

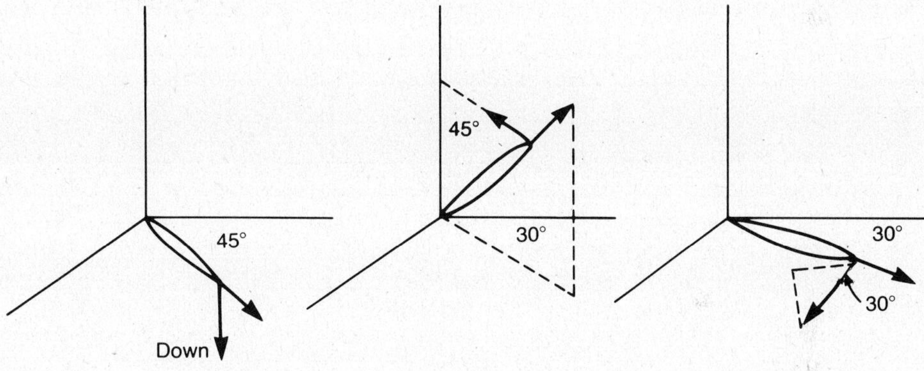

(a) (b) (c)

8.5. Calculate the projected coordinates of the closest point on the cube in figure 7.8 for each of the orientations in problem 8.4. Assume that the location is the origin.

8.6. Implement a complete perspective projection program by combining the procedures in the text and the ones you wrote in problem 8.1. Use the cube in figure 7.8 to test it. Change the coordinates to reasonable values for your system.

8.7. What would the rotation matrices yield when an observer faces away from an object?

REFERENCES

Carlbom, I., and Paciorek, J. "Geometric Projection and Viewing Transformations." *Computing Surveys 1*(4), 1978, 465–502.

Foley, J. D., and Van Dam, A. *Fundamentals of Interactive Computer Graphics.* Reading, Mass.: Addison-Wesley, 1982, pp. 279–295.

Harrington, S. *Computer Graphics: A Programming Approach.* New York: McGraw-Hill, 1983, chapter 8.

Chapter 9

Hidden Line Removal

When you have finished this chapter, you will be able to limit the display of an object to those parts that are visible to the viewer.

Objectives

1. To be able to distinguish between front and back faces of a given object.
2. To be able to determine how much of a given object is blocked from an observer's view by another object.
3. To be able to use the foregoing conditions to project only the visible parts of a scene.

The one obvious flaw in the projection routines we have developed so far is that all parts of an object, even those we normally cannot see, are projected onto the screen. The image, called a **wire frame drawing**, is suggestive of an object whose edges are wire and whose surfaces are invisible. This effect can be very disturbing. Complex objects are projected as a jumble of line segments, and even simple images can play optical tricks on the observer (figure 9.1). To improve the realism of the projected image, we must develop methods whereby only the visible parts of an object appear on the screen. This is called **hidden line removal**. From a programming standpoint, this is a tall order; removing hidden lines is rather taxing on a computer's resources.

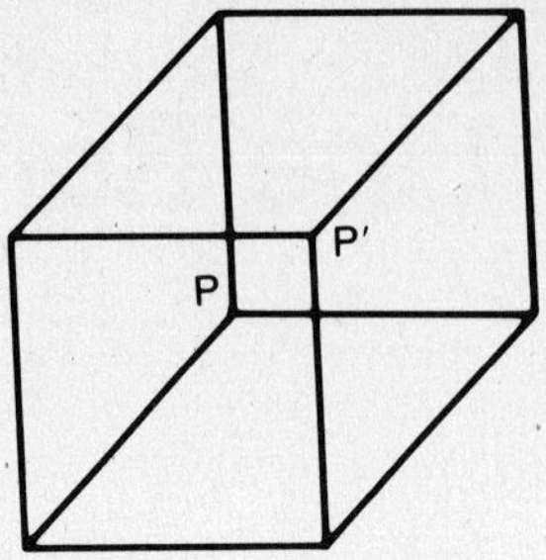

Figure 9.1 Which point is in front—P or P'?

(Actually, the only computer that does it easily is the human brain.) In this chapter, we shall investigate a straightforward method for removing hidden lines.

BACK FACES

In any collection of objects, about half of the surfaces face away from a given observer. These surfaces, called **back faces**, cannot be seen by the observer. Removal of back faces is an important first step, because they represent the majority of the faces that cannot be seen.

How can we tell that a face cannot be seen? We have already determined a method for specifying the orientation of a surface. We connect the vertices in a counterclockwise order, as indicated in figure 7.5, and then take a cross product. The result is a normal, **N**, that points in a direction outward from the object. Let us first consider a parallel projection, where the projector is represented by

$$\mathbf{V} = xd\mathbf{i} + yd\mathbf{j} + zd\mathbf{k}$$

The scalar product $\mathbf{N} \cdot \mathbf{V}$ will determine how the surface faces with respect to the observer. Recall that the dot product of two vectors, such as **N** and **V**, is

$$\mathbf{N} \cdot \mathbf{V} = |N| \cdot |V| \cos(\theta)$$

where θ is the angle between **N** and **V**. When a normal is on side A (see figure 9.2), the corresponding surface is not visible to the observer. For this situation, $\cos(\theta)$ is negative. Hence, a negative dot product of projector and normal indicates an unseen surface.

For the perspective case, the line of sight is assumed to be in the positive y-direction. Hence, when we take $\mathbf{N} \cdot \mathbf{V}$, we must use

$$\mathbf{V} = -\mathbf{j}$$

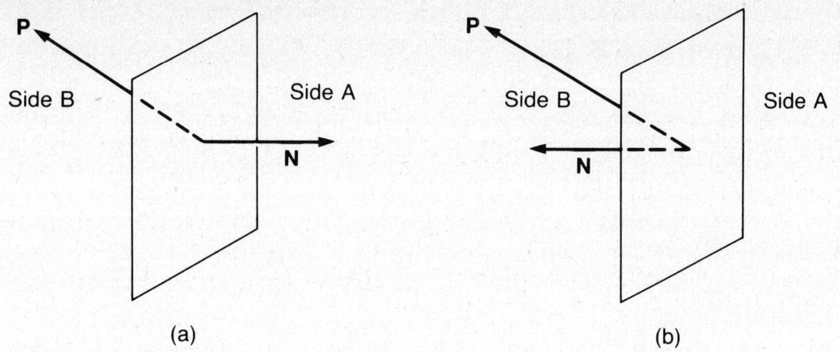

Figure 9.2 (a) If side A is the outside face, it is not visible ($\mathbf{P}\cdot\mathbf{N} < 0$). (b) If side B is the outside face, it is visible ($\mathbf{P}\cdot\mathbf{N} > 0$).

PROGRAMMING BACK FACE REMOVAL

We can include back face removal in our general projection scheme by adding only one procedure, which basically consists of two steps:

1. Calculate the dot product for each side.
2. If the dot product is negative, put a notation in the linked list that that particular side is not to be projected.

We get the normal to a face by picking the first three vertices off the list, then making two vectors from them. The cross product of these two vectors is the normal, whose dot product we then take with the projector.

Program 9.1: Back Face Removal

Assumptions. Linked list with usual pointer notation. Beginning of face n marked by $bg[n]$; end marked by $e[n]$. Coordinates of the three vertices are $ex[n]$, $ey[n]$, $ez[n]$, $n = 1 \rightarrow 3$. Projection direction *xd, yd, zd.*

```
PROCEDURE ELIMFACE;
VAR
  m,n:integer;
  ex,ey,ez: array[1..20] of real;
  dot,dotz,doty,dotz:real;

BEGIN {1}
  FOR m := 1 to numsides DO
  BEGIN {2}
```

```
      p := bg[m];
    FOR n := 1 to 3 DO
    BEGIN {3}
      ex[n] := p^.x;
      ey[n] := p^.y;
      ez[n] := p^.z;
      p := p^.adr
    END; {3}
  doty := yd*((ex[3]-ex[2])*(ez[2]-ez[1])-(ex[2]-ex[1])
    *(ez[3]-ez[2]));
  dotx := xd*((ey[2]-ey[1])*(ez[3]-ez[2])-(ey[3]-ey[2])
    *(ez[2]-ez[1]));
  dotz := zd*((ex[2]-ex[1])*(ey[3]-ey[2])-(ex[3]-ex[2])
    *(ey[2]-ey[1]));
  dot := dotx + doty + dotz;          {this is dot product of}
  IF dot < 0                          {projector and normal}
  THEN
    BEGIN {4}
      p := bg[m];
      WHILE (p <> e[m]) and (p <> NIL) DO
        BEGIN {5}                     {turn pen off for all}
         p^.penstatus := off;         {records of back face}
         p := p^.adr
        END {5}
    END {4}
    END {2}
  END; {1}
```

LINES BLOCKED BY ANOTHER OBJECT

When one object is located in front of another, the front object can block some part of the rear object. Removing those hidden lines is much more difficult than back face removal. To explain the process clearly, we will outline the general strategy, examine the unfamiliar steps in more detail, and then consider the programming itself. We assume that we have two cubes, as shown in figure 9.3. They will be projected onto the *x–z* plane using a parallel projection. The following is the general approach to removing the unwanted lines:

1. Remove the back faces of each object.
2. Determine which object is in front and which is in the rear. In figure 9.3, object *A* is in front.
3. Project the front object (figure 9.4).

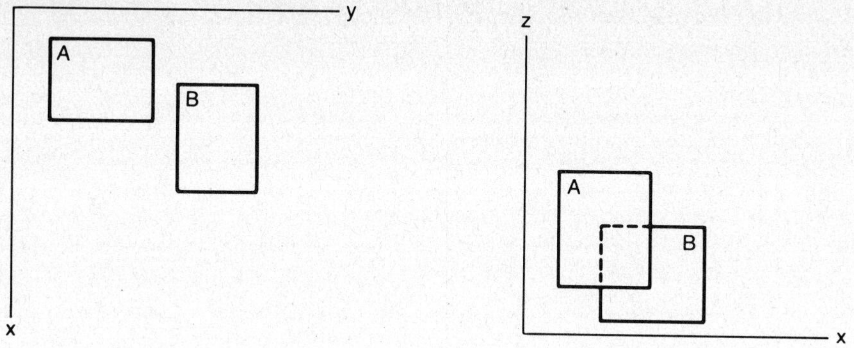

Figure 9.3 Top and front view of two cubes. Cube A is in front of cube B.

4. Determine the outer limits of the front object's projected area (figure 9.5).
5. Determine any intersections of the projections of the rear object's edges with the front object's projected area.
6. Plot those parts of the projection of the rear object that are outside the determined perimeter (figure 9.6).

With this overall outline in mind, we can turn to a more detailed examination of each step. We already know how to eliminate back faces, so we can start with the second step.

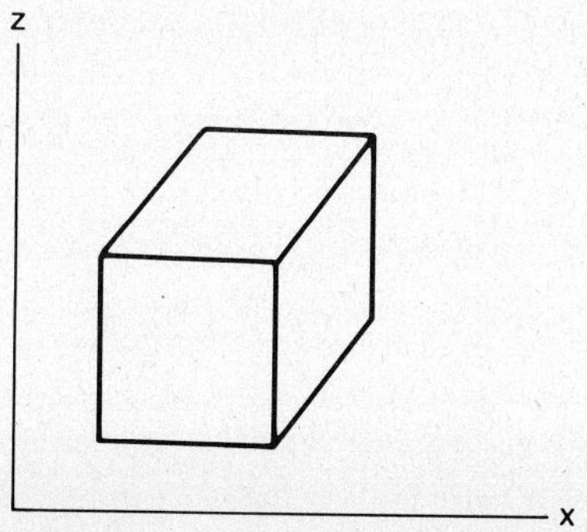

Figure 9.4 Cavalier projection of the front object (cube A in figure 9.3).

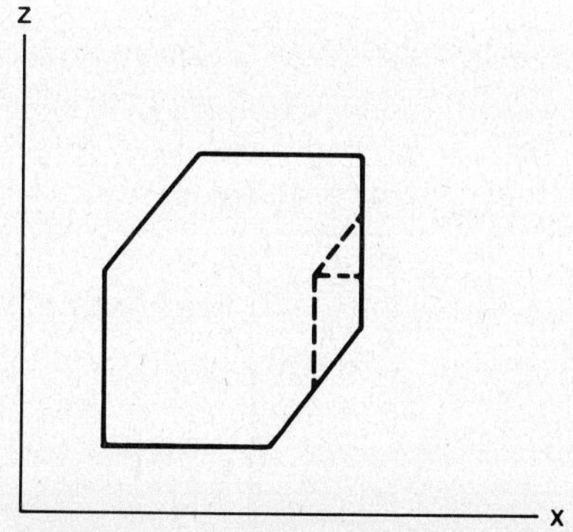

Figure 9.5 Total projected area of the front object. Dashed lines show what part of the rear object this area blocks.

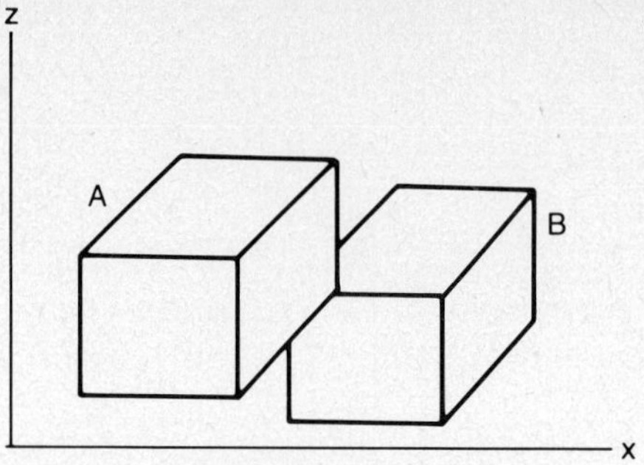

Figure 9.6 Final plot of the two cubes in figure 9.3.

Determining the Front Object

By *front object*, we mean the object that has the potential to hide part of the other object. Let us first consider figure 9.7, which shows two objects and two possible directions of projection. If we choose direction A as the projector, object A' has the potential to hide object B'. Hence, A' is considered the front object. If we choose direction B, object B' can hide object A', and thus B' must be considered the front object. Of course, it is easy for us to see this, but how can the computer make the choice? Consider the additional information shown in figure 9.8, which is the same as figure 9.7, except that we have drawn a plane that separates the two objects and is perpendicular to the x–y plane. Note that we have drawn two normals to the separating plane that pass through the centroids of the objects. These normals provide the crucial means for determining which object is in front: If the dot product of a normal and the direction of projection is positive, then the object whose centroid was used to draw that normal is in front.

The plane we added is called a **separating plane**. Actually, any plane that accomplishes the same objective is a separating plane. We chose a

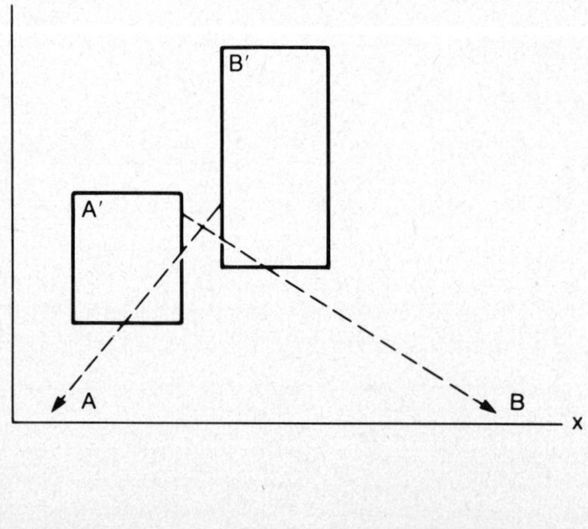

Figure 9.7 Determining which object is in front depends on the projection direction: A' is in front if A is the projector; B' is in front if B is the projector.

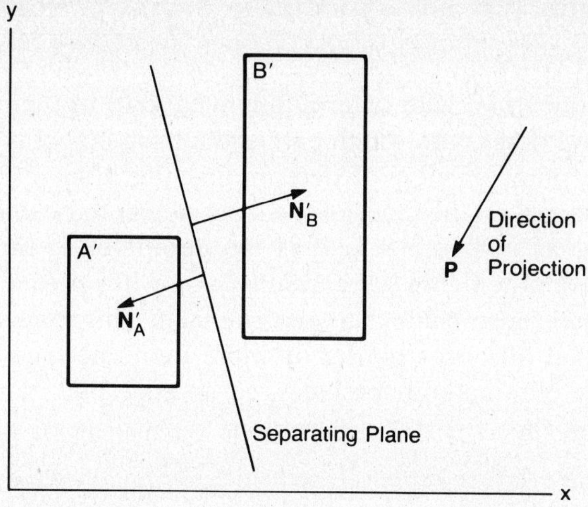

Figure 9.8 For this direction of projection, A' should be in front. The test is $\mathbf{N}' \cdot \mathbf{P}$. Here $\mathbf{N}'_A \cdot \mathbf{P} > 0$ and $\mathbf{N}'_B \cdot \mathbf{P} < 0$.

special case here to simplify the task of finding the normals. From figure 9.8, we see that our plane can be considered a line in the x–y plane. We need the coordinates (x_i, y_i) of the intersection of the normal and the plane. Since the intersection is on the line $y = mx + b$, we can write

$$y_i = mx_i + b$$

From the formula relating the slopes of perpendicular lines, we know that the slope of the normal is $-1/m$. Hence:

$$-1/m = (y_C - y_i)/(x_C - x_i)$$

where C represents the centroid. By solving these two equations, we can get the values of x_i and y_i:

$$x_i = [m(y_C - b) + x_C]/[1 + m^2]$$

$$y_i = [m^2(y_C - b) + mx_C]/[1 + m^2] + b$$

The normal vector is then

$$\mathbf{V} = (x_C - x_i)\mathbf{i} + (y_C - y_i)\mathbf{j}$$

Note that this analysis does not hold if the separating plane is parallel to the y–z plane. (This would be a vertical line in the diagram, such as $x = x_P$). Then the normal vector is simply:

$$\mathbf{V} = (x_C - x_P)\mathbf{i}$$

Determining the Total Projected Area of the Front Object

We are ultimately concerned with determining what part of the rear object is blocked from view; we don't care which part of the front object is responsible. Therefore, from the point of view of determining the hidden lines, we can consider the projection of all the faces of the front object to be one contiguous patch on the screen, as in figure 9.5. It is the perimeter of this patch that interests us. If you examine figure 9.9 carefully, you will see that an edge that belongs to the perimeter also belongs to just one face. This may seem strange in view of the fact that all edges border on more than one face. Remember, though, that we have eliminated back faces, so an edge that is common to a back face and a front face fits this description. We will need a list of these critical edges.

Determining Inside and Outside Points

Look at figure 9.9 again. The arrows indicate how the turtle moves when it draws each face. If you eliminate the inside edges and then examine the edges that compose the perimeter, you can see that the turtle moves counter-clockwise around the perimeter. This is very significant. If a point is inside the projected area, it is *always* to the left of the turtle. We cannot say this for an outside point. To determine which is which, we resort once again to vectors. In figure 9.10a, point A is inside the area, and point B is outside. In figure 9.10b, we have drawn three vectors from the starting point of the edge: **TH**, the edge vector; **TA**, a vector to the inside point; and **TB**, a vector to the outside point. The cross product of the edge vector with **TA** points out of the screen (the $-\mathbf{j}$ direction), for *all* edge vectors. This is not true for an outside point. Thus, by examining the sign of an easily calculated quantity, a cross

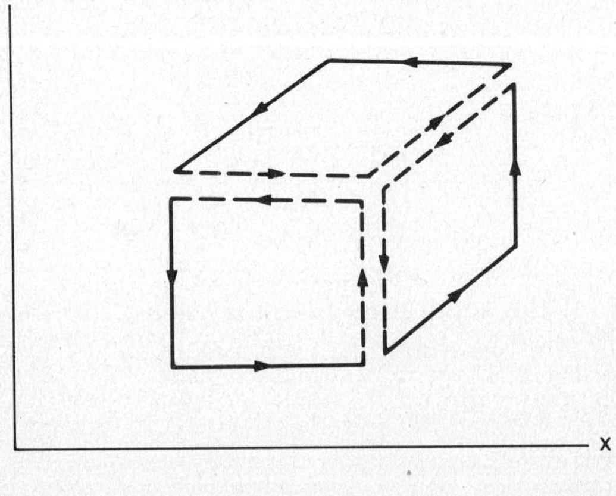

Figure 9.9 Edges that belong to the perimeter of the projected area border on only one face. Here, solid lines indicate a border on one face; dashed lines indicate a border on two faces.

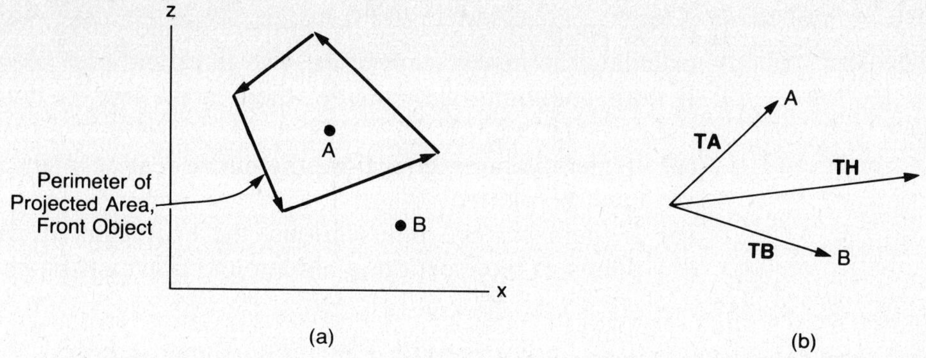

Figure 9.10 (a) A point inside the area is always to the left of the turtle. (b) **TH** × **TA** points out of the page, regardless of edge vectors used. For **TH** × **TB**, the result points into the page in at least one case. This provides a convenient test for inside versus outside points.

product, we can determine whether or not a vertex is inside or outside the area taken up by the front object.

Determining Intersections of Rear Edges with the Front Object Projection

In chapter 6, we went through the steps necessary to determine whether two line segments intersect. Let us concentrate here on what the intersection possibilities are. After we check the endpoints of a given rear edge, we have four possibilities, as shown in figure 9.11:

1. If both endpoints are inside the perimeter, the edge is entirely out of view; we don't plot it.

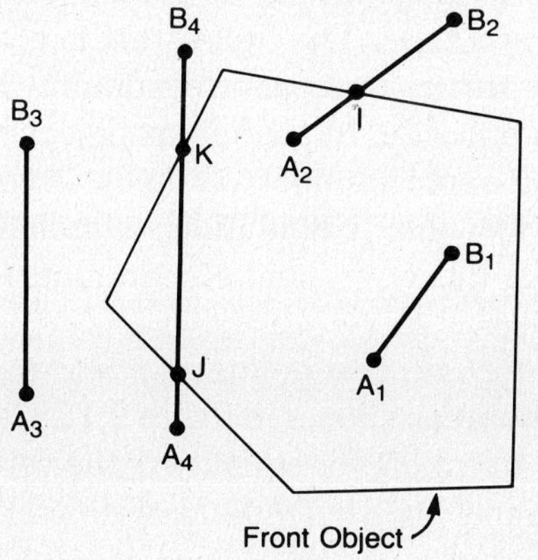

Figure 9.11 Segments JK, A_2I, and A_1B_1 are hidden by the front object.

2. If one endpoint is inside the perimeter (and one outside), we must calculate the intersection of the two lines and plot accordingly.
3. If both endpoints are outside, there are either no intersections or two.
   (a) If there is no intersection, the entire rear segment is visible and must be plotted.
   (b) If there are two intersections, the line segment joining the two points of intersection is hidden and must not be plotted.

PROGRAMMING CONSIDERATIONS FOR TWO OBJECTS

To demonstrate the programming for one object blocking another, we will consider a parallel projection of two cubes. We will assume that a linked list has been established with each cube in a separate segment, the beginning and ends of which are pointed to by the usual pointers. For reasons that will become apparent shortly, we have added another field, *switch*, to our record structure. It now looks like this:

```
newdisplay = RECORD
               segnum:INTEGER;
               side: INTEGER;
               x:REAL;
               y:REAL;
               z:REAL;
               penstatus:(on,off,erase);
               switch:0..1;
               adr: ^display
               END;
```

The first step, finding a centroid, is a little more complex than we might initially expect. We cannot simply average all the vertices in a list. Recall that we enter the vertices for one side at a time. The first vertex is entered twice—once as the starting point for the turtle, once as its endpoint. Furthermore, each vertex borders on more than one side. In a complex object, we cannot be sure that each vertex is used the same number of times. Hence, we must search the list and, at least for this calculation, eliminate unwanted duplications. Then we can average the x-, y-, and z-coordinates as called for by the definition of the centroid.

In the following procedure, we use two pointers, p and q, to check for duplicate vertices. They initially point as shown in figure 9.12a. The idea is to move q step by step down the list, checking for equality of the vertices in p and q at each step. If an equality is found, the *switch* field of p is set to 0. Then p

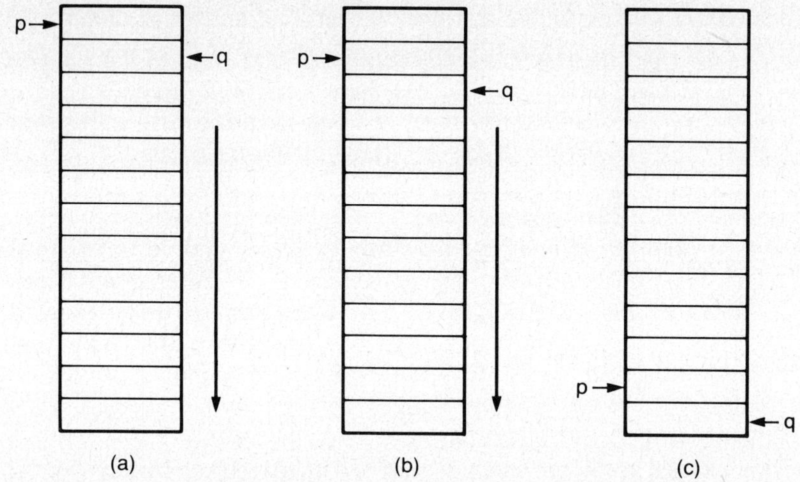

Figure 9.12 Eliminating duplicate vertices on a linked list. (a) The pointer p remains fixed while q moves down the list. (b) If a duplicate is found, or if q reaches the end without finding a duplicate, p and q are reset. (c) The process is repeated until both pointers have advanced as far as they can go. Before any pointers are reset, duplicate vertices are marked, as described in the text.

and q are reset to the positions shown in figure 9.12b and the process is repeated. If q gets to the end of the list and no equality is found, nothing happens to the *switch* fields; p and q are simply reset as in figure 9.12b. Eventually, p and q reach the end of the list (figure 9.12c), with all duplicate vertices marked by *switch* fields of 0. Then the centroid coordinates are calculated as simple averages.

Program 9.2: Finding a Centroid

Assumptions. Linked list with structure of *newdisplay*. Object n has *numsides*[n] sides. Pointer $bg[k, n]$ points to the beginning of the kth side of the nth object. Pointer $e[k, n]$ points to the end of the kth side of the nth object.

```
PROCEDURE CENTROID;
VAR n,count:INTEGER;

BEGIN {1}
  FOR n:= 1 to objects DO
   BEGIN {2}
    p:= bg[1,n];
    q:= p^.adr;
```

```
REPEAT
  IF (p^.x = q^.x) AND (p^.y = q^.y) AND (p^.z = q^.z)
  THEN BEGIN {3}      {if two vertices have same coordinates,}
         p^.switch := 0;    {eliminate one of them}
         p := p^.adr;     {then reset pointers}
         q := p^.adr
         END {3}
  ELSE IF  q = e[numsides[n],n]      {if a duplicate can't be
                                      found with the}
        THEN BEGIN {4}      {current value of p, and q has}
               p := p^.adr;      {reached its limit, reset the
                                  pointers}
               q := p^.adr
               END {4}
  ELSE q := q^.adr      {if no duplicate, but q not at end of list
                         then move only q up one record}
UNTIL p = e[numsides[n],n];
xct[n] := 0;      {centroid coordinates are xct[n],etc.}
yct[n] := 0;
zct[n] := 0;
count := 0;
p := bg[1,n];
WHILE p <= e[numsides[n],n] DO
   BEGIN {5}
    IF p^.switch = 1      {don't count duplicate vertices in this
                           sum}
    THEN BEGIN {6}
           xct[n] := xct[n] + p^.x;
           yct[n] := yct[n] + p^.y;      {sum of x, y, and z
                                          coordinates}
           zct[n] := zct[n] + p^.z;
           count := count + 1;
           p := p^.adr
           END {6}
    ELSE p :=p^.adr
  END; {5}
xct[n] := xct[n]/count;      {divide sums by count to get
                              centroid}
yct[n] := yct[n]/count;      {coordinates}
zct[n] := zct[n]/count
 END {2}
END; {1}
```

In the following procedure, the centroid of the object in the first segment is used to form the dot product (discussed earlier in the chapter). If the dot product is positive, the front object is in the first segment; otherwise, it is in the second segment. In the procedure, the dot product is called *test*. The integers g and h are used to indicate the segment numbers of the front and rear objects, respectively. For example, if the front object is in the first segment, $g = 1$ and $h = 2$.

Program 9.3: Finding the Front Object

Assumption. Centroid of the object in the first segment is known. Separating plane can be represented by a line identified by *slope* and *int.*

```
PROCEDURE FRONT;
VAR xi,yi,test:REAL;

BEGIN
  xi:= (slope*(yct[1] - int) + xct[1])/(1 + sqr(slope));
  yi:= slope*xi + int;
  test:= (xct[1] - xi)*xd + (yct[1] - yi)*yd;
  IF test > 0     {test = dot product of separating plane normal and
                   the direction of projection}
  THEN BEGIN
        h := 2;     {if test > 0, then object in first
                     segment is in front}
        g:= 1
        END
  ELSE BEGIN
        h:= 1;     {otherwise, object in second segment is in front}
        g:= 2
        END
END;
```

Once the front object is determined, it should be drawn.

The next procedure determines which edges comprise the perimeter of the projected front object. We have noted that the perimeter consists of edges that border on only one face. How can we determine this from a list of vertices? We start by setting two pointers, r and u, to the first two records in segment g (figure 9.13a). These are the endpoints of an edge. We do the same with two other pointers, p and q, which are the endpoints of another edge. We move the pair p and q through the list, one record at a time, checking for duplicate edges. From figure 9.9, we can see that duplicate edges are drawn in opposite directions, so we look for the following equalities:

Coordinates in r = coordinates in q

Coordinates in u = coordinates in p

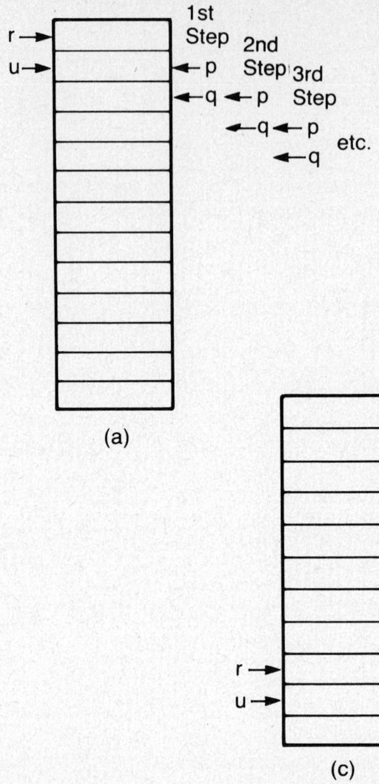

Figure 9.13 Eliminating duplicate line segments from a list. The endpoints of one segment are pointed to by r and u; the endpoints of another segment are pointed to by p and q. (a) The p-q pair moves down the list. (b) If a duplicate segment is found, or if the p-q pair reaches the end of the list without finding a duplicate, the pairs are reset. (c) The process is repeated until the pointers have advanced as far as they can go. Before any points are reset, duplicate line segments are marked, as described in the text.

If these conditions are true, we set the field *penstatus* to off in the r and p records. Then the pointers are reset as in figure 9.13b and the process is repeated. If p and q reach the end of the list and no duplicate edges are found, *penstatus* is left alone and the pointers are simply reset as in figure 9.13b. After the last possibility is checked (figure 9.13c), the list ends up modified so that only the initial endpoints of perimeter edges have *penstatus* = *on.*

Program 9.4: Finding the Perimeter of the Front Object

Assumptions. Same as those of CENTROID. For front object, segment number is g.

```
PROCEDURE PERIMETER;
VAR test1,test2:BOOLEAN;

  PROCEDURE MOVEALL;        {this is what we mean by "reset all
                             pointers"}
   BEGIN
    r := r^.adr;       {advance r and u each one record}
    u := r^.adr;
    p := u;      {reset p and q to one record past r and u,}
    q := p^.adr      {respectively}
   END;

BEGIN {1}
  r := bg[1,g];       {point r and u to first and second records}
  u := r^.adr;
  p := u;      {point p and u to second and third records}
  q := u^.adr;
  REPEAT
    IF r^.penstatus = off       {if pen is off in this record, then}
    THEN MOVEALL       {reset all pointers}
    ELSE IF p^.penstatus = off       {if pen is off in this record}
         THEN IF q = e[numsides[g],g]       {reset pointers if q is
                                              at end}
                THEN MOVEALL
                ELSE BEGIN {2}
                       p := p^.adr;       {if q not at end, move p
                                            and q}
                       q := p^.adr       {ahead by one record}
                       END {2}
         ELSE BEGIN {3}       {however, if pens are on . . . }
                test1 := (r^.x = q^.x) AND (r^.y = q^.y) AND
                (r ^.z = q ^.z);
                test2 := (u^.x = p^.x) AND (u^.y = p^.y) AND
                (u^.z = p^.z);
                IF test1 and test2       { . . . and identical line
                                           segments are found}
                THEN BEGIN {4}
                       r^.penstatus := off;       {turn off pen in these
                                                    records}
                       p^.penstatus := off;
                       MOVEALL       {and reset all pointers}
                       END {4}
         ELSE BEGIN {5}
                IF q = e[numsides[g],g]       {if pens are on and
                                                there is}
                THEN MOVEALL       {no equality, either reset all}
```

```
                    ELSE BEGIN {6}      {pointers if q is at end, or}
                         p := p ^.adr;     {advance only the p-q pair}
                         q := p ^.adr
                         END {6}
                         END {5}
                         END {3}
UNTIL u ^.adr = e[numsides[g],g]
END; {1}
```

Now we are ready for the most complex part: the procedure INSIDE, which determines which parts of the rear object, if any, are blocked by the front object. Specifically, INSIDE modifies the rear object's list so that the only records with *penstatus=on* are those containing initial points of line segments that lie outside the front object's perimeter. INSIDE uses two local procedures:

> CHECKIT: This determines whether endpoints of rear object edges are inside or outside the perimeter.
>
> INTERSECT: This determines the intersection coordinates of a rear object edge and the perimeter.

INSIDE proceeds essentially as follows: For each edge of the rear object, the endpoints are passed to CHECKIT to see if they are inside or outside the perimeter. If both endpoints are inside, the *switch* field of each record is set to 0. (INSIDE temporarily uses *switch*, rather than *penstatus*, to mark unwanted points. It initially sets all *switch* fields to 1.) If both points are outside, the *switch* fields are left alone (but see problem 9.7). If one point is inside and the other outside, then the edge must intersect the perimeter. Its endpoint coordinates are passed to INTERSECT, which calculates the intersection coordinates and creates a new record to hold them. The new record is inserted in the list between the records holding the endpoints (figure 9.14). If the initial endpoint is outside, the *switch* field of the new record is set to 0. This will prevent the turtle from drawing between the intersection point and the inside point (figure 9.15a). On the other hand, if the initial point is inside, then the *switch* field of the new record is set to 1. This will enable the turtle to draw from the intersection point to the outside point (figure 9.15b). INSIDE checks all edges of the rear object in this way. When it is finished, all *penstatus* fields of the rear object's list whose *switch* fields are 1 are set to *on*. All other *penstatus* fields are set to *off*. When you examine INSIDE in detail, keep the following in mind:

1. INSIDE uses pointers p and q to point to endpoints of a perimeter edge, and r and u to point to endpoints of a rear object edge.

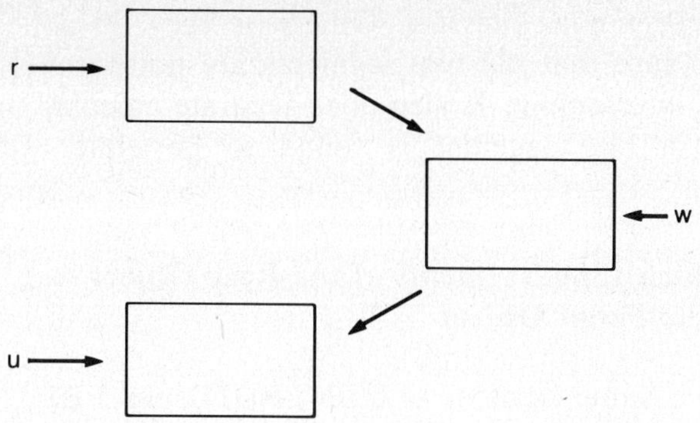

Figure 9.14 Adding a record for an intersection point. If a line segment from the rear object intersects the perimeter of the front object when projected, a new record, *w*, must be created between the records containing the segment's endpoints, *r* and *u*. After creation of the new record, *r* points to *w* and *w* points to *u*.

2. The variables *test1* and *test2* in CHECKIT are the cross products that correspond to **TH** $\times$ **TA** (or **TH** $\times$ **TB**) of figure 9.10.
3. The intersection of two arbitrary line segments is calculated in INTERSECT as follows. The equations for the two lines passing through the segments are solved for their intersection point (xint,yint). If these coordinates are between the endpoints of both segments (conditions denoted by the Boolean variables B1, B2, etc),

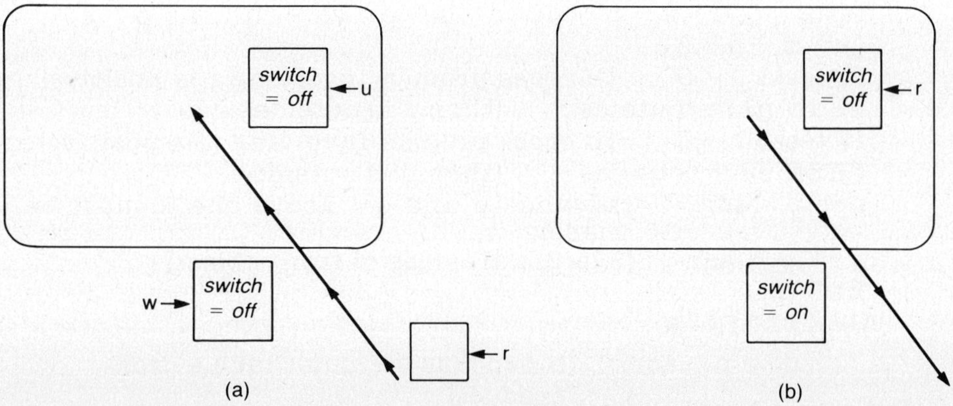

Figure 9.15 Setting *switch* for the new record. (a) *w* ^ *.switch* must be set to *off* so that no plotting takes place inside the perimeter. (b) *w* ^ .switch must be set to *on* to ensure plotting to the endpoint pointed to by *u*. Note that *switch* for both inside endpoints is set to *off*.

then the two segments intersect. Otherwise they do not. INTERSECT makes sure that the two segments are not parallel before it calculates an intersection. It also does separate calculations for the cases where a line segment is found to be either vertical or horizontal.

Program 9.5: Determining Which Line Segments of the Rear Object Are Blocked by the Perimeter of the Front Object

Assumptions. Same as those of CENTROID and PERIMETER.

```
PROCEDURE INSIDE;
VAR p1,p2:string;

PROCEDURE CHECKIT;       {checks whether r and u are inside or
                          outside}
VAR test1,test2:REAL;    {the front object's perimeter}
  BEGIN {1}
    p1 := 'inside';
    p2 := 'inside';
    p:= bg[1,g];       {p and q point to line segments of the front
                        object}
    q:= p^.adr;
    REPEAT
      IF p^.penstatus = on
      THEN     {test1 and test2 are cross products—see text}
       BEGIN {2}
       test1 := (r^.x - p^.x)*(q^.z - p^.z) - (q^.x - p^.x)*
          (r^.z - p^.z);
        test2 := (u^.x - p^.x)*(q^.z - p^.z) - (q^.x - p^.x)*
        (u^.z - p^.z);
        IF test1 >= 0      {if cross product involving r is positive}
        THEN p1 := 'outside';      {then r is outside}
        IF test2 >= 0      {if cross product involving u is positive}
        THEN p2 := 'outside';      {then u is outside}
        p:= p^.adr;       {advance p and q— above check must be
                           made}
        q:= p ^.adr       {against all sides of front object}
        END {2}
       ELSE BEGIN {3}
             p := p^.adr;      {if pen was off, don't take a cross
                                product}
             q := p ^.adr
             END {3}
    UNTIL p = e[numsides[g],g]
```

```
      END; {1}

   PROCEDURE INTERSECT;     {calculates intersection coordinates
                             if CHECKIT found on inside and
                             one outside point}

   VAR k1,k2:REAL;
     B1,B2,B3,B4,B5,B6,B7,B8,B9:BOOLEAN;
   BEGIN {1}
     p := bg[1,g];
     q := p^.adr;     {p and q point to perimeter segment endpoints}
     REPEAT     {r and u point to rear object endpoints}
       B9 := true;
       IF p^.penstatus = on
       THEN{*}
        BEGIN {2}
   IF q^.x = p^.x     {if perimeter line segment is vertical}
   THEN IF u^.x = r^.x     {and rear line segment is vertical}
         THEN B9 := false     {and intersection is impossible}
         ELSE BEGIN {3}     {but if rear segment is not
                              vertical . . . }
                k2 := (r^.z - u^.z)/(r^.x - u^.x);
                xint := q^.x;     { . . . this is the intersection}
                yint := u^.z + k2*xint - k2*u^.x
                END {3}
   ELSE IF r^.x = u^.x
        THEN BEGIN {4}     {if only the rear segment is
                              vertical . . .}
                k1 := (q^.z - p^.z)/(q^.x - p^.x);
                xint := r^.x:     { . . . this is the intersection}
                yint := p^.z + k1*xint - k1*p^.x
                END {4}
        ELSE BEGIN {5}
               k1 := (q^.z - p^.z)/(q^.x - p^.x);
               k2 := (r^.z - u^.z)/(r^.x - u^.x);
               IF k2 = k1     {if both segments have the same
                                 slopes . . . }
               THEN B9 := false     { . . . intersection is}
                                    {impossible}
               ELSE BEGIN {6}
                 xint := (p^.z - k1*p^.x - u^.z + k2*u^.x)/
                         (k2 - k1);
                 IF k1 = 0     {this finds intersection if segments}
                 THEN yint := q^.z     {are neither vertical
                                         nor parallel}
                 ELSE IF k2 = 0
```

```
            THEN yint := r^.z
            ELSE yint := u^.z + k2*(xint - u^.x)
            END {6}
        END; {5}
B1 := (xint> = u^.x) AND (xint <= r^.x);        {intersection
                                                  coordinates}
B2 := (xint <= u^.x) AND (xint >= r^.x);        {must be
                                                  between}
B3 := (yint >= u^.z) AND (yint <= r^.z);        {segment
                                                 endpoints for}
                                                 these}
B4 := (yint <= u^.z) AND (yint >= r^.z);         conditions to
                                                {be true}
B5 := (xint >= p^.x) AND (xint <= q^.x);
B6 := (xint >= q^.x) AND (xint <= p^.x);
B7 := (yint >= p^.z) AND (yint <= q^.z);
B8 := (yint <= p^.z) AND (yint >= q^.z);
IF B9 AND (B1 OR B2) AND (B3 OR B4) AND (B5 OR B6) AND
  (B7 OR B8)
THEN BEGIN {7} {if above is true, segments intersect . . . }
        new(w);
        w^.x := xint;      { . . . so create a new record, put in the
                             coordinates}
        w^.z := yint;      {of the intersection, point r to w and
                            w to u, then}
        r^.adr := w;       {advance p and q}
        w^.adr := u;
        p := p^.adr;
        q := p^.adr
        END {7}
ELSE BEGIN {8}        {if conditions are not met, just advance
                       p and q}
       p := p^.adr;     {and try the next side}
       q := p^.adr
       END {8}
     END {2}
  ELSE BEGIN {9*}       {if pen in record p was off, don't do any
                         analysis}
         p := p^.adr;    {just go to the next side}
         q := p^.adr
         END {9}
  UNTIL p = e[numsides[g],g]
END; {1}

BEGIN     {main routine}
```

```
r := bg[1,h];      {point r and u to rear object line segment}
u := r^.adr;
p := bg[1,h];      {for the rear object's records . . . }
WHILE (p <> e[numsides[h],h]) and (p <> NIL) DO
  BEGIN {1}
    IF p^.penstatus = on      { . . . turn switch to 1 for all records
                               with pen on}
    THEN p^.switch := 1       {switch used temporarily to mark
                               records}
    ELSE p^.switch := 0;
    p := p^.adr
  END; {1}
p := bg[1,g];      {point p back to front object}
REPEAT
    IF r^.penstatus = on      {do for a rear line segment that is to
                               be projected}
    THEN BEGIN {2}
      CHECKIT;
      IF (p1 = 'inside') AND (p2 = 'inside')
      THEN BEGIN {3}
             r^.switch := 0;      {both endpoints inside? turn them
                                   off}
             u^.switch := 0;
             r := r^.adr;
             u := r^.adr
             END {3}
      ELSE IF (p1 = 'outside') AND (p2 = 'outside')
            THEN BEGIN {4}
                   r := r^.adr;      {both endpoints outside?}
                   u := r^.adr       {leave them alone}
                   END {4}
        ELSE IF p1 = 'inside'
              THEN BEGIN {5}        {r inside and u outside?}
                     INTERSECT;       {find intersection, turn r off}
                     r^.switch := 0;       {turn w on, advance r
                                            and u}
                     w^.switch := 1;
                     r := u;
                     u := r^.adr
                     END {5}
        ELSE BEGIN {6}        {r outside and u inside?}
              INTERSECT;       {find intersection, turn u off}
              u^.switch := 0;       {turn w off, advance r and u}
              w^.switch := 0;
              r := u;
```

```
                u := r ^ .adr
                END {6}
            END {2}
        ELSE BEGIN {7}        {was pen off in r? just go to next rear
                               line segment}
            r := r ^ .adr;
            u := r ^ .adr
            END {7}
UNTIL r = e[numsides[h],h];
p := bg[1,h];
WHILE (p < > e[numsides[h],h]) and (p < > NIL) DO
  BEGIN {8}
    IF p ^ .switch = 1       {go over all records in rear list, set pen
                              to on if switch was 1}
    THEN p ^ .penstatus := on
    ELSE p ^ .penstatus := off;
    p := p ^ .adr
  END {8}
END; {main routine}
```

To write a complete program incorporating hidden line removal, use the procedures just developed (in conjuction with previous ones) as follows:

ELIMFACE (for both objects)

CENTROID

FRONT

TRANSFORM (for both objects)

DRAWIT (for front object)

PERIMETER

INSIDE

DRAWIT (for rear object)

The details are left as an exercise (problem 9.3). Note that when we worked out ELIMFACE, TRANSFORM, and DRAWIT, we were dealing with only one object. Make sure that your versions of these procedures can deal with both objects as needed.

PROBLEMS

9.1. Given the cubes in figure 9.16, solve the following, assuming a cavalier projection, with $A = 30^\circ$.

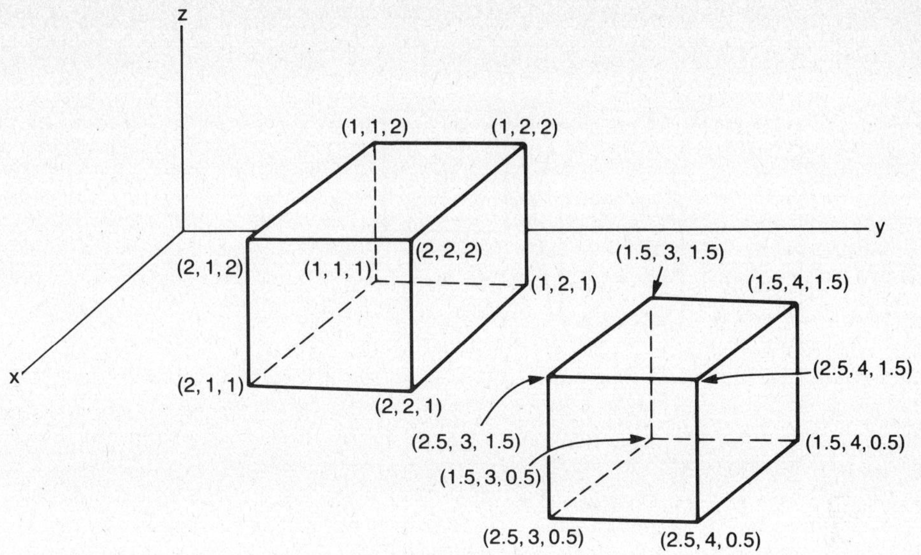

Figure 9.16 Construction for problems 9.1 and 9.3.

(a) Find the centroid of each cube.

(b) Pick a separating plane that is parallel to the *x–y* plane. Write the expressions for the two normals that pass through the centroids.

(c) Show explicitly that one of the objects is in front by performing the dot product test.

(d) Repeat parts (b) and (c) for a plane that is not parallel to the *y–z* plane, but is perpendicular to the *x–y* plane.

(e) Pick an edge of the front object whose projection is one of the front edges that comprises the perimeter of the total projected area. Calculate the projected coordinates of the endpoints. Draw the vector representing the turtle's direction for that segment.

(f) Pick any vertex on the rear cube and calculate its projected coordinates.

(g) Use the cross product test outlined in the chapter to determine whether this point is hidden or in view.

9.2. Comment on this apparent paradox: For the two cubes in figure 9.17, the choice of which object is in front seems to depend on the choice of separating plane. If separating plane *A* is used, cube *A* comes out in front. If separating plane *B* is used, cube *B* comes out in front.

9.3. Implement a complete hidden line removal program that includes a choice of parallel or perspective projection. Test the program on the cubes in figure 9.16.

9.4. Can a separating plane intersect any of the vertices on an object? Explain fully.

9.5. Suppose that the separating plane is not perpendicular to any of the coordinate planes.

(a) Qualitatively describe the problem of finding the two normals.

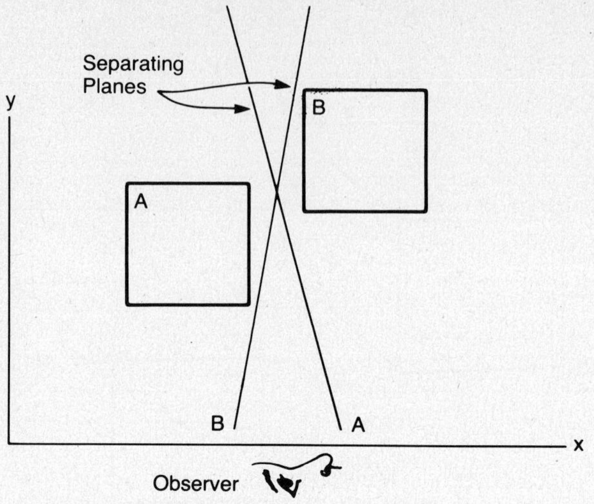

Figure 9.17 Geometry for problem 9.2.

(b) Derive (or look up) the formulas appropriate to the solution of part (a). Modify the Pascal procedures accordingly.

9.6. Explain clearly the role of the field *switch* in the addition of the record *w* to the rear object's list. Could we have gotten along with just PENSTATUS?

9.7. As it stands, the procedure INSIDE cannot eliminate hidden lines like this:

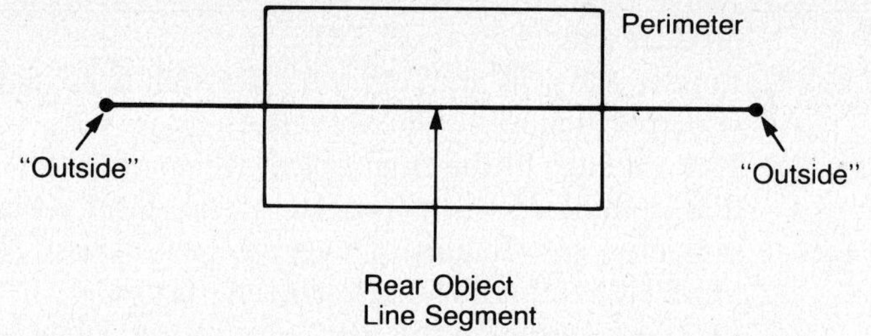

Modify the appropriate part(s) of INSIDE so that it can do so.

9.8. For the house you drew in problem 7.9, eliminate any faces you cannot see.

REFERENCES

Harrington, S. *Computer Graphics: A Programming Approach.* New York: McGraw-Hill, 1983, chapter 10.

Meyers, R. *Microcomputer Graphics.* Reading, Mass.: Addison-Wesley, 1982, chapter 7.

Rost, R. J. "Hidden Surface Elimination the Easy Way." *Creative Computing*, February 1984, 189–196.

Seppi, K. D. "Simplified Hidden Line Removal." *Journal of Pascal and Ada*, January/February 1983, 21–25.

Sutherland, I.E.; Sproull, R. F.; and Schumacker, R. A. "A Characterization of Ten Hidden Surface Algorithms." *Computing Surveys 6*(1), March 1974, 1–55.

Appendix A

Mathematics Review

The study of computer science requires a reasonable facility with mathematics in general and a knowledge of certain mathematical topics in particular. We assume that you meet the former requirement and can use that facility to rectify any deficiencies in the latter requirement. This appendix reviews a variety of mathematical topics with which you should be familiar.

ANALYTIC GEOMETRY

We begin our discussion with an assumption—that you have a good intuitive concept of what a point and a line are. Our only concern about a point is specifying its location on a flat surface (the screen). We can take two perpendicular lines (**axes**), one horizontal and the other vertical, and call their point of intersection the **origin**. Any point can be specified as being x units from the origin parallel to the horizontal axis and y units from the origin parallel to the vertical axis. The quantities x and y are called **coordinates**; the location of the point is denoted by the shorthand (x, y). The grid shown in figure A.1 is called a **Cartesian coordinate system**.

Lines

Consider the line passing through (x_1, y_1) and (x_2, y_2) in figure A.2. We define the slope, m, of the line as

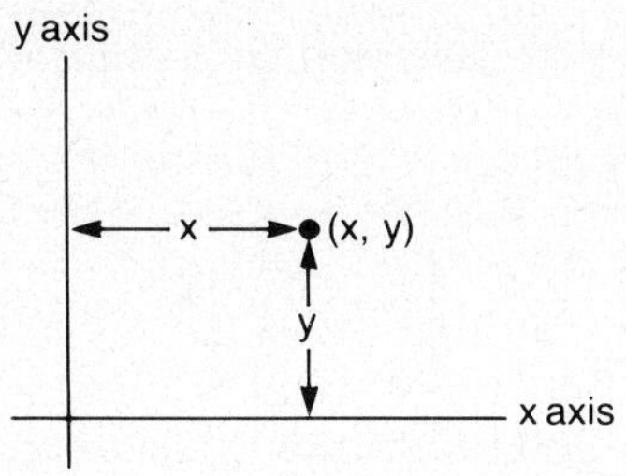

Figure A.1 Cartesian coordinate system.

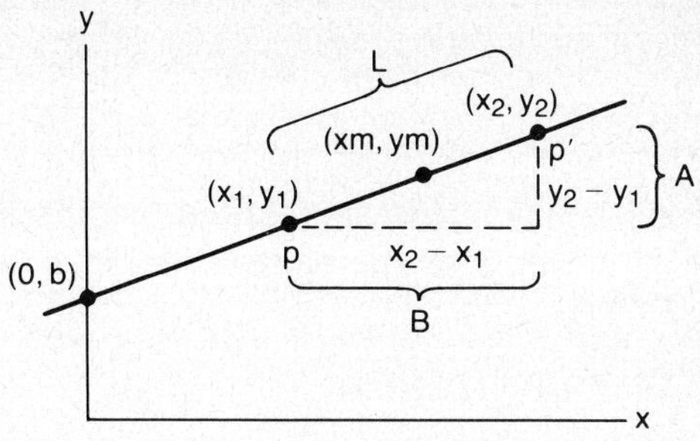

Figure A.2 Line and line segment parameters: $m = (y_2 - y_1)/(x_2 - x_1)$; $xm = (x_1 + x_2)/2$; $ym = (y_1 + y_2)/2$; $PP' = \sqrt{(x_2 - x_1)^2 + (y_2 - y_1)^2}$.

$$m = (y_2 - y_1)/(x_2 - x_1) \tag{A.1}$$

Consider any other point (x, y) that is also on the line. We can calculate the slope twice, once using (x, y) and (x_1, y_1) and then using (x_1, y_1) and (x_2, y_2). Since they are part of the same line, these expressions must be the same. Hence:

$$(y - y_1)/(x - x_1) = (y_2 - y_1)/(x_2 - x_1)$$

Multiplying both sides by $x - x_1$ yields:

$$y - y_1 = (y_2 - y_1) \cdot (x - x_1)/(x_2 - x_1) \tag{A.2}$$

This is called the equation of the line. Note that the only variables are x and y; everything else is a known constant.

Any relationship between certain known parameters (in the foregoing case, the coordinates of the known points) and an arbitrary point on the line can serve as an equation of the line. For example, equation (A.2) can be rewritten:

$$y - y_1 = m \cdot (x - x_1) \tag{A.3}$$

This is a relation between an arbitrary point (x, y), the slope, m, and a particular point (x_1, y_1). It is therefore an equation of a line. On the other hand, equation (A.1) cannot be the equation of a line. The relation does not involve an arbitrary point (no x and y in the equation).

One important parameter of a line is the so-called **y-intercept**—the place where a line (except a vertical one) crosses the y-axis. By definition, its x-coordinate is zero; its y-coordinate is called b. Using these values for x and y in equation (A.3), we get:

$$b = y_1 - mx_1$$

Then we can write yet another equation of a line:

$$y = mx + b \tag{A.4}$$

Hence, the equation of a line can be written several ways. The only difference is in the makeup of the known parameters: two points, a point and the slope, or the slope and the y-intercept.

Line Segments

Since the CRT screen is finite and a line is infinite, it is really line *segments* that interest us. A line segment is simply the part of a line between two endpoints, such as (x_1, y_1) and (x_2, y_2). It has a slope whose formula should look familiar:

$$m = (y_2 - y_1)/(x_2 - x_1)$$

However, a line segment has two important attributes that are not associated with lines: midpoint and length. The x-coordinate (or y-coordinate) of the midpoint is the average of the x-coordinates (or y-coordinates) of the endpoints:

$$(x_m, y_m) = [(x_1 + y_1)/2, (x_2 + y_2)/2]$$

The length can be calculated by applying the Pythagorean theorem to the parameters in figure A.2. This theorem states that

$$L^2 = A^2 + B^2$$

Using the coordinates of the endpoints of A and B in this equation, we get:

$$L^2 = (y_2 - y_1)^2 + (x_2 - x_1)^2$$

This is called the distance formula, and is usually written as:

$$L = [(y_2 - y_1)^2 + (x_2 - x_1)^2]^{1/2}$$

It is also useful to know whether two segments are perpendicular. This can be determined by a simple test. Consider any two perpendicular segments. We can move the pair so that their intersection point is at the origin (figure A.3); this doesn't change their relationship (they are still perpendicular), but it makes the calculations easier. We can also draw the vertical line from A to B, as shown. This gives us a triangle whose right angle is at the origin. From the distance formula, we can write:

$$(x - 0)^2 + (mx - 0)^2 + (x - 0)^2 + (nx - 0)^2 = (x - x)^2 + (mx - nx)^2$$

Expanding and canceling leaves us with

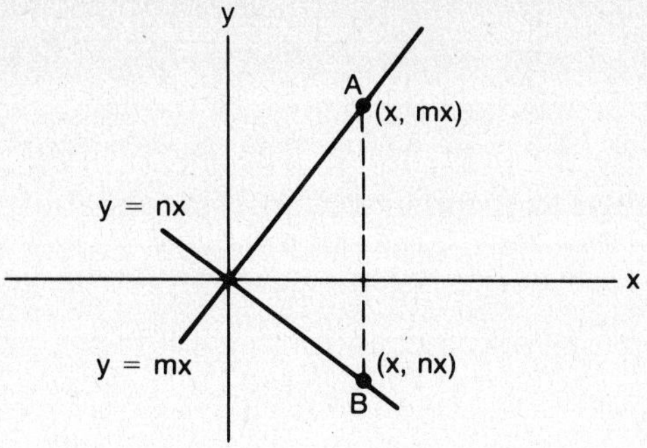

Figure A.3 Geometry for perpendicular line derivation.

$$2x^2 = -2mnx^2$$

Hence:

$$mn = -1$$

Thus, if two lines are perpendicular, one slope is the negative reciprocal of the other.

Conic Sections

Consider a piece of cardboard in the shape shown in figure A.4a. If it is rotated about the vertical axis, a three-dimensional shape called a **right**

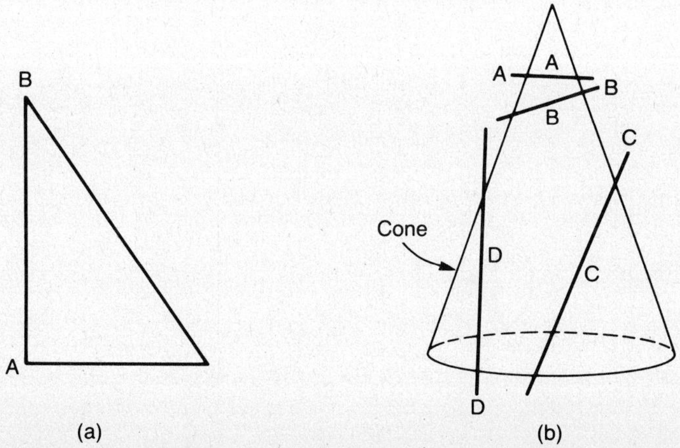

Figure A.4 Conic sections. (a) Rotate about AB to produce right circular cone. (b) Conic sections produced by indicated slices; A, circle; B, ellipse; C, parabola; D, hyperbola.

circular cone results. If we now slice the cone with a knife, a new surface is created. That surface is bounded by a curve called a **conic section.** How we slice the cone (figure A.4b) determines the nature of the conic section. Each conic section has an equation to describe it. The same principles that we applied to a line can be applied to a conic section. The equation is a relation between an arbitrary point on the curve and known parameters. In the discussions that follow, we will describe those parameters and show the important steps in the derivations of the equations (we'll leave out the tedious algebra).

Circles A circle is a curve whose points are all equidistant from a common point called a **center.** The distance from the center to the curve is called a **radius.** We can use the distance formula to calculate the length of the radius drawn in figure A.5:

$$R^2 = (x - h)^2 + (y - k)^2$$

This is the equation of a circle. It is a relation between any point (x, y) and the parameters radius and center.

Example. A circle has a radius of 5 and its center is located at (12, 7). Its equation is

$$5^2 = (x - 12)^2 + (y - 7)^2$$

In this example, we could have expanded and rearranged so that the equation became

$$0 = x^2 + y^2 - 24x - 14y + 168$$

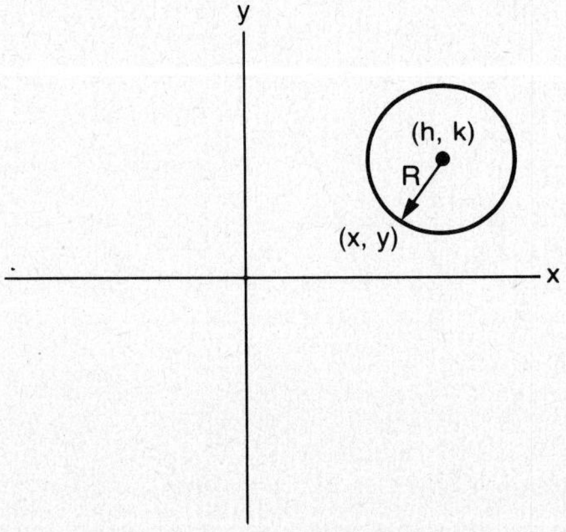

Figure A.5 A circle with its center at an arbitrary point.

However, this form is not desirable, because it does not allow us to recognize immediately the coordinates of the center or the radius.

Parabolas Figure A.6a shows a parabola and names various elements needed to define it. The two most important elements are a line—the **directrix**—and a point—the **focus**—neither of which is on the curve. The parabola consists of points that are equidistant from the directrix and the focus. Using the distance formula on DC and CF, we have:

$$[x-(h-p)]^2=[x-(h+p)]^2+(y-k)^2$$

After expanding and canceling, we get:

$$(y-k)^2=4p(x-h)$$

Note that all we need is the distance from the focus to the vertex and the coordinates of the focus. For parabolas that open in the negative x-direction

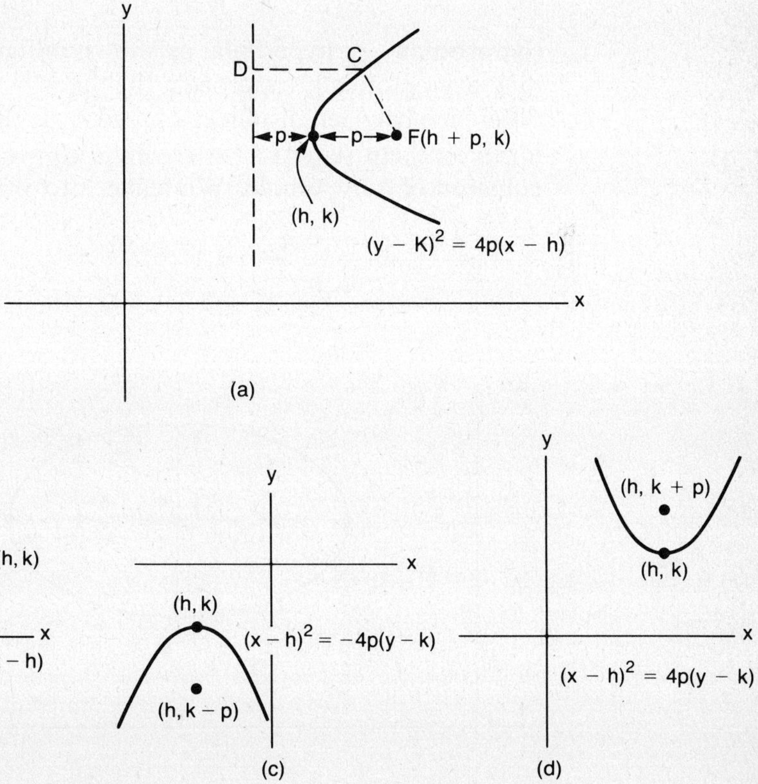

Figure A.6 (a) Geometry for the parabola derivation in text; F = focus, C = point (x, y) on the curve. (b), (c), (d) Other parabolas.

(and y-directions), the formulas have similar patterns. Consult figure A.6 for details.

Ellipses An ellipse (figure A.7) has two foci that play a role analogous to that of the center of a circle. In an ellipse, the distance from one focus to a point P on the curve plus the distance from P to the other focus is a constant. Using the distance formulas on these distances, we get:

$$[x-(h-c)]^2+(y-k)^2+[x-(h+c)]^2+(y-k)^2=\text{a constant}$$

What is the constant? If we choose P to be at V, then the dashed lines are $a+c$ and $a-c$, which add up to $2a$. A great deal of algebra is needed to show that the equation of an ellipse is:

$$\frac{(x-h)^2}{a^2}+\frac{(y-k)^2}{b^2}=1$$

The derivation makes use of the fact that $c^2=a^2-b^2$, a relation that becomes obvious when P is chosen to be at $(0, b)$.

Hyperbolas A hyperbola, as shown in figure A.8, consists of two branches that asymptotically approach the lines $y=\pm(b/a)x$. In a hyperbola, the difference between distances L_1 and L_2 is the constant $2a$. Virtually the same algebraic steps required to derive the ellipse formula are required to derive the equation of a hyperbola. We leave it to you to grind out the solution:

$$\frac{(x-h)^2}{a^2}-\frac{(y-k)^2}{b^2}=1$$

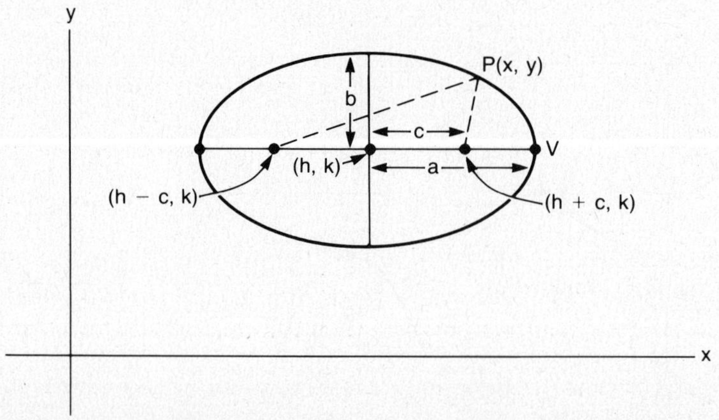

Figure A.7 An ellipse. The sum of the distances represented by the dashed lines is always the same.

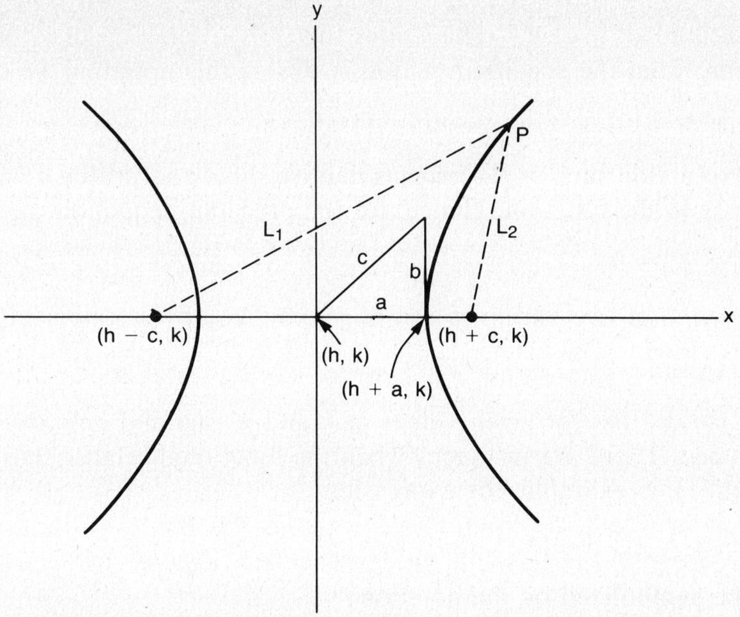

Figure A.8 A hyperbola. The difference of the distances represented by the dashed lines is always the same.

FUNCTIONS AND TRIGONOMETRY

You should already be familiar with the basic concept of a function. A function is essentially an equation that relates two or more variables and follows certain rules. Consider an equation relating x and y. If a given value of x leads to one and only one value of y, then we say that y is a function of x. For the equation

$$y = x^2$$

y is a function of x, because any value of x produces one and only one value of y. If we rewrite the equation to look like this:

$$x = \sqrt{y}$$

it might appear that x is a function of y. However, when $y = 4$, x could be either $+2$ or -2. Thus, a given value of y produces more than one value of x.

For convenience, we use the following shorthand notation to indicate the general case of a functional relationship:

$$y = f(x)$$

which is read "f of x." This states that y is a function of x, but it does not indicate what the specific function is. Using this notation, we can write

$$f(x) = x^2$$

An expression such as $f(3)$ means that we should substitute a 3 wherever an x appears in the function. Hence, for the preceding equation:

$$f(3) = 3^2 = 9$$

A function of two variables can be symbolized by a statement like this:

$$z = f(x, y)$$

This means that for given values of x and y, one and only one value of z is produced. There are instances when the functional relationship is a bit more specific. For example, the expression

$$z = 3(x + y)^2 + 2(x + y) + 12$$

can be symbolized by the notation

$$z = f(x + y)$$

This *cannot* be written as $f(x) + f(y)$. To convince yourself of this, consider the simple function

$$f(x) = x^2$$

We can easily see that $f(3) + f(3) = 18$, whereas $f(3 + 3) = f(6) = 36$.

Trigonometric Functions

Consider a circle of radius $R = 1$ whose center is at the origin (figure A.9). We have drawn a radius to an arbitrary point (x, y). It should be evident that a given angle θ is associated with a unique pair of coordinates (x, y). In fact, both x and y are functions of θ. These functions are so well known that they are given names: $x = \cos(\theta)$ and $y = \sin(\theta)$. Graphs of these functions are shown in figure A.10. Most high-level computer languages can evaluate these functions for all values of θ.

It is useful to look at sin and cos another way. For angles less than 90 degrees, we can represent $\sin(\theta)$ and $\cos(\theta)$ in terms of a right triangle (figure A.11). We can see that

$$\sin(\theta) = B/C$$

$$\cos(\theta) = A/C$$

Therefore, we can express the two perpendicular sides of a triangle in terms of the hypotenuse and θ:

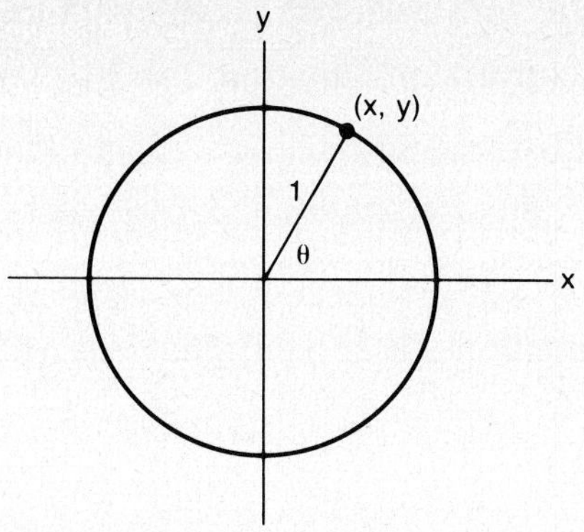

Figure A.9 Definition of cos and sin function: $\cos(\theta)$ is defined as the x-value; $\sin(\theta)$ is defined as the y-value.

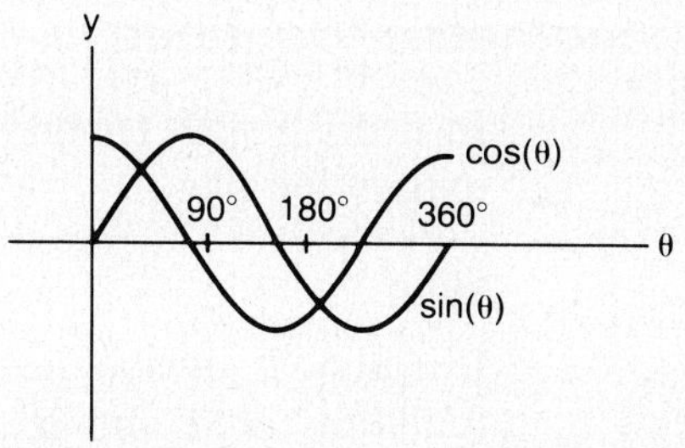

Figure A.10 Graphs of $\sin(\theta)$ and $\cos(\theta)$.

$$B = C\sin(\theta)$$
$$A = C\cos(\theta)$$

Radians

We all know that a circle is divided into 360 equal parts called degrees. This number seems logical because we are so used to it. Actually, it is arbitrary. We could divide a circle into any number of equal parts. One measure of angles that is not arbitrary, however, is the **radian**. If we mark off an arc length equal to the radius of the circle (figure A.12), the angle subtended is one radian. For an arbitrary arc length S, the angle is

$$\theta = S/R$$

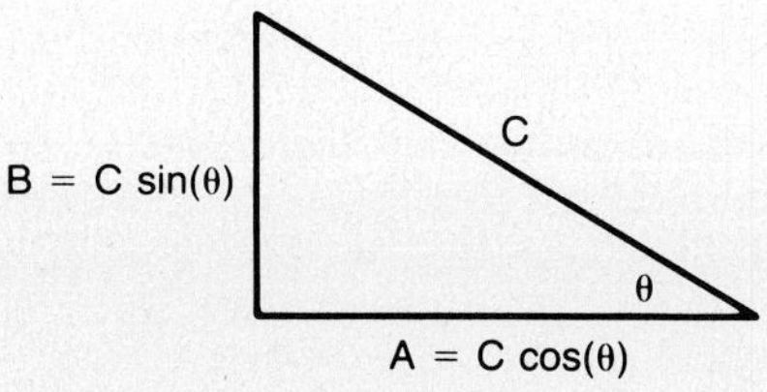

Figure A.11 The sin and cos functions in terms of a right triangle.

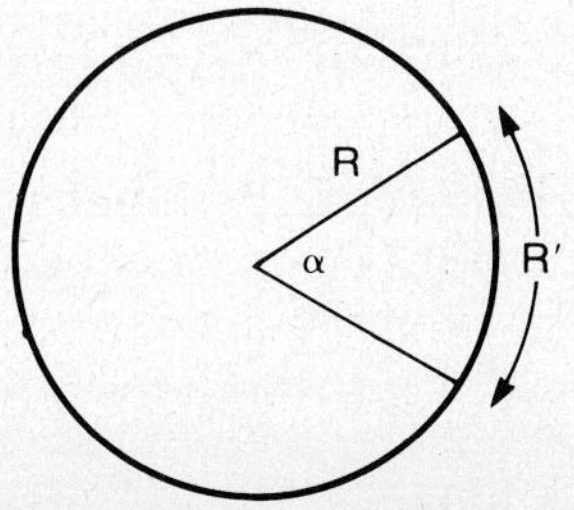

Figure A.12 Definition of a radian. One radian is the angle subtended by an arc length equal to the radius, R. Here, $\alpha = 1$ radian.

Since the circumference of a circle is $2\pi R$, there must be 2π radians per 360 degrees, yielding the following conversion equation:

$$\theta\,(\text{radians})/\theta\,(\text{degrees}) = 2\pi/360 = \pi/180$$

Trigonometric Identities

In dealing with trigonometric functions, it is likely that you will run into an expression like

$$\sin(A + B)$$

It is almost always desirable to rewrite such an expression in terms of known functions of A and B alone. From our discussion of functions, you should realize that we *cannot* write

$$\sin(A + B) = \sin(A) + \sin(B)$$

Therefore, we must derive a correct expression. Consider two angles, A and B, as shown in figure A.13. (Note that two angles are labeled A. We made use of the fact that $A + \alpha = 90°$.) Using the right triangle versions of the sin and cos definitions, we can write

$$\cos(A) = IF/IE, \qquad \sin(A) = FE/IE$$
$$\cos(B) = IE/IC, \qquad \sin(B) = EC/IC$$

We can also write an expression for $\sin(A + B)$ from the definition:

$$\sin(A + B) = (EF + ED)/IC = EF/IC + ED/IC$$

Since

$$EF = IE \sin(A) \quad \text{and} \quad ED = EC \cos(A)$$

we can write

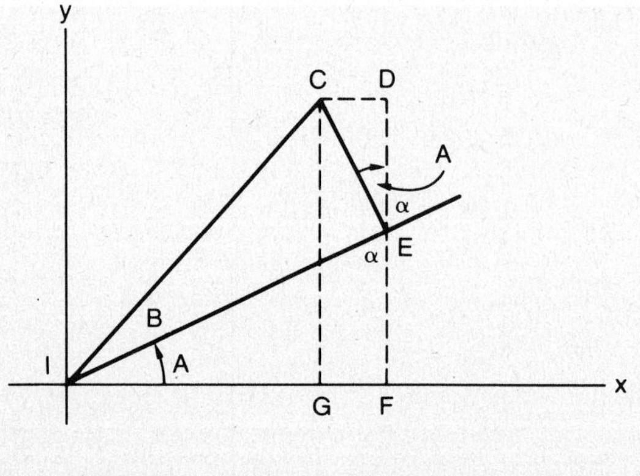

Figure A.13 Geometry for $\sin(A + B)$ and $\cos(A + B)$ derivations.

$$\sin(A + B) = (IE/IC)\sin(A) + (EC/IC)\cos(A)$$

Substituting for the two fractions, we get:

$$\sin(A + B) = \cos(B)\sin(A) + \sin(B)\cos(A)$$

Using a similar approach, we can derive the formula for $\cos(A + B)$:

$$\cos(A + B) = (IF - GF)/IC = (IF - CD)/IC = IF/IC - CD/IC$$

Now, since

$$IF = IE\cos(A) \quad \text{and} \quad CD = CE\sin(A)$$

we have:

$$\cos(A + B) = (IE/IC)\cos(A) - (CE/IC)\sin(A)$$

Again substituting for the two fractions, we get:

$$\cos(A + B) = \cos(B)\cos(A) - \sin(B)\sin(A)$$

The formulas just derived are called **identities** because they hold for any value of A and B.

VECTORS

The quantities we have been using up to now, such as angles, lengths, and coordinates, are all classified as **scalars**. A scalar is a quantity that has only magnitude. For some quantities, however, stating the magnitude is not enough. For example, a car stuck in the mud might require a force with a magnitude of 200 pounds to set it free. However, applying that force downward from the roof would not be too productive! Obviously, the direction also matters. A quantity that is characterized by both magnitude and direction is called a **vector**.

We normally symbolize a vector by an arrow (figure A.14). The length of the arrow is proportional to the magnitude of the quantity; the direction is that pointed to by the arrow. Note the labeling *head* and *tail* and the use of a boldface letter to symbolize that something is a vector.

A vector is considered equal to another vector if the two have the same magnitude and the same direction. A vector is the negative of another vector if the magnitudes are the same but they point in opposite directions.

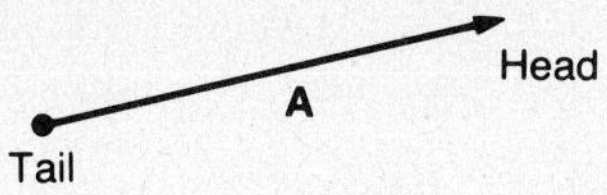

Figure A.14 Vector representation.

Addition and Subtraction of Vectors

To add two vectors (figure A.15a) we first move the tail of one to the head of the other (without changing any directions). Then we draw an arrow from the tail of the unmoved vector to the head of the moved vector (figure A.15b). A consequence of this definition is that any vector can be thought of as the sum of one vector parallel to the x-axis plus one vector parallel to the y-axis.

The *difference* of two vectors, such as **B** − **A**, is found by reversing the direction of **A** and *adding* the two vectors (figure A.15c).

Multiplication of Vectors

When a vector is multiplied by a scalar, its magnitude changes, but not its direction. Two vectors can be multiplied, but the rules governing this differ from the usual multiplication rules.

The **scalar (dot) product**, denoted by **A · B**, is a scalar whose magnitude is the product of both magnitudes and the cosine of the angle between the vectors (Figure A.16a):

$$\mathbf{A} \cdot \mathbf{B} = |\mathbf{A}| \cdot |\mathbf{B}| \cos(\theta)$$

From this we can conclude that the dot product of two perpendicular vectors is zero, while the dot product of two parallel vectors is the product of their magnitudes.

The **vector (cross) product** of **A** and **B** (Figure A.16b) is denoted by **A × B**. It is a vector whose magnitude and direction are determined as follows:

Magnitude: $|\mathbf{A}| \cdot |\mathbf{B}| \sin(\theta)$

Direction: Rotate **A** into **B** through the smaller angle. Curl the fingers of the right hand in the direction of this rotation. The thumb, when extended, points in the direction of the cross product.

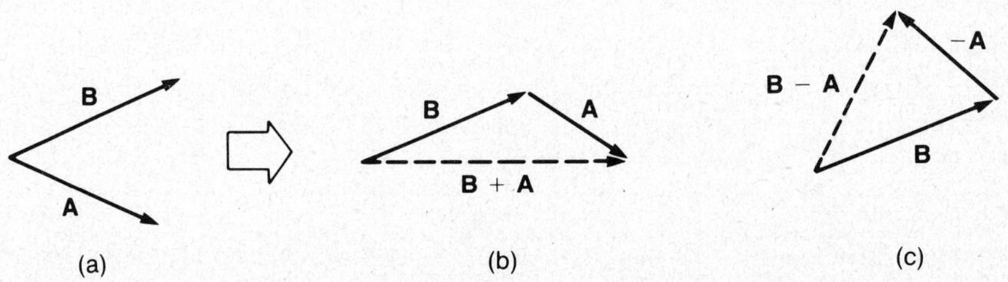

Figure A.15 (a) Two vectors ready to be added or subtracted. (b) Addition. (c) Subtraction.

Figure A.16 Vector multiplication. (a) Dot product: $\mathbf{A}\cdot\mathbf{B} = |\mathbf{A}|\,|\mathbf{B}|\,\cos(\theta)$. (b) Cross product: $|\mathbf{A}| \times |\mathbf{B}| = |\mathbf{A}| \times |\mathbf{B}|\,\sin(\theta)$; $\mathbf{A} \times \mathbf{B} \perp \mathbf{A}$.

Note that if two vectors are parallel, their cross product is zero. If two vectors are perpendicular, the magnitude of the cross product is the product of the two magnitudes.

Unit Vectors

A unit vector is a vector whose magnitude is one. The concept of a unit vector is quite useful. Any vector **V** can be written as a product of a scalar whose magnitude is the same as **V** times a unit vector pointing in the direction of **V**. Figure A.17a shows two very special unit vectors, **i** and **j**. By convention, these point along the *x*-axis and along the *y*-axis, respectively. Since a vector can be thought of as a vector parallel to the *x*-axis plus one parallel to the *y*-axis, we can write an arbitrary vector **V** in the following form:

$$\mathbf{V} = a\mathbf{i} + b\mathbf{j}$$

where *a* and *b* are precisely the scalars needed to make the vectors on the right add up to **V**. Figure A.17b shows an example of this representation.

The beauty of this arrangement is its convenience for doing some of the operations just described. For example, in adding two vectors

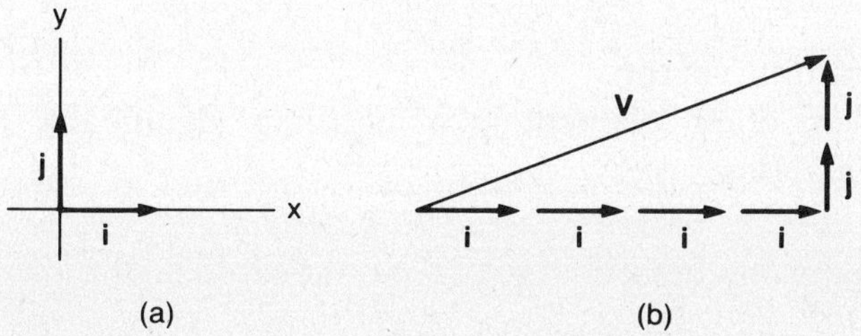

Figure A.17 (a) Unit vectors in the direction of coordinate axes. (b) A vector **V** represented as a sum of unit vectors.

$$\mathbf{V} = a\mathbf{i} + b\mathbf{j}$$
$$\mathbf{W} = c\mathbf{i} + d\mathbf{j}$$

we simply add the separate x and y components to get x and y components of the sum:

$$\mathbf{V} + \mathbf{W} = (a + c)\mathbf{i} + (b + d)\mathbf{j}$$

The dot product $\mathbf{V} \cdot \mathbf{W}$ is really the sum of four dot products:

$$\mathbf{V} \cdot \mathbf{W} = a\mathbf{i} \cdot c\mathbf{i} + a\mathbf{i} \cdot d\mathbf{j} + b\mathbf{j} \cdot c\mathbf{i} + b\mathbf{j} \cdot d\mathbf{j}$$

All we have here are dot products of parallel and perpendicular vectors. The perpendicular vectors drop out, leaving only $a\mathbf{i} \cdot c\mathbf{i} + b\mathbf{j} \cdot d\mathbf{j}$. Hence:

$$\mathbf{V} \cdot \mathbf{W} = ac + bd$$

Matrices

A matrix is a rectangular array of numbers used as a shorthand for representing certain information. The following are two examples of matrices:

$$\begin{pmatrix} 2 & 4 & 7 \\ 1 & 0 & 8 \end{pmatrix} \qquad \begin{pmatrix} 1 & 3 & -2 \\ 0 & -1 & 4 \\ 8 & 3 & 9 \end{pmatrix}$$

The dimensions of the matrix on the left are two **rows** by three **columns**. The matrix on the right, which has three rows and three columns, is called a square matrix. Sometimes a matrix has only one row:

$$\begin{pmatrix} 1 & 4 & 3 \end{pmatrix}$$

This is called a **row vector**. If a matrix has only one column:

$$\begin{pmatrix} 2 \\ 4 \\ 7 \end{pmatrix}$$

it is called a **column vector**.

The position of an element in a matrix is significant. For example, consider the equations

$$2x + 5y = 9$$
$$x - 3y = 2$$

If we want a matrix to represent the coefficients of the variables as they appear in the equation, we would write

$$\begin{pmatrix} 2 & 5 \\ 1 & -3 \end{pmatrix}$$

It would be wrong to write

$$\begin{pmatrix} 2 & 1 \\ 5 & -3 \end{pmatrix}$$

Multiplication of Matrices

The real convenience of matrices for our purposes is their use in multiplication. Explaining matrix multiplication is much more tedious than actually doing it. Let us first list the steps necessary to multiply two matrices; then we will see what they mean in actual examples:

1. Check whether the matrices can be multiplied. Two matrices can be multiplied only if the number of columns of the first matrix equals the number of rows of the second.
2. Determine the dimensions of the product matrix. The product matrix has the same number of rows as the first matrix and the same number of columns as the second.
3. Fill in the elements of the product matrix. The element in the nth row and mth column of the product matrix is the sum of the products of the nth row of the first matrix and the mth column of the second.

Example

$$\begin{pmatrix} 1 & 2 & 7 \end{pmatrix} \times \begin{pmatrix} 4 \\ 1 \\ 5 \end{pmatrix}$$

First, we check whether these matrices can be multiplied. The number of columns of the first matrix (three) is the same as the number of rows of the second. Thus, they can be multiplied. Next, what will the dimensions of the result be? It will be one row and one column. The only element we must fill in is the sum of the products of the row and column. That is done as follows:

$$\text{Sum of products} = (1 \times 4) + (2 \times 1) + (7 \times 5)$$

Hence, the product matrix has one element whose value is 41.

Example

$$\begin{pmatrix} 2 & 3 & 6 \\ 4 & 1 & 8 \end{pmatrix} \times \begin{pmatrix} 2 & 2 & 4 & 2 \\ 6 & 1 & 0 & 0 \\ 1 & 1 & 2 & 1 \end{pmatrix}$$

The number of columns of the first matrix equals the number of rows of the second. Hence, these matrices can be multiplied. The result will have two rows and four columns. We have calculated three of the eight elements of the result.

$$\begin{pmatrix} 2 & 3 & 6 \\ 4 & 1 & 8 \end{pmatrix} \begin{pmatrix} 2 & 2 & 4 & 2 \\ 6 & 1 & 0 & 0 \\ 1 & 1 & 2 & 1 \end{pmatrix} = \begin{pmatrix} \cdots & \cdots & 20 & \cdots \\ 22 & \cdots & \cdots & 16 \end{pmatrix}$$

The first row, third column $= (2 \times 4) + (3 \times 0) + (6 \times 2)$. Similarly, the second row, fourth column $= (4 \times 2) + (1 \times 0) + (8 \times 1)$, and the second row, first column $= (4 \times 2) + (1 \times 6) + (8 \times 1)$.

Example

$$\begin{pmatrix} 4 \\ 1 \\ 5 \end{pmatrix} \times \begin{pmatrix} 1 \\ 2 \\ 7 \end{pmatrix}$$

This cannot be done, because the number of columns of the first matrix does not equal the number of rows of the second.

Example

$$\begin{pmatrix} 1 & 2 \\ 4 & 8 \end{pmatrix} \begin{pmatrix} 1 & 1 \\ 1 & 1 \end{pmatrix} = \begin{pmatrix} 3 & 3 \\ 12 & 12 \end{pmatrix}$$

but

$$\begin{pmatrix} 1 & 1 \\ 1 & 1 \end{pmatrix} \begin{pmatrix} 1 & 2 \\ 4 & 8 \end{pmatrix} = \begin{pmatrix} 5 & 10 \\ 5 & 10 \end{pmatrix}$$

In general, we cannot reverse the order of matrix multiplication.

Determinants

A *second-order determinant* is a 2×2 array symbolized as follows:

$$\begin{vmatrix} a & b \\ c & d \end{vmatrix}$$

It has a numerical value that can be calculated according to the relation

$$\begin{vmatrix} a & b \\ c & d \end{vmatrix} = ad - cb$$

A *third-order determinant* is a 3 × 3 array symbolized as follows:

$$\begin{vmatrix} a_1 & a_2 & a_3 \\ b_1 & b_2 & b_3 \\ c_1 & c_2 & c_3 \end{vmatrix}$$

It can be reduced to a sum of three second-order determinants:

$$\begin{vmatrix} a_1 & a_2 & a_3 \\ b_1 & b_2 & b_3 \\ c_1 & c_2 & c_3 \end{vmatrix} = a_1 \begin{vmatrix} b_2 & b_3 \\ c_2 & c_3 \end{vmatrix} - a_2 \begin{vmatrix} b_1 & b_3 \\ c_1 & c_3 \end{vmatrix} + a_3 \begin{vmatrix} b_1 & b_2 \\ c_1 & c_2 \end{vmatrix}$$

Each second-order determinant can be evaluated as indicated earlier. Determinants are useful as shorthand ways of representing certain quantities.

Appendix B

Additional p-System Graphics Commands

The IBM version of Turtlegraphics is more extensive than the abbreviated system introduced in chapter 2. It includes functions and procedures for choosing colors, dealing with individual pixels, storing and retrieving images, and drawing with different turtles. The purpose of this appendix is to discuss the proper use of these additional features.

FIGURES

In the IBM system, the area in which a turtle roams is called a **figure**. Until now, the only figure we have used has been the screen, with all drawing done by only one turtle. Actually, there can be more than one figure, and each can have its own independent turtle. This feature enables the user to make different drawings and display them on the screen at will. The general procedure for working with more than one figure is as follows:

1. Inform the system that a new figure is desired.
2. Specify that drawing commands are to be sent to the new turtle, not to the old one.
3. Draw the desired image in the new figure using the usual turtle commands.
4. Display the new image on the screen.

The first step is accomplished through the use of a function that creates a rectangular drawing area and assigns an identification number to it. The function, called CREATEFIGURE, has the following format:

```
CREATEFIGURE(W,H:real):integer;
```

where W = width of the figure, specified by the user
H = height of the figure, specified by the user

The integer returned by the function is the identification number of the figure.

Example. If we write:

```
I := CREATEFIGURE(50,80);
```

a drawing area is created whose lower left corner is at (0, 0) and whose upper right corner is at (50, 80). The dimensions are in the units of the display scale in effect at the time the figure is created. This figure is identified by the variable I. Note that we need not be aware of the numerical value of I, just the fact that the variable I contains the identification number of the figure. However, it is important to know that, for the screen, $I = 0$.

The second step is quite simple: we invoke the procedure

```
ACTIVATETURTLE(I);
```

which sends all turtle commands to the turtle associated with figure I. It also deactivates the previously active turtle. To get back to the screen's turtle, we simply write

```
ACTIVATETURTLE(0);
```

For the third step, now that we have set up a figure and activated a turtle, we can apply the usual rules to draw an image. Before doing so, however, we must specify a pen color and a pen mode for the new figure. Otherwise, they will default to 0 and the figure will remain blank. The palette need not be specified if the current value is acceptable. Finally, as noted earlier, the value of the display scale in effect when CREATEFIGURE is invoked must be accepted.

The last of the four steps is accomplished by a procedure that selects a figure and transfers it pixel-by-pixel to the screen. With this procedure, called GETFIGURE, the user can choose the point on the screen where the lower left corner of the figure is to be placed. GETFIGURE has the following format:

```
GETFIGURE(source:integer; cx,cy:real; mode:integer);
```

where *source* = identification number of the desired figure
cx = screen *x*-coordinate of lower left corner of figure
cy = screen *y*-coordinate of lower left corner of figure
mode = an integer that determines how the pixel transfer takes place (see later discussion of *mode*)

Example. Assuming the 50 by 80 figure created in the earlier example, the statement

```
GETFIGURE(1,20,40,1);
```

places figure *1* on the screen so that its lower left corner is at (20, 40) and its upper right corner is at (70, 120). The 1 in the parameter list—the *mode*—is explained below.

It should be noted that *cx* and *cy* are in units of the current display scale. It is strongly recommended that this be changed (if necessary) to the display scale in effect at the time of creation.

The parameter *mode* in the procedure GETFIGURE can take on integer values from 0 to 4, with meanings as follows:

mode = 0: No operation is performed.
mode = 1: Each pixel in the figure is substituted for the corresponding pixel on the screen.
mode = 2: Each pixel in the figure that is not part of the figure's background replaces the corresponding pixel on the screen. (In other words, only the part of the figure that was drawn on by the turtle is transferred.)
mode = 3: This is similar to the *mode* = 2. If a pixel in the figure was written on by the turtle, it will be transferred to the screen, provided that the corresponding screen pixel is of the screen's background color. (In other words, if a screen pixel was written on by the screen's turtle, the corresponding pixel from the figure will not be transferred.)

mode = 4: This is identical to *mode* = 2, except that the screen pixel is complemented.

The usual choice is *mode* = 1 until you have spent some time thinking about the others.

It is not necessary to activate a turtle and give it drawing commands to create an image on a particular figure. The procedure PUTFIGURE allows us to transfer a portion of the screen to a figure. The area transferred is identical in size and shape to the figure. PUTFIGURE has the following format:

```
PUTFIGURE(destination:integer; cx,cy:real; mode:integer);
```

where *destination* = identification number of the receiving figure
cx = *x*-coordinate of lower left corner of the part of the screen that gets transferred
cy = *y*-coordinate of the same part of the screen
mode = an integer (see preceding procedure)

Example. Assuming the previous 50 by 80 figure, the statement

```
PUTFIGURE(I,30,30,1);
```

takes the portion of the screen from a lower left corner of (30, 30) to an upper right corner of (80, 110) and transfers it to figure *I* pixel-by-pixel.

When a figure is created, space is reserved for it in the memory. The more figures you create, the more memory is taken up, and there is a very real possibility that you can run out of memory. The easiest way to avoid this is to eliminate a figure when it is no longer needed. This can be done using a simple procedure called DELETEFIGURE, which has the form

```
DELETEFIGURE(I:integer);
```

where *I* is the identification number of the figure to be deleted.

STORAGE AND RETRIEVAL OF FIGURES

The IBM system provides four functions that allow the user to store and retrieve figures to and from a disk file. The basic ideas of these functions are easy to understand. Figures in a disk file are stored sequentially and are identified by index numbers indicating their position in the file. Index numbers are assigned during the process of storage. When the user wishes to retrieve a figure, he or she specifies the appropriate index. Keep in mind that the number that identifies a figure in a disk file is not the same number that identifies it in memory.

Storing Figures

Two steps are needed to store a figure on disk. The first is to create a disk file. To do this, we invoke a function called WRITEFIGUREFILE, which is the functional equivalent of opening a file for writing. Its form is

```
WRITEFIGUREFILE(filename:string):integer;
```

Here, *filename* is the name we wish to give to the disk file. The system then adds the suffix .FOTO to it. The integer that the function returns indicates whether there was an error in the creation of the file (0 = no error, but see table B.1). If a file of a different name is already open for writing, it is closed before the new one is opened.

Example. The statement

```
J := WRITEFIGUREFILE('#4:PIC');
```

TABLE B.1 I/O ERROR MESSAGES

Message	Meaning
0	No error
1	Bad block, parity error (CRC)
2	Bad device number
3	Invalid I/O request
4	Data-com timeout
5	Volume is no longer on-line
6	File is no longer in directory
7	Bad file name
8	No room insufficient space on volume
9	No such volume on-line
10	No such file on volume
11	Duplicate directory entry
12	Not closed: attempt to open an open file
13	Not open: attempt to access a closed file
14	Bad format: error in reading real or integer
15	Ring buffer overflow
16	Volume is write-protected
17	Invalid block number
18	Invalid buffer

creates a file on the disk in the left drive called PIC.FOTO and assigns one of the integers defined in table B.1 (0, we hope) to *J*.

The second step in storing figures involves a function called STOREFIGURE, which does two things at once: it stores the figure on the disk *in the file that is currently open*, and it assigns the figure an integer that indicates its position in the file. STOREFIGURE has the form

```
STOREFIGURE(I:integer):integer;
```

where *I* is the identification number of the figure to be stored. The integer that this function returns is the position of the figure in the file. The first figure is assigned the index 0.

Example. Assuming the call to WRITEFIGUREFILE in the preceding example, the statement

```
P := STOREFIGURE(I);
```

stores the figure identified by the integer *I* in the file called PIC.FOTO and assigns it the number *P* as its position in that file. Note that the figure is identified in the memory by *I* but in the disk file by *P*.

Retrieving Figures

Two steps are involved in retrieving figures. The first is to identify the name of the disk file from which we wish to retrieve a figure. We do this with a function called READFIGUREFILE, which basically opens a file for reading. It has the form

```
READFIGUREFILE(filename:string):integer;
```

Here, *filename* is the name of the disk file (specifying the suffix .FOTO is unnecessary). The function returns the same type of result as WRITEFIGUREFILE—an integer that indicates a possible error in opening the file. If a file is already open for reading, it is closed before the new one is opened.

Example. Assuming that a file called SHOW.FOTO exists on the disk in the right drive, the statement

```
L := READFIGUREFILE('#5:SHOW');
```

opens SHOW.FOTO for reading. If there was no error in opening the file, *L* will be assigned the value 0.

The actual retrieval of the figure is accomplished by a function called LOADFIGURE, which selects the desired figure from the disk file and loads it into memory. LOADFIGURE has the following format:

```
LOADFIGURE(position:integer):integer;
```

Here *position* is the figure's identification in the disk file. The integer that the function returns is the retrieved figure's new identification number in the memory.

Example. Assuming that SHOW.FOTO has been opened for reading, the statement

```
Q := LOADFIGURE(P);
```

selects the figure identified by*P* in the file SHOW.FOTO and loads it into memory under the identification number *Q*. Be careful when you are storing and retrieving in the same program. A file that is open for writing (as a result of WRITEFIGUREFILE) must be closed before it can be reopened for reading. Unfortunately, there is no *close* statement for .FOTO files. Therefore, it is necessary, first, to execute WRITEFIGUREFILE using a dummy filename. Then you can read from the original file name.

A Sample Program Illustrating Figures and Files

This program first draws a diagonal line across the screen. Then it creates a 50 by 50 area ("figure") and draws a diagonal line across it. It opens a file on the disk called test 1.foto and stores four copies of the figure in that file. Then it recalls the copies of the figure from the disk and puts them one by one across the bottom of the screen. Note that a piece of the original diagonal file is erased. This is because the blank portion of the 50 by 50 figure overlays that part of the diagonal line.

PRESS RETURN AFTER THE ORIGINAL DIAGONAL IS DRAWN, AND AT THE END OF THE RUN

```
PROGRAM DEMO;

USES IBMSPECIAL,TURTLEGRAPHICS;
VAR
```

```
    a,b,index,ii,jj,cc,i,j,mode:integer;
    color:integer;
    seed:array[1..5] of integer;
    x,y,lx,ly,ux,uy:real;

  BEGIN
    DISPLAYSCALE(0,0,320,200);
    PALETTE(1);
    PENCOLOR(1);
    PENMODE(1);
    MOVETO(320,200);      {draw a diagonal line across the entire
                           screen}
    i := CREATEFIGURE(50,50);      {create a 50 by 50 drawing area
                                    identified by i}
    ACTIVATETURTLE(i);       {send subsequent drawing commands
                              to area i}
    FILLSCREEN(i,0);      {clear area i}
    PENMODE(1);
    PENCOLOR(1);
    MOVETO(50,50);      {draw a diagonal line across area i}
    READLN;      {pause, then press return to continue}

    jj := WRITEFIGUREFILE('test1');      {create a file called
                                          test1.foto on disk}

    FOR color := 1 to 4 DO
      seed[color] := STOREFIGURE(i);      {store four copies of area i
                                           in test1.foto
                                           these will be labelled
                                           seed[1] --> seed[4]}
    jj := WRITEFIGUREFILE('test2')      {create a file called
                                         test2.foto, the real
                                         purpose of which is to close
                                         test1.foto}
    cc := READFIGUREFILE('test1');      {open test1.foto for reading}
    FOR color := 1 to 4 DO
      BEGIN
      ii := LOADFIGURE(seed[color]);      {load 50 by 50 area into
                                           memory}
      GETFIGURE(ii,color*60,10,1)      {place 50 by 50 area on the
                                        screen so
                                        that lower left corner is at
                                        color*60,10}

      END;
      READLN;
```

```
    VIDEOMODE(2)
END.
```

COLOR

If you have a color monitor, you can take advantage of the system's ability to specify both background and drawing colors. If we consider a blank pixel to be black, there are eight possible colors: black, blue, green, red, yellow, cyan, magenta, and white. As we shall see, however, the system can display only four of these colors at a time.

Background Color

The default background color is black. To change this, there is a procedure called BKGNDCOLOR, which has the following format:

```
BKGNDCOLOR(color1:fourbits);
```

where the type *fourbits* = 1 . . . 15. The following list indicates what the various integers mean:

1 = blue

2 = green

4 = red

8 = high intensity

Any combination of these values can be used; for example, a value of 12 would give a high-intensity red.

Drawing Color

Two procedures affect the color of the turtle's pen. The first is PALETTE, which selects a predetermined set of four colors. The format of this procedure is

```
PALETTE(color2:onebit);
```

where type *onebit* = 0 . . . 1. For *color2* = 0, the turtle can draw in four colors:

PENCOLOR = 0: background color

PENCOLOR = 1: green

PENCOLOR = 2: red

PENCOLOR = 3: yellow

For *color2* = 1, the color choices are as follows:

PENCOLOR = 0: background color

PENCOLOR = 1: cyan

PENCOLOR = 2: magenta

PENCOLOR = 3: white

More on PENMODE

There are two pen modes we have not discussed: PENMODE(3) and PENMODE(4). In PENMODE(3), the turtle draws whatever color has been selected. However, when it comes to a pixel that is not of the background color, that pixel is left alone. IBM refers to this feature as *underwriting*. With PENMODE(4), the turtle changes the color of each pixel that it crosses to the opposite color.

Single-Color Figures

It is possible to light all the pixels in a figure with the same color using a single procedure—FILLSCREEN—which has the following format:

```
FILLSCREEN(figure, color:integer);
```

Example. Assuming a choice of PALETTE(1), the statement

```
FILLSCREEN(I,2);
```

causes all the pixels in figure *I* to light up magenta.

INDIVIDUAL PIXEL COMMANDS

There are four functions and one procedure that deal with individual pixels on the screen. The first three functions require no arguments: TURTLEx has no arguments and returns a real value that is the *x*-coordinate of the *current* turtle position. TURTLEy is the same as TURTLEx, but it returns the *y*-coordinate. TURTLEANGLE returns the direction, in degrees, in which the current turtle is facing.

The function READPIXEL returns an integer that is the color of a specified pixel. The format is

```
READPIXEL(figure:integer; x,y:real):integer;
```

Example. The statement

```
c := READPIXEL (I,x,y);
```

determines the color of the pixel at (*x, y*) on figure *I* and assigns its integer value to *c*.

The procedure SETPIXEL allows you to set a particular pixel to a desired color. Its format is

```
SETPIXEL(figure:integer; x,y:real; color:integer);
```

Example. The statement

```
SETPIXEL(0,50,35,2);
```

sets the pixel on the screen (that is, figure 0) at (50, 35) to either red or magenta, depending on the choice of PALETTE.

THE VIEWPORT PROCEDURE

Turtlegraphics has a built-in procedure called VIEWPORT that does not conform to the definition of a viewport given in chapter 6. This "viewport" does *not* map a window to a specified area of the screen. Rather, it cuts off all screen information outside the specified boundaries. The format of this procedure is

```
VIEWPORT(xmin,ymin,xmax,ymax:integer);
```

The parameters (*xmin,ymin*) are coordinates of the lower left corner of the "viewport"; (*xmax, ymax*) are the coordinates of the upper right corner.

Example. Assume that the statement

```
VIEWPORT(30,30,80,100);
```

is executed. If a line is drawn from (20, 50) to (40, 50), only the portion from (30, 50) to (40, 50) will show. If the viewing area is subsequently expanded by the statement

```
VIEWPORT(10,10,80,100);
```

the part of the line that was originally missing will still be missing. Information that is outside the "viewport" is lost forever.

VIEWPORT affects only the screen, not other figures.

Appendix C

Turbo Pascal

Turbo Pascal is a Pascal compiler that runs under PC DOS rather than the p-System. Although Turbo's graphics commands (available starting with version 2.0) are primitive compared to Turtlegraphics, the system as a whole has been widely praised, especially for its compilation speed and its low price. The following discussion first will cover two of the graphics modes, then will demonstrate how Turbo draws an image. We will also take a quick look at how Turbo reads and writes disk files.

SCREEN MODES

Turbo has four different screen modes:

1. Text
2. Medium-resolution monochrome graphics
3. Medium-resolution color graphics
4. High-resolution monochrome graphics

Only the last two are of interest to us here.

Medium-Resolution Color Graphics

For the IBM PC, medium resolution means 320 pixels horizontally by 200 pixels vertically. The medium-resolution color mode is selected by invoking the built-in procedure `GRAPHCOLORMODE`, with no parameters. This also clears the screen. In this mode, a drawing can be made in three colors, with a fourth color serving as the background. The set of four colors is called a **palette**. Four different palettes are available; they are summarized in table C.1. The notation *Background* in the table represents a choice of sixteen background colors, which are listed in table C.2. (Light colors are obtained by increasing the intensity of the beam for dark colors. If your monitor does not respond to the intensity signal, only the eight dark colors will show up.)

Palettes are selected by invoking the built-in procedure `PALETTE(p)`, where $p = 0 \ldots 3$, as listed in table C.1.

Background color is selected by invoking the built-in procedure `GRAPHBACKGROUND(g)`, where $g = 0 \ldots 15$, as listed in table C.2.

Example C.1. The program segment

```
GRAPHBACKGROUND(1);
PALETTE(2);
```

selects a blue background and allows a choice of light green, light red, or yellow as the drawing color.

The parameters p and g default to 0 if no choice of `PALETTE` or `GRAPHBACKGROUND` is specified.

High-Resolution Monochrome Graphics

In the high-resolution mode, the screen is 640 pixels wide by 200 pixels high. It is selected by invoking the built-in procedure `HIRES`, with no parameters. `HIRES` also clears the screen. In this mode, the graphics memory is devoted to coordinate information, so nothing is left for color information. This has two consequences:

1. Only one background color, black, is available.
2. Only one drawing color, selected from the sixteen in table C.2, can be used at any given time.

TABLE C.1 PALETTES AND THEIR COLORS

	Color number			
Palette	0	1	2	3
PALETTE(0)	Background	Green	Red	Brown
PALETTE(1)	Background	Cyan	Magenta	Light gray
PALETTE(2)	Background	Light green	Light red	Yellow
PALETTE(3)	Background	Light cyan	Light magenta	White

TABLE C.2 BACKGROUND (AND HiRes) COLORS

0 = Black	8 = Dark gray
1 = Blue	9 = Light blue
2 = Green	10 = Light green
3 = Cyan	11 = Light cyan
4 = Red	12 = Light red
5 = Magenta	13 = Light magenta
6 = Brown	14 = Yellow
7 = Light gray	15 = White

The choice of drawing color is made using the procedure HIRESCOLOR(*g*), where $g = 0 \ldots 15$ and is selected from table C.2. Note that the choice of drawing colors for the high-resolution mode is exactly the same as the choice of background colors for the medium-resolution mode.

Example C.2. The program segment

```
HIRES;
HIRESCOLOR(5);
```

selects the high-resolution mode and a drawing color of magenta. The background is automatically black.

DRAWING COMMANDS

Turbo's coordinate system, shown in figure C.1, takes a bit of getting used to. Turbo's drawing ability is rather limited: it can plot a point and draw a line between two endpoints. To plot a point, the user invokes the built-in procedure PLOT(x,y,c), where *x* and *y* are the screen coordinates. The

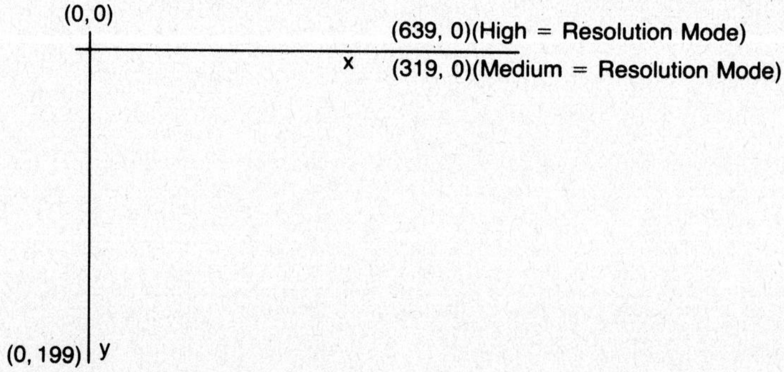

Figure C.1 Coordinate system for Turbo graphics screens.

variable c has different meanings, depending on the mode. For the medium-resolution mode, c is one of the four palette colors.

Example C.3. The program segment

```
GRAPHCOLORMODE;
GRAPHBACKGROUND(4);
PALETTE(3);
PLOT(30,60,3);
```

selects the medium-resolution color mode and a red background, then plots a white point at $x = 30$ and $y = 60$.

Example C.4. If the last line of example C.3 were

```
PLOT(30,60,0);
```

the point $x = 30$ and $y = 60$ would be plotted with the background color. Thus, plotting with $c = 0$ erases what was plotted previously.

In the high-resolution mode, c can be 0 or 1. If $c = 1$, the point is plotted using the current HIGHRESCOLOR. If $c = 0$, the point is erased.

Example C.5. The program segment

```
HIRES;
HIRESCOLOR(7);
PLOT(55,10,1);
```

selects the high-resolution mode and plots a blue point (on a black background) at $x = 55$ and $y = 10$.

To connect two points with a straight line, the user invokes the built-in procedure DRAW(x1,y1,x2,y2,c), where (x_1, y_1) and (x_2, y_2) are the coordinates of the endpoints, and c has the same function it has in PLOT.

Example C.6. The program segment

```
HIRES;
HIRESCOLOR(2);
DRAW(0,0,639,199,1);
```

selects the high-resolution mode and draws a green diagonal across the screen.

Example C.7. The program segment

```
GRAPHCOLORMODE;
DRAW(0,0,639,199,1);
DRAW(0,199,639,0,2);
```

selects the medium-resolution color mode and, by default, PALETTE(0), with a black background. Then it draws two diagonal lines—first a green one, then a red one.

Suppose that we change the palette in the middle of a drawing. Then all existing lines change color according to the definition of the color number in the new palette. For example, a change to PALETTE(1) in the example C.7 would change the green line to cyan and the red line to magenta. The same idea holds true for the HIRES mode. A change in HIRESCOLOR causes previously drawn lines to appear in the new color.

Two final notes are necessary here. Turbo can be returned to the text mode with the command TEXTMODE. Also, the screen-clearing command, CLRSCR, will not work in the graphics modes. You must use GRAPHCOLORMODE or HIRES to clear the screen.

TURBO PASCAL FILE HANDLING

Turbo Pascal handles disk files pretty much as described at the beginning of chapter 5, but with a few minor differences. The best way to understand these differences is with the aid of two programs:

```
PROGRAM NUMBERONE(Input,Output);
  VAR
    int:FILE OF INTEGER;
    n:INTEGER;
  BEGIN
    ASSIGN(INT,'b:TEST1.DAT');
    REWRITE(int);
    FOR n := 1 TO 100 DO
      WRITE(int,N);
    CLOSE(int)
  END.
```

This program writes 100 integers to a file called TEST1.DAT, located on drive *b:*. The ASSIGN statement associates the internal and external file names. In the p-System, this is done by the REWRITE statement. In Turbo, the REWRITE statement opens the file for writing and sets the pointer to the beginning of the file. The WRITE statement does the actual writing of the 100 integers to the file. If we were doing this in the p-System, we would have used the statement PUT(int). Finally, the file is closed with the CLOSE statement, but the word LOCK is not needed.

```
PROGRAM NUMBERTWO(Input,Output);
VAR
  int:FILE OF INTEGER;
  a:ARRAY[1..100] OF INTEGER;
  n:INTEGER;
BEGIN
  ASSIGN(int,'b:TEST1.DAT');
  RESET(int);
  FOR n:= 1 TO 100
    READ(int,A[N]);
  CLOSE(n)
END.
```

This program reads 100 integers from the file TEST1.DAT, located on drive *b:*, into the variables *a*[1] through *a*[100]. The ASSIGN statement has the same function it has in the preceding program, while RESET opens the file for reading and sets the pointer to the beginning of the file. In the p-System, RESET alone would have accomplished as much. The READ statement reads the 100 integers into the array. In the p-System, we would have used GET(int). The file is closed as it is in the first program.

INDEX